The Book of Brilliant Hoaxes

Simon Rose

First published in Great Britain in 1995 by
Virgin Books
an imprint of Virgin Publishing Ltd
332 Ladbroke Grove
London W10 5AH

A catalogue record for this book is available from the
British Library.

ISBN 0 86369 975 8

Typeset by Litho Link Ltd, Welshpool, Wales, UK
Printed and bound in Great Britain by Cox & Wyman Ltd,
Reading, Berks.

Many now know that Simon Rose is the Sixth Man. Fewer know that he was election agent to Plaid Cymru in Putney in the 1979 General Election.

On the international scene, he is one of our leading Middle-Eastern peace brokers and has long since been a close friend of the Dalai Lama, on whose cricket team he regularly plays No. 5. Professional jealousy cost him the 1994 Nobel Peace Prize and still fuels the rumours that dog him; for his part, he maintains that he was nowhere near the Berlin Wall when it came down.

A black belt in marital arts and the only man to be the subject of eleven answers in Trivial Pursuit, Simon Rose originally planned to be a film star, but his career stalled when he lost the lead role in *Raiders of the Lost Ark* after an argument with Steven Spielberg over whether *Citizen Kane* or *It's a Wonderful Life* was the greatest film ever made. How ironic that it should be Harrison Ford who is now tipped to play Rose in the movie of his life.

As the inventor of the Coco Pop, Simon Rose is a wealthy man. Sadly, he is unwelcome in many financial circles for starting the panic on Black Monday, precipitating the stock market crash. Only last year did he admit that the panic was because he'd locked his keys in his car.

The Guinness Book of Records is considering his claim to be the most fertile man in Britain. According to the Child Support Agency, he is the father of 138 children and, for two years, escaped detection as the bigamous husband to Siamese twins.

His one unfulfilled ambition is to find a cure for the common cold – and then hide it.

Contents

Introduction

Hoaxes are nothing new. Since the dawn of man, people have been pulling each other's legs and playing practical jokes and pranks on each other. And great fun such frivolity is too, always providing that you're not the unfortunate victim.

History is full of hoaxes and hoaxers, both real and fictitious: The Trojan Horse; The Man Who Never Was; Baron Münchausen; *The Hitler Diaries*; Till Eulenspiegel; The Bermuda Triangle; Tom Keating; The Return of Martin Guerre; Milli Vanilli and so on.

But those are not really the sort of hoaxes this book is about. I can't get terribly excited about serious scams and swindles, the type of hoaxes done to enhance someone's professional reputation or to make them some money. I might admire the work that went into creating 60 volumes of *The Hitler Diaries*, but it's not the sort of thing that will send me off into helpless laughter whenever I think of it.

Nor do I include episodes like Orson Welles' famous Mercury Radio Theatre broadcast of *War of the Worlds*, which sent America into a panic in 1938. True, it is quite amusing now to think of people shoving their furniture onto their cars and grannies escaping cities at the idea of a Martian invasion. But Welles never meant it to be a hoax, as is clear if you listen to the beginning of the broadcast. It's also worth remembering that when *War of the Worlds* was broadcast in 1949 in Quito, Ecuador, there was a far less amusing panic which ended with the radio station being set alight and the deaths of twenty people.

No, the hoaxes that I have written about are those inspired by sheer mischief; the pranks and japes that are carried out for pure devilment. The truly great hoaxers are the ones who can make people laugh at their activities or, at the very least, raise a smile at the thought of them.

It would be nice to say that I have always been a hoaxer myself, but I'm too much of a wimp to do more than dream them up. Perhaps I came to practical joking too early in life? My grandfather had a joke shop, but my taste for trying out the stock waned when I discovered that I could never 'get' him with his own rubber spiders or fake ink-bottle spills. With the exception of 'Magic Ear', a spoof of the *Magic Eye* books on my radio programme on London Newstalk Radio, the nearest I have come to perpetrating a hoax was when I was election agent to a friend standing for Plaid Cymru in Putney in the 1979 General Election, the only time the party has ever fought a seat outside Wales. Eh? 41 votes actually, since you ask.

But that doesn't stop me admiring others who think up wacky, weird and wonderful tricks to play. Whether they're called hoaxes, practical jokes, shenanigans, hacks or pranks, it is sad that so many people profess to despise such frivolity, believing such activities beneath them. Well, these antics weren't too base for the likes of Mark Twain, Max Beerbohm, General Ulysses S. Grant, Virginia Woolf, Wolfgang Amadeus Mozart, David Niven, Abraham Lincoln, Jonathan Swift or King George VI, so who are they to be so snooty?

In these stuffy strait-laced, straight-faced days, when everything and everybody is taken far too seriously, we need a little more hoaxing to brighten up our lives and to shake up those who make our lives miserable. Why keep such a life-enhancing activity to just one day? Let us spread the happiness of 1 April throughout the year, using hoaxes and pranks to cheer us up, prick pomposity, debunk reputations and deflate bureaucracy.

We should not forget, either, that practical joking really can have a practical side to it. Hoaxers, as many of the examples here show, often serve to keep corporations on their toes and punish them for their indifference to the public. In the case of the *War of the Worlds*, it even helped the authorities learn how better to prepare for a future real emergency.

I offer you this selection of my favourite hoaxes in the hope that they might make you smile or laugh or, even better, inspire you to conjure up your own.

THANKS

Many people helped me to track down stories for the book. Among those I cannot thank enough are Amanda Jane Doran and Miranda Taylor at the *Punch* Library, WCRS (for the BMW ads), Alan Coren, Jeremy Beadle, Michael Bentine, Norman Murphy, Michael Meyer, David Thomas, Gail Renard, Mitchell Symons, Patrick Walsh, Steve Penk, Carol and her colleagues at Southfields Library, Peter Dennis, Steve Williams, Clive Bull, Paul Merton, John Lloyd, Gill Steene, Roy Hudd, Andrew Best, Michael Bywater, Nicole Aragi, John Whitney and Lois Rathbone.

Appeal

I am collating hoaxes and practical jokes for another book along the same lines and would welcome any examples (preferably with provenance) that you think might tickle readers' fancies.

There are several hoaxes that I am particularly keen to track down, such as the Rosebowl hoax, the Caltech prank involving the Hollywood sign, details of the turfing of Oxbridge college JCRs and the story of the hoaxer who sent letters purporting to come from the electricity company to the inhabitants of a skyscraper in New York. These told some residents they must keep their lights on for a specified period and others that they must keep their lights off. The lights spelt out a certain four letter word many storeys high.

If Robert Redford or Paul Newman are reading this, I would also love to hear details of the practical jokes the pair of you are reputed to play on each other on your birthdays.

Please send them to me c/o:

Virgin Publishing Ltd
332 Ladbroke Grove
London
W10 5AH

1

The Great Jokers

HORACE DE VERE COLE

Although some of the most inspired hoaxes were mere one-offs, there have been a few men whose place in history is assured by devoting their lives to the practical joke. Curiously, most of their names begin with the letter 'H', for reasons which I have yet to fathom. It bothered me for some time that there was only one important exception. As a consequence, I was tempted to leave the great Alan Abel out of this chapter altogether for reasons of neatness. But instead I have now taken to affecting an accent like Parker in *Thunderbirds*, referring to him as 'H'Alan H'Abel'.

Greatest of all hoaxers was undoubtedly Horace de Vere Cole. A wealthy Londoner of Irish descent and the son of a major, Cole left school at eighteen and went to fight in the Boer War, returning when his career was cut short by deafness. He was an amateur poet and over his life built up a substantial collection of modern paintings. He was well-connected, his sister marrying Neville Chamberlain.

Despite Cole's pre-eminence in his field, the Greater London Council shamefully refused to dedicate one of their blue plaques to him, showing their complete disdain for one of the nobler arts, preferring instead to remember stuffy politicians, painters, poets, philosophers and countless others who the majority of Londoners could not relate to. No wonder the GLC is no more.

1

Baldness Be My Friend

It was Cole who once sent four bald acquaintances to the theatre to a performance of a play he hated. The seats were in the front row and, just as the performance was about to start, the four removed their hats. The audience in the circle roared with laughter. On the men's heads were painted the letters 'S ... H ... I ... T'.

If Baby I'm the Bottom ...

Another time Cole sent out handsomely printed invitations to a great event at a town hall. There was only one thing connecting each guest and it was not immediately apparent.

Cole himself chose not to turn up, instead preferring to imagine the scene as all those who did attend began introducing themselves, with Mr Higginbottom shaking hands with Mr Winterbottom and Mr Shufflebottom saying, 'How do you do?' to Mr Ramsbottom. Every single one of those invited had 'Bottom' in their names.

The Great String Gag

For a truly great hoaxer like Horace de Vere Cole, even a gentle stroll to the shops for a humble ball of string was rife with possibilities. On one occasion, when he was walking home after buying a ball of twine to hang some pictures, Cole saw a stuffy-looking gentleman approaching him. On the spur of the moment, he introduced himself, claiming to be part of a surveying team. Unfortunately, lamented Cole, his colleague had been taken ill and he was at a loss to know what to do. Would the stranger be good enough to spare him just a few moments of his time?

Bristling with self-importance, the chap condescended to help and was asked to hold on to the end of the string, which Cole then unrolled as he walked backwards around the corner, supposedly to carry out some measurements.

2

It was his intention to tie the other end of the string to something fixed like a doorknob and then simply to disappear. But when he saw another well turned out gentleman coming towards him, a man of Cole's sparkling inventiveness couldn't resist the temptation to top the gag. Claiming as before to be surveying the area, he begged the new arrival for just a few moments' assistance. Would he mind terribly just holding on to the string while he concluded his calculations? Again the man agreed.

Cole then vanished, leaving the pair standing there, each tightly grasping one end of a piece of string.

The Road from Zanzibar

It was Cole who was responsible for perhaps the most famous hoax there has ever been, convincing the Navy to play open house to what they imagined was the Sultan of Abyssinia and his entourage. Most bizarrely of all, the group included Virginia Woolf.

Cole had had a dry run for this prank while an undergraduate at Cambridge. The Sultan of Zanzibar was in the country and Cole persuaded the mayor of Cambridge that the Sultan's uncle was very keen to see around the city and its colleges. Cole and three of his fellow students donned beards, make-up and an approximation of Zanzibar's national costume and found themselves being taken on a personal tour of the university by the mayor himself, a tour that culminated in a grand dinner. By the end of the day Cole and his friends were heartily sick of the Zanzibar national anthem.

The only fly in the ointment came when the mayor insisted on seeing them on to the train to London himself, leaving them to find their way back to Cambridge from the next station on the line. Even though Cole ensured that the hoax soon came to light, he was not sent down, the university authorities feeling it better to sweep the whole embarrassing thing under the carpet.

3

Several years later, Cole decided that the time was right for a similar impersonation, but on a grander scale. He aimed high, possibly as high as he could. For the target of Cole's prank was to be the pride of the Royal Navy, HMS *Dreadnought*, moored at Weymouth. It is difficult now to understand just how important this battleship was to the country. Its launch in 1906 had been a decisive moment in the escalation of naval armaments that led to the First World War. Considered to be the world's most powerful battleship, only a fool or a genius could possibly believe that they could gain access to it.

Many of Cole's friends understandably thought him a fool and would have nothing to do with his idea. But he did manage to persuade a handful of acquaintances, among them Duncan Grant, the artist, and Adrian Stephen, who had been part of the Zanzibar hoax. When they found they couldn't persuade anyone else they wanted to join their party, Stephen suggested his sister Virginia, later to become Virginia Woolf. As if it wasn't complicated enough that Virginia was quite obviously not a man, it transpired that William Fisher, the Admiral of the Fleet's Chief of Staff, was the cousin of Virginia and Adrian Stephen.

On 10 February 1910, the fourth anniversary of the *Dreadnought*'s launching, the conspirators went to the theatrical costumier Clarksons to be made up. While Cole donned top hat and tails to play Herbert Cholmondley of the Foreign Office and Adrian Stephen sported a moustache and bowler hat as the group's German interpreter, the others blackened their faces, stuck on false beards and dressed in flowing African robes and turbans. Once disguised, they were satisfied that it was nearly impossible to tell that Virginia was a woman. The 'Abyssinians' were warned not to eat or drink or their faces would show streaks and the beards begin to peel off. Sadly for them, unlike Cole they had had no time for breakfast that morning.

At Paddington the station-master, amazed to find royalty visiting the terminus, hurriedly arranged a reception for them, giving 'interpreter' Adrian Stephen, a chance to try out his act. Unfortunately, Stephen hadn't been able to find any books on the Abyssinian language. The nearest thing he had been able to unearth was a booklet produced by the Society for the Propogation of the Gospel in Swahili.

Cole arranged for a friend to send a telegram to the Admiral of the Fleet, purporting to come from the head of the Foreign Office, informing him that: 'PRINCE MAKALEN OF ABYSSINIA AND SUITE ARRIVE 4.20 TODAY WEYMOUTH. HE WISHES TO SEE DREADNOUGHT. REGRET SHORT NOTICE. FORGOT WIRE BEFORE. INTERPRETER ACCOMPANIES THEM. HARDING. FOREIGN OFFICE.' The recipients were sent into such a fluster that they did not notice that Hardinge's name was misspelt.

The Admiral did the 'Lion of Judah' proud. There was a red carpet to welcome them at Weymouth station. The party were greeted formally on the platform, then taken to waiting cars. From the quayside, a steam launch took them to the *Dreadnought* to meet Admiral Sir William May. Stephen and Cole had trouble containing their laughter when they were played on to the battleship, not with the Abyssinian national anthem, but with the nearest thing the band had been able to find, which turned out to be the anthem of Zanzibar, the tune they had grown so tired of on their previous stunt.

It was a near miracle that the conspirators escaped detection, particularly as Adrian and Virginia Stephen's nightmare came true and they found themselves being introduced to their own cousin. Fortunately, they were not recognised, although Stephen nearly had a fit soon afterwards when he was told that there was a man in the fleet who spoke fluent Abyssinian! Again, luck was with the conspirators, for the chap turned out to be away on leave.

It was not long before Stephen ran out of phrases in Swahili and he had to switch to Latin and Greek, quoting passages from the *Aeneid* and Homer but concealing the source by mispronouncing it terribly. The 'Abyssinians' contented themselves with chanting 'bunga bunga' at anything that amazed them.

At one point it began to rain, threatening the group's make-up. Luckily, the Admiral agreed with Cole's proposal that, as natives of a hot climate, they would be far more comfortable viewing the ship's interior. Lunch for the party was refused by Cole, who claimed that it would be impossible to prepare a meal at such short notice that would accord with the Abyssinians' religious beliefs.

It appears that the Admiral offered the visitors a salute by the *Dreadnought*'s guns but Stephen, by now eager to leave before they were exposed and concerned at the trouble the Navy had gone to, turned it down, claiming that as the French fleet had not given them one, nor should the Royal Navy.

Fortunately for the starving Abyssinians, the Admiral had arranged for them to travel back to London in a special railway coach. Unfortunately Cole delayed their meal by claiming to the stewards that the Royal Party could only be served if white kid gloves were worn. Only when they left Reading, where train staff had rushed off to the town to buy the necessary gloves, could they finally eat.

The conspirators had earlier agreed among themselves that if they were successful, the whole thing would be kept a secret. They were therefore horrified when Cole leaked news of the hoax to the Press, together with a photograph they had had taken of themselves at its conclusion. It was now far from a secret. The *Daily Mirror* carried the story on the front page and questions were asked in Parliament about the Navy's appallingly lax security.

MPs were presumably comforted by the First Lord of the Admiralty's assurances that, according to Hansard, 'No flags were hoisted or salutes fired and no special train was ordered.' As to the question of 'whether it is not a fact that these gentlemen conferred the Royal Abyssinian Order on the Admiral, who wrote to the King to know whether he could wear it?' the response from the Lord was that it was quite untrue.

There was talk of prosecuting the conspirators, until it was realised that the most serious offence they had committed was to have sent a telegram under a false name.

The officers and sailors on the *Dreadnought* found their lives made a misery by the hoax. Whenever they went on shore, they were taunted by children who followed them shouting out 'bunga bunga'. The phrase soon cropped up with regularity in music-hall acts.

William Fisher and a couple of his fellow officers sought out Cole so that they could avenge the honour of the Navy. The smooth-talking Cole persuaded them that he would take his punishment, to be administered with a cane, only if he could cane the man who flogged him with exactly the same force afterwards. As a result, he got not six of the best, but six of the least – tiny taps that caused little pain but which, apparently, were enough to satisfy the Navy's honour.

In later years Virginia Woolf appears to have relished being one of the conspirators. In a biography of Woolf, she is said to have made a Women's Institute helpless with laughter at her account of the affair. But while she joined out of a sense of fun, she claimed in the end, mainly because of Cole's behaviour, that it simply showed how silly men could be. She pointed out that as a result of it, the rules about telegrams were changed so that it would be almost impossible to repeat such an incident. In that way, she said, she had actually been of help to her country. In addition, of course, naval security became very much tighter.

Bizarrely, papers were released by the Public Record Office in 1990 that showed that Admiral William May had received a letter from the Admiralty on the day after the visit of Cole and his friends, saying that 'a man of the name of Cole' had told the Foreign Office that the visit was a hoax. Initially, says the letter, 'the inclination of the FO was to regard the man as mad', but they thought the Admiralty should be informed. The man who wrote the letter and who investigated the incident was Assistant

Secretary Graham Greene, uncle of the novelist who was himself, as we shall see later, a keen practical joker.

Cole's Venice Honeymoon

Cole had promised his first bride, Denise Daly, that he would give up practical joking once the marriage ceremony had taken place. But if she had expected him to change the habits of a lifetime, the end of March was perhaps not the most sensible time to have chosen for the wedding, nor Venice the most sensible place to have picked for the honeymoon.

Cole stole away to the mainland on the last evening of the month with a set of fire tongs and a pair of suitcases lined with newspaper. There he paid a visit to a riding stables before returning to Venice. That night, while the city slept, he took his cases – now full – to the beautiful St Mark's Piazza.

The following morning, April Fools' Day 1919, was a day long-remembered by the inhabitants of Venice. For, impossible though it seemed, there was clear evidence that horses had visited the square in the night and, what's more, a considerable number of them. There was horse dung everywhere.

Mr and Mrs Cole's marriage did not last.

Or Forever Hold His Tongue

Cole's friends were understandably nervous whenever they were part of some solemn occasion that Cole knew about. One of them was petrified in advance of his wedding, believing that despite his promises to the contrary, Cole would not possibly allow the ceremony to pass without trying some jape or other.

Mercifully, everything went smoothly. The bride turned up, nobody challenged the marriage, the rings were exchanged, the register was signed and the happy couple walked down the aisle together and into the sunshine.

Just as the groom relaxed and the photographer

prepared to take the pictures, a well-built woman threw herself at him. Distraught, she screamed that he should not forget the years they had spent together and that, when his bride tired of him, he should know that she would always be there, waiting for him.

In tears, she departed, recovering just in time to collect her cheque from her employer for the hour, Horace de Vere Cole.

Stop That Man

Cole once got into a heated argument with Conservative MP Oliver Locker-Lampson, a man with a singular lack of sympathy for the less fortunate. He refused to give any credence to Cole's belief that the very act of imprisonment was enough to turn an honest man into a criminal.

He made a mistake in telling Cole that, 'A truly innocent man would no sooner be arrested on a London street than I.' With hardly a moment's thought, Cole undid his watch-chain and popped his watch into Locker-Lampson's pocket. When Cole suggested that the two of them have a race, the egotistical MP readily agreed.

After starting off neck and neck Cole dropped back a few paces and began screaming, 'Thief! Thief! That man's pinched my watch.'

Locker-Lampson was grabbed by a couple of decent citizens. They then summoned a policeman who found Cole's watch in Locker-Lampson's pocket and took the pair to the local police station.

Some reports say that Locker-Lampson spent the night in the cells. Others seem more believable in claiming that the policeman soon realised that the thing had been a prank and that it was instead Cole who spent the night in clink, before being charged £5 for a breach of the peace.

Goodbye Piccadilly

Perhaps the neatest day in Cole's hoaxing career came when he chanced upon a group of workmen digging up part of Piccadilly. He apologised for interrupting them, telling them that he was a professor at London University and that he had heard that as a rag week stunt some of the students intended disguising themselves as policemen and ordering the hole in the road to be filled in. Although sneaking was an un-British thing to do, he felt that it was his responsibility to warn them about such a silly prank. He begged them to consider the charitable intent of the students and the high spirits under which they had no doubt conceived the idea.

Cole then marched round to the nearest police station, still posing as a professor. He confessed to the officer on duty that, as a rag week stunt, some of the students had disguised themselves as workmen with the intention of digging up Piccadilly. Although the high jinks of rag week were all in a good cause, he couldn't help feeling that the students had gone too far. He was sure, however, that he could rely on the discretion of the police to bring such silliness to a halt in good time.

The police were soon on the scene, trying to stop the workmen who they were convinced were students from digging up the road. For their part, the workmen were having no truck with the students dressed as policemen trying to stop them doing their job. A scuffle began which quickly brought traffic in Piccadilly to a complete standstill. The disruption soon spread, causing havoc throughout the West End for much of the day.

HUGH TROY

Although an illustrator of some renown, true aficionados of Hugh Troy recognise that he was one of the greatest practical jokers of all time. Like Cole, Troy was at his most active in the thirties. Weirdly, he ended his professional life working for the CIA.

Don't Sit Under the Cherry Tree

Troy's first recorded exploit was as a schoolboy in the twenties when, in advance of his neighbours returning to

10

the States from a long tour of Europe, he and his brother wired dozens of apples to their cherry tree.

It was only after the victims had invited most of the inhabitants of the town to witness what appeared to be a miracle in their garden that they noticed the wires.

It is said that while still a teenager, Troy also invented the gag of putting a sign saying 'Jesus Saves' outside a bank.

The Absent-Minded Professor

Troy became a student at Cornell, where he took advantage of one of the more absent-minded professors who was in the habit of wearing rubber galoshes over his shoes in wet weather. Troy borrowed these one day and used his artistic skills to paint them in the form of human feet. Once his work had dried, he covered it up again with lamp-black, essentially water-soluble carbon, which was the same colour as the original galoshes.

As the professor walked across the campus, the rain washed the lamp-black off, giving the appearance that he was making his way home in his bare feet.

The Great Rhinoceros Panic

It was Troy who created The Great Rhinoceros Panic while he was at Cornell. One summer he acquired a rhinoceros foot wastepaper basket and, never one to waste a good prop, he stored it away until winter.

After a snowfall, he weighted the foot with bits of metal while pieces of rope were attached to each side. Troy and a fellow student then walked slowly across the campus at night, lowering and raising the foot at the requisite intervals to create rhinoceros prints in the snow.

The following morning, there was considerable bewilderment at Cornell for an animal, clearly of some considerable size, had apparently wandered unseen through the campus during the night. The tracks led down to the frozen Beebee Lake and then out on to the ice to a point where there was a large hole, presumably where the animal had fallen in. Their amazement grew still further when the teachers in the zoology faculty announced that the animal prints were that of a rhinoceros. The lake fed the local water supply and when the newspaper carried the story, much of the town gave up drinking water. Some of those who didn't swore blind they could taste the rhinoceros in it.

Troy only leaked the fact that it was a hoax when a group of local citizens planned to dredge the lake.

You Can't Park That Bench There, Mate

One of Troy's favourite stunts was to sneak a park bench that he had bought and paid for into Central Park with a friend.

When they saw a policeman approaching, the pair would pick it up and sprint away, only to find themselves collared and charged for stealing a park bench. They waited until they were in the station house before producing the receipt for the bench, protesting with considerable indignation about the policeman's infringement of their rights.

There's a Hole in My Avenue

Troy moved to New York when he graduated. Echoing Horace de Vere Cole's earlier Piccadilly stunt, he and four friends dressed as labourers and made their way to Fifth Avenue. They marched out into the middle of the street, surrounded themselves with 'Men Working' signs and began to dig. One policeman even stood by them for a while, helpfully diverting the traffic.

They stopped to have lunch at a fashionable hotel restaurant nearby, ignoring the disapproving glances of other diners and convincing the head waiter that their presence was a prank set up by the manager.

By the time they had finished, they had created a hole five feet deep measuring eight feet by six feet, right in the middle of one of New York's busiest streets. They knocked off work at the end of the day, by which time the traffic snarl-up was appalling. It was only the next day that the authorities realised that whoever had been digging up the street had no business being there in the first place.

Some sources claim that Horace de Vere Cole carried out a similar prank, persuading a group of workmen he encountered having a break to march with him to Piccadilly where he ordered them to begin digging. Helped by friendly coppers who diverted the traffic, Cole let them knock off for the day only once there was a massive crater in the middle of the street. A different group of workmen would return to complete the job the next day, Cole assured them.

Only late on the morrow did it occur to somebody that the work was very far from being 'official'. It took far longer to fill the hole than it had taken to dig it and it was some time before order could be restored and the traffic chaos that had blighted the West End was brought under control.

I can't believe that Cole carried this off as well as the student rag week stunt. I prefer to believe in the latter, which strikes me as being one of the most perfect practical jokes that can be imagined.

The Army's War on Flies

During World War II, Troy served as an officer in the American Army. It was not long after he started officer training that he became irritated at the degree of bureaucracy involved in waging the war. His means of protesting was to add to it, printing up forms on which officers could report on the success of the fly papers that were liberally distributed about the base's buildings.

The forms required the officer to inform the Pentagon just how many fly papers were being used, where they were located and the numbers of flies being caught on each over set periods. Troy slipped the forms in with the usual mound of papers he had to fill in and was delighted to be quizzed by other officers about them soon afterwards. They had been admonished for not having returned their fly paper forms. Troy expressed astonishment that they hadn't been filling them out before now. He gave them a handful of copies of the forms he had knocked up and watched as they scuttled back to their offices to try to catch up with all the back paperwork.

It is said, although it seems rather fanciful, that the use of the forms spread to other bases and that, long after the war had ended, officers throughout the American armed services were still filling in their *Fly Papers, Use Of* forms.

THEODORE HOOK

Theodore Hook was an early nineteenth-century novelist, dramatist and composer. He became editor of *John Bull*, an early predecessor of magazines like *Private Eye*, and was the model for Mr Wagg in Thackeray's *Vanity Fair*. He was also an inveterate practical joker. He once went up to a pompous-looking gentleman in the street and, bowing extravagantly, said: 'I beg your pardon, sir, but are you anyone in particular?'

On another occasion, he strode on to the stage of a theatre in mid-performance, handing the leading actor a letter and telling him that he had inherited a fortune.

Two Men in a Boat

Hook was once rowing up the Thames on a fishing trip in the company of the comic actor Charles Matthews when he became irritated by a sign at the bottom of someone's garden prohibiting unauthorised landings. They rowed to the shore, moored their boat and pretended they were surveying the lawn, counting out their steps and using fishing line in place of a tape measure.

The houseowner, an Alderman, demanded to know what they were doing. Hook claimed to be working for a canal company which was about to begin work on a new canal. It would, said Hook sadly, cut through the Alderman's lawn but they could probably arrange for a tunnel to take it underneath the house itself.

After much blustering, the Alderman invited the pair to dinner, entertaining them lavishly in the hope that they would be able to persuade the canal company to change the intended route. Only as the port was being passed around did Hook own up to the deception.

The Berners Street Hoax

Theodore Hook is best remembered, however, as being the perpetrator of what must surely rank as the most elaborate hoax ever. Although the exact details differ in almost every account, it would appear that while strolling through London in 1809 with fellow playwright Samuel Beazley, Hook's companion remarked on the quietness of the street through which they were passing. Hook wagered a guinea that within the week, he could make it the most talked about spot in London.

The house they were standing by was number 54, Berners Street, just north of Oxford Street. Mrs Tottenham, a widow, had until that moment led a quiet, secluded life. Hook changed all that. It took the writing of around a thousand letters, but he did it.

He and Beazley took a room in a lodging house across the street the following week and watched, entranced, as a dozen chimney sweeps arrived, followed by twenty wagons, each loaded with a ton of coal. Then came cartloads of furniture, a hearse accompanied by funeral coaches, assorted medics and a midwife, cartloads of beer, clocks, carpets, potatoes and even a pipe organ with half a dozen men to install it. Also answering apparent summonses from number 54 were coachmakers, clockmakers, wigmakers, opticians and a variety of other tradespeople. A selection of domestic staff arrived hoping to take up one of the positions that had been advertised.

Before long carts were overturned and fights broke out. The street was sheer pandemonium, with a throng of spectators adding to the confusion. But there was more to come. Mere tradespeople weren't enough for the devilish Hook, who had also written to a selection of dignitaries, informing them that Mrs Tottenham was on the point of disposing of her considerable fortune. Among those turning up were the Lord Mayor of London, the Archbishop of Canterbury, the Governor of the Bank of England and the Lord Chief Justice. To cap it all, the Duke of York then arrived, together with an escort of cavalry befitting his position as Commander-in-Chief (some say the Duke of Gloucester, but why spoil the story by downplaying it?); he had been informed that one of his mistresses lay dying there.

Hook was for a time the most unpopular man in London, so much so that he considered it prudent to leave the capital for a time. His escape gave the language a new expression: 'To hook it.'

Hook had, however, won his bet and the Prince Regent was apparently so tickled by reports of the hoax that he gave him a job as Accountant-General and Treasurer in Mauritius, with the handsome salary of £2000 a year. Sadly, Hook was later held to be responsible when a deputy embezzled some money and he ended up in clink for a couple of years.

BRIAN G. HUGHES

New York box manufacturing magnate Brian G. Hughes demonstrated a considerable talent not only for business, but also for practical jokes.

Take My Umbrella . . . Please

One of Hughes' perennial favourites was also extremely simple to bring off. He would go into a bar on a rainy day, hang up his rather expensive umbrella, and wait for some desperate umbrella-less soul to walk off with it. Hughes apparently never grew tired of watching what happened when the victim opened it outside. Instead of being sheltered from the rain, they would be deluged with bits of paper saying 'This Umbrella Stolen from Brian Hughes'.

(In London in the fifties, Lt Col. Derek Monckton of the General Staff Office used to leave a beautiful furled umbrella hanging on the back of his door. On occasion it was borrowed by a desperate clerk who would find, on opening it in Whitehall, that all the spokes fell out. Monckton kept the sabotaged brolly there solely for that purpose.)

Hughes the Public Benefactor

But I digress. Hughes once announced that he was going to donate a piece of prime Brooklyn real estate to the city for use as a public park. The city authorities went out of their way to praise his generosity – until they found out that the land measured only eight feet by two feet.

The Rare Dublin Brindle Alley Cat

Hughes showed up the cat fraternity in New York when he bought an alley cat for ten cents, fed it on top-grade steak for a few weeks and paid to have it groomed.

Sure that the judges knew far less about cat breeding than they claimed, Hughes entered the now beautiful moggie into New York's annual cat show in Madison Square Garden under the name of Nicodemus, proclaiming it to be one of the very few existing examples of the Dublin Brindle breed.

It was awarded first prize.

The First Reetsa in Captivity

Hughes invented an imaginary expedition to South America, the purpose of which was to capture a Reetsa before the species became extinct. He managed to increase public interest in the expedition steadily until eventually he announced that one had been captured.

Through the Press, Hughes revealed that the creature would be brought back to New York and large crowds thronged the dockside to catch a glimpse of it. Hughes himself led it down the gangplank – backwards. Not everyone was amused when they reversed the spelling of Reetsa.

Are You Yonkers?

One of Hughes' favourite pranks was to create a traffic jam simply by taking his time getting on a bus. He would pretend to be deaf and dumb and, making sure no passengers could slip on behind him, would write out a note for the driver saying, 'Does this car go to Yonkers?'

The driver would have to write out that it didn't, only to get a note back from Hughes asking where he *could* get a bus for Yonkers. With traffic getting increasingly restless behind the stationary bus, the driver would feel obliged to write out detailed directions for getting to Yonkers by bus.

Hughes would pick the note up and read it carefully, before saying to the driver loudly and clearly: 'That's funny. I had it on good authority that *this* bus went to Yonkers.'

Bearing in mind New Yorkers' famed quick tempers, Hughes was presumably quite a brave man.

ALAN ABEL

'Alan Abel, a writer, musician and film producer who specialised in satire and lampoons, died of a heart attack yesterday at Sundance, a ski resort near Orem, Utah, while investigating a location for a new film. He was 50 years old and lived in Manhattan and Westport, Conn.'

This obituary, in the *New York Times* on 2 January 1980, was a hoax. Alan Abel was very much alive and well and up to his old tricks, having arranged for his skis to be discovered on the ski slopes and for the paper's diligent fact-checkers to be led on a wild-goose chase. Abel claimed to find it fascinating to read the letters of condolence, thus learning who his true friends were.

Dignity for Animals

Alan Abel is the king of modern hoaxers. It all began back in the mid-fifties when Abel, then a New York advertising executive, was held up on a Texas road by a herd of cattle crossing. When a bull suddenly decided to exercise his droit de seigneur in the middle of the road, Abel noticed that some of the other motorists behaved almost as if the copulating couple were human, averting their eyes and pretending not to notice anything untoward was happening.

He quickly wrote a short comic story, 'The Society for Indecency to Naked Animals', about a wealthy man whose legacy was 'to be spent solely for promoting decency and morality through SINA'. Sadly, every magazine Abel submitted it to turned it down.

Four years later Abel was in a hotel room watching a particularly boring pedant bang on about his pet peeve on *The Today Show* when he realised that there was a chance of bringing SINA to life. He dashed off a letter, ostensibly from G. Clifford Prout, Jr, the President of SINA, claiming that he spoke 'to quite a few women's groups who are upset over all the animal nudity in the world. They feel it is driving young people to an early ruin.'

Today's researchers bit at Abel's lure. Abel needed a frontman quickly, and he asked Buck Henry, later to write and act in movies such as *The Graduate* and *Short Cuts*, but then unemployed, to take on the job of impersonating Prout.

So it was that on 27 May 1959 'Prout' and Abel appeared on *Today*, with Prout pleading with decent Americans to put an end to the 'lewd, naked animals' that were left to roam around cities and the countryside and to join the campaign to clothe, for the sake of decency, all animals taller than four inches or longer than six inches. 'Why do cows have their heads down in fields? Not because they're grazing, but because they're hanging their heads in shame.'

Why should animals be denied the same privilege that humans had, they demanded to know, having clothes to hide their nakedness? Claiming that his father's endowment meant that no donations or membership fees were needed, Prout implored anyone wanting to join SINA to write to an address in New York City. The television station was inundated with letters and phone calls, with sackloads of mail soon turning up at the address given.

Although many letters attacked the preposterousness of SINA, a surprising number wanted to jump aboard the SINA bandwagon. Most astonishing of all to Abel was the fact that absolutely everyone took it seriously, whether they were for it or against it. He decided that instead of letting the hoax lie, he would see what happened if he ran with it. Its success far exceeded any possible expectations he had.

Abel and Henry produced leaflets, a logo and a SINA song. While Prout was inundated with calls to appear on television and radio, Abel issued a stream of press releases. He hired people to march in front of the White House with placards and he set up a phone line with the number MOrality-1-1963. One of their press releases talked about the 'presence of 825,000 nude dogs and cats on the West Coast. Los Angeles County in particular has been declared a moral disaster area by SINA National Headquarters and decent citizens are urged to clothe their pets and protect their children from the sight of naked animals.'

He then sent SINA members official-looking summonses which they could hand to animal owners who had the audacity to walk in public with their naked pets. He had the SINA marching band parade through the streets, playing an alarming array of instruments, very badly. According to Abel, 'While it was horrible to hear and ridiculous to see because we were carrying the American flag and looking serious, everyone along the way applauded.'

After SINA received 40,000 letters in the first two years of its life, Vice-President Abel decided to go on a publicity tour of the West Coast. He gave a summons to the guard at San Simeon, William Randolph Heart's mansion with its extensive collection of wild animals, was photographed trying to put trousers on a deer called Bambi in San Francisco's Golden Gate Park Zoo and complained to the head of RCA about the nakedness of Nipper, the dog on the company's record labels.

At one point, the Internal Revenue Service demanded that SINA pay taxes on the £40,000 that Prout Sr had left his son. When Abel's excuses wouldn't fob them off any more, they visited the organisation's offices. In reality, this was nothing more than a broom cupboard in an office block which was used as a receptacle for the large quantity of mail. Through the keyhole could be glimpsed a picture of a dog with trousers on.

When the IRS discovered that SINA operated from a cupboard they got really excited, believing that they had stumbled across a massive case of fraud. In the end, the IRS realised that SINA was a hoax and preferred to leave Abel alone rather than risk making fools of themselves.

Only after Buck Henry had appeared on prime-time CBS news in 1962, being interviewed by the illustrious Walter Cronkite, did the SINA hoax begin to unravel. Although Henry gave a superlative performance as Prout, accompanying his rendition of the SINA marching song on ukelele, he was no longer the unemployed actor he had been three years earlier. Now he was being seen regularly on TV on *The Garry Moore Show*. Unfortunately, *The Garry Moore Show* was a CBS production and Abel realised that to prolong the hoax would jeopardise Henry's job.

Even after SINA had been exposed as a sham, there was life in it yet. One of Abel's lectures was released as a record, a regular newsletter was produced and Abel and his wife Jeanne still occasionally lobbied politicians to clothe animals.

Was it all so ridiculous? Back in 1837, the British Captain Frederick Marryat wrote in his *Diary in America* of the horror of Americans for the word 'leg'. They thought the word terribly indelicate, and preferred 'limb', even when referring to the legs of a table or piano. At one establishment for the education of young ladies, he wrote, the headmistress had dressed all four 'limbs' of a piano in 'modest little trousers, with frills at the bottom of them'. It caused much amusement in Britain at the time, but may in fact have been a spoof – an early version of SINA perhaps.

New York Needs a Mother

With the success of SINA behind him, Abel spent more and more of his time on hoaxes, proving time and time again how true it is that you can fool some of the people any time you want to. He claims to be continually astounded at the average American's total lack of irony. Abel has now turned his hoaxing abilities into a profession, charging companies to carry them out to help with publicity campaigns.

In 1964, Abel aimed for the White House although even he can't have thought that his candidate, the Bronx housewife Yetta Bronstein, would have posed much of a problem to the runaway favourite Lyndon Johnson. His wife Jeanne posed as Yetta, a mumsy type who admitted to knowing nothing about politics but who made that her platform, saying that it was about time governments talked in language ordinary people could understand. She wanted the White House to put a suggestion box on the railings on Pennsylvania Avenue; to only appoint people to the cabinet who had already learned to live with failure; and to lower the voting age to eighteen to give juvenile delinquents something to do. She also planned to put a naked Jane Fonda on stamps, partly as a way to raise money but 'also to give a little pleasure for six cents to people who can't afford *Playboy*'. Her catchy campaign slogan was VOTE FOR YETTA AND WATCH THINGS GET BETTA. She was not nominated.

The following year, Yetta stood for Mayor of New York City, rallying supporters with the cry, 'New York needs a mother.' This time she was a candidate and, although she didn't win, she tried once again for President in 1968, doing no better than four years earlier.

Air on a G-String

In the mid-sixties, the boundaries of sex and censorship were being pushed backwards rapidly. Shortly before the musical *Hair* exposed the public to nudity on the legitimate stage for the first time, a cellist, Charlotte Moorman, had been arrested by the vice squad and convicted of indecent exposure. Her avant-garde concert at the packed Carnegie Hall, *Opera Sextronimique*, had featured her playing topless in a gas mask, with two propellers attached to her breasts.

The mood was right for Abel to enter the fray in 1967. He sent out press releases heralding the American tour of the French chamber group, The Topless String Quartet, 'France's first gift to America since the Statue of Liberty'. Comprising of three violinists and a cellist, instead of the more usual combination, Abel claimed that the toplessness of Madeleine Boucher, Michele Andréa, Maria Tronchet and Gretchen Gansebrust improved the tone of the instruments and that the members of the group were hoping to attract people to their concerts who would normally only listen to pop music.

As with SINA, Abel was getting ahead of himself. But he still managed to convince a *New York Post* reporter that the quartet was genuine, for a piece appeared under the heading 'Bach, Beethoven, Brahms and Bosoms'. It claimed that although topless waitresses, suddenly popular in San Francisco, had been banned in New

York, the French Topless String Quartet would circumvent this by appearing in private, invitation-only, concerts in the city.

After the piece appeared, Abel was inundated with press enquiries. Once again deciding to run with the hoax, Abel and Jeanne chose four models who posed topless in white long skirts and cummerbunds together with their instruments. Bizarrely, the photos also included a topless, bald man billed as Jacques Goldetsky, a pianist. When the *San Francisco Chronicle* ran the photo, other papers having decided against it, Abel was once more swamped with interview requests. When *Life* magazine mentioned the quartet in an issue about the way in which nudity was sweeping the country, giving Abel's address, he received sackfuls of requests for photographs.

To top it all, one of the letters he got was from the great Frank Sinatra, who wanted to sign the group to record on his Reprise label.

Don't Get Mad – Get Even

Abel is perhaps unique among the great practical jokers in that he has been able to make a career out of it without turning it into a TV show. He now teaches seminars on practical joking for 'revenge or self-defence' under the title 'Don't Get Mad – Get Even'. Among other things, he advises people how to get money from debtors who are slow in paying up. 'Say a company owes you $30,000, and they're dragging their feet. Have friends all over the country send a dollar or two to the company, each with a note saying that they heard on a local call-in radio show that the company was strapped for cash and was making a public appeal to pay off their debt to you. Make sure someone writes a note saying, "I'm on welfare, but I believe in honesty. Here's a dollar." It's quicker than hiring a collection agency, and it never fails,' says Abel.

Abel still carries out hoaxes from time to time. It was he who convinced the Washington press that Salman Rushdie was making a surprise visit to the city. He sent out faxes to various newsrooms just twenty minutes before Rushdie was due to appear at the Radisson Hotel. Reporters were sent straight over there, some being withdrawn from a press conference given by Nancy Reagan.

Arriving at the Radisson, the reporters became increasingly annoyed at the delay caused by Rushdie's bodyguards. Not only were the journalists examined with metal detectors, but they were also given a fiercely probing body search by two women karate experts clad in black catsuits. Suddenly Rushdie, or rather a lookalike, appeared with a girlfriend, arguing about whether or not he should abandon all the secrecy. They raced off into a limousine, with the Press giving chase. The whole thing was watched from the wings by the amused Abel.

Amin the Mood for Love

Abel rented a suite at the New York Plaza, installed an Idi Amin lookalike and invited 150 members of the Press to the former dictator's wedding, Amin having recently been expelled from Uganda. Abel made it abundantly clear that Amin was trying to get US citizenship by marrying an American woman. In addition to the reporters, representatives of the FBI and the State Department turned up to witness an obviously coerced woman being married by a clearly intoxicated judge. While the bride and groom argued, Pinkerton agents kept anyone from getting too close.

Other Abel stunts include the announcement of a concert by the Australian All-Dog Symphony Orchestra; passing himself off as Howard Hughes behind a layer of bandages; and making up the win of $35 million in the New York lottery by Lee Chirillo, a woman who celebrated her good fortune by throwing money out of her window. The latter, in 1990, was covered on its front page by the *New York Daily News*.

To Abel's mind, practical jokes should be just that – practical. 'They should help you get what you want. The way I see it, it's better to give ulcers than to get them.'

BARRY HUMPHRIES

So convincing are his creations of Dame Edna Everage and Sir Les Patterson that one could argue that Barry Humphries' professional career has been entirely based upon practical jokes.

He has always been a keen exponent of the art away from the stage too, going right back to his days at art school in Melbourne. He had a fascination with Dadaism and he and some of his fellow students mounted a series of 'impractical jokes, that is to say, jokes that had no rationale, or even satiric point, so they defied explanation'. In his autobiography, *More Please*, Humphries relates the following stories.

Mr Malouf

Although Humphries is proud that these examples of street theatre pre-date *Candid Camera* by some years, he admits that some were deeply misanthropic. Unfortunately, the funniest also happens to be the most misanthropic of all. The group selected as their victim a man named Malouf who kept a small shop near the college campus. It was, apparently, 'the euphony and novelty of his name' that appealed to them.

Malouf's shop contained a wide range of merchandise, but the Dadaists concentrated on just one item. Each day, at a set time, one of them would go into the shop and buy one bar of Lux soap. The routine was exactly the same every day. Mr Malouf would put the change on the counter, it would be scooped up and then the buyer would walk towards the exit, leaving the soap behind. Mr Malouf would yell out, 'Hey, you've forgotten your soap!' only to receive the reply, 'I don't want the soap, I just want to buy it!'

'We would then leave,' says Humphries, 'and join our accomplices, convulsed with childish laughter. This simple but radical variation on a fundamental commercial principle was repeated countless times until Mr Malouf ceased, at last, to mention our failure to take the goods we had paid for.' From time to time, they would enlist a stranger to go in and buy the soap for them. But any joy Mr Malouf might express that he had finally found somebody to take a bar of Lux soap out of the shop would disappear when he heard the final phrase, 'I don't want it, I just want to buy it.'

When the group noticed that Mr Malouf was returning the bar of soap to the stock and that it was now getting rather grubby, they played their *coup de grâce*. One day, having paid for the soap, Humphries actually took it out of the shop with him. But he ran back just a minute later saying, 'I'm sorry. I forgot to leave the soap.'

It was the last time he entered the shop. For what he had taken back was not the soap at all. They had substituted a slab of cooking lard for the soap, identical in size, and concealed in a Lux wrapper.

As with all great practical jokes, it is the contemplation of what might happen that provides the greatest joy. 'We conjectured it would be this that in the normal course of his business Mr Malouf would ultimately sell. The customer would have discovered under unpleasant circumstances, in the bathtub or shower, the inadequacy of his purchase, and would have irately complained to Mr Malouf. He, in turn, relieved to have, at last, an explanation of the strange events in his shop, and assuming a *rational explanation*, would then have unwrapped every cake of soap on his shelves.'

Humphries concludes that, 'We were not surprised to learn soon after that Mr Malouf, severely depressed, had closed his business and moved to another district.' Now he realises that it was a 'not very sensitive thing to do when one considers the feelings of the shopkeeper'. He has kept the name of Malouf alive, though, inventing a Malouf Memorial Library and a Malouf concerto. Over 30 years later the introduction to Les Patterson's *The Traveller's Tool* was written by one Professor Malouf.

A Nice Bit of Chicken

Another piece of Humphries' street theatre involved him disguising himself as a tramp who rummaged around in litter bins. He would plant something like a cooked chicken and a bottle of bubbly in a bin near a bus queue.

'The large queue of staid travellers were at first repelled and alienated by a filthy scavenger and then astonished by the delicious trophies he fished out of the refuse. Wandering away swigging champagne and gnawing on a drumstick I always noticed that a few people detached themselves from the queue and peeked curiously into the bin searching for treasures for themselves.'

Although Humphries realised that more sensible observers would realise that the whole thing had been set up, he liked to think that they would also be asking themselves why he had gone to the trouble of planting them. 'It was a question without an answer.'

Please Give Up Your Seat

As with so many other practical jokers, trains have been a great inspiration to Humphries. On several occasions, his friend John Perry would enter a carriage composed mainly of middle-aged ladies who had been shopping. He had his leg in a plaster cast and wore a neck brace. With his dark glasses, he gave the impression of being blind. Invariably somebody would stand and give him their seat if there was not one free.

After a while, Perry would bring out an old Pianola roll and pretend to read it as if it were Braille, muttering to himself as he did so.

That was the cue for Humphries to appear, clad in black coat and black hat, with long unkempt hair, rings on his fingers and carrying a stick. He would waste no time in making himself as objectionable as possible. Despite the No Smoking signs, he would light up a foul-smelling Turkish cigarette and produce a German newspaper which he would read loudly.

Humphries would glare at Perry from time to time. Then, at the next station, he would suddenly get to his feet, grab the roll of Braille from him and rip it into pieces. Humphries would then start hitting Perry's plaster with his stick, before snatching off his glasses and breaking them underfoot, all the while swearing in cod German mixed with plain English phrases like, 'You blind, crippled Australian bastard.'

Nobody ever moved to help the chap. They were probably too staggered to do so. Nor was there ever a problem with Humphries making his escape, leaving Perry to travel onwards, muttering 'forgive him, forgive him'. At a station further down the line, he would hobble off and join Humphries in the car. 'Our theory,' says Humphries, 'was that events of sufficient strangeness and violence, such as this, would change the lives of those who witnessed them and provide them, perhaps with their most indelible, if mysterious memories.'

The Ashburton Line Affair

In something he refers to as 'The Ashburton Line Affair', Humphries sat himself in a non-smoking first-class compartment on an early morning Melbourne suburban train. At each stop, a waiter resplendent in uniform would pass in a course of breakfast: first it would be grapefruit, then at the next station the cornflakes would come through the window, then the bacon and eggs and finally the coffee.

Not a word passed between Humphries and the waiters. The effects on the other passengers in the compartment is not hard to imagine.

While acting at Stratford East under the direction of Joan Littlewood in the play *A Kayf Up West* Humphries would travel back on the Underground in the company of Jeffrey Bernard. He found considerable enjoyment in asking East-Enders on the tube if they could direct him to the buffet car. In retrospect, he admits, this always seemed more amusing once they had had a few drinks.

Pass the Sick Bag

Humphries was able to enliven the long air journey between Australia and Britain, which he made frequently, with another of his most famous practical jokes. It involved the purchase beforehand of a quantity of Heinz Russian salads. This delicacy is comprised largely of bits of mayonnaisey potato with a few peas and fragments of carrots thrown in. It was the closest approximation Humphries could find to human vomit.

Swallowing a little first, he would feign sudden illness and chuck the salad up into a sick bag. Even that simple act would make other hitherto calm passengers feel slightly queasy. But that was nothing as to their feelings when Humphries would make use of the cutlery provided by the airline for the meal and scoop the salad out of the bag into his mouth, eating it with considerable relish.

He didn't confine himself only to aeroplanes when carrying out this joke, but would sometimes deposit some Russian salad on a pavement. 'Disgusted pedestrians were already giving it a very wide berth, holding their breaths and looking away with watering eyes. Not I, as I knelt beside one of the larger puddles, curdled and carrot-flecked. Drawing a spoon from my top pocket I devoured several mouthfuls, noticing out of the corner of my eye, and with some satisfaction, several people actually being sick at the spectacle.'

Only once, he claims in his autobiography *More Please*, was he ever approached by a policeman while doing this. It was in Fleet Street in the 1960s and, perhaps not too surprisingly, the man 'was too profoundly nauseated to take my name, and as he stood gagging on the salad-splattered pavement I made my escape.'

2

Literature

The Swift Death of Mr Partridge

Jonathan Swift is now best known for having written *Gulliver's Travels*, a book actually taken seriously at the time by many people, thanks to its title page which maintained that the book was a true account of 'Travels into Several Remote Nations of the World.'

Not only a satirist, but also the dean of St Patrick's Cathedral in Dublin, Swift was outraged by the hugely popular almanacs that a former cobbler, John Partridge, produced each year. According to the *Dictionary of National Biography*, Partridge's predictions 'carried the phraseology of equivocation . . . to a pitch of rare perfection'. Packed full of astrological mumbo-jumbo and ads for patent medicines, Partridge's *Merlinus Liberatus* irritated Swift by telling of a future heavily slanted towards the interests of the Whigs, who he hated for their attacks on the Church. Noting Partridge's frequent challenges to his rivals to beat his predictions, Swift set to work.

In 1707, using the pseudonym of Isaac Bickerstaff, Swift produced an almanac with the title *Predictions for the Year 1708* which claimed to be 'written to prevent the people of England from being further imposed upon by vulgar almanac makers'. Bickerstaff said that unlike the vague prophecies offered by other almanacs, he would make much more precise predictions. As biased as Partridge's work, but in the other direction, Bickerstaff's most notable prediction was about John Partridge himself. 'I have consulted the star of his nativity by my own rule, and find he will infallibly die upon 29 March next, about 11 at night, of a raging fever.'

On the 30 March, a pamphlet appeared with the title: *The Accomplishment of the first of Mr Bickerstaff's Predictions. Being an account of the Death of Mr Partridge, the almanac-maker upon the 29th inst.* Lamenting the fact that Bickerstaff was four hours adrift with the time of Partridge's death, it offered, in some considerable detail, an eyewitness account of Partridge's dying hours, which included a deathbed confession from Partridge that he was an imposter.

The pamphlet fooled everybody. The Company of Stationers, the body that controlled publishing, struck Partridge's name from their register and took legal action to make sure that no more almanacs could be published with his name. The man's wife was assumed to be a widow and was inundated with condolences. The Spanish Inquisition even ordered Bickerstaff's works to be burnt, as such accurate forecasts were obviously the work of the devil.

Partridge's attempts to prove that he was alive provided considerable amusement to the reading classes, with Swift fanning the flames by producing another pamphlet by Bickerstaff attacking Partridge's ludicrous attempts to prove that he was still living. It took him some six years to recover the sales he had lost as a result of Swift's efforts.

The Plagiarising Pope

In those days, writers had to be terribly careful of letting people see their work in advance of publication, for literary pirating was rife. When Alexander Pope read to Jonathan Swift a passage from *The Rape of the Lock*, he was overheard by another friend, Thomas Parnell, a man with a prodigious memory.

Parnell crept off and, able to recall Pope's work with clarity, translated it into Latin, setting it down on parchment. Emboldened by Swift's favourable response,

Pope later decided to read his new work to a wider group of friends. He was understandably dismayed when Parnell said that it seemed terribly familiar and disappeared for a while before returning with a dusty old piece of parchment which bore an uncanny resemblance to what Pope was trying to pass off as an original piece of writing. Pope was horrified that such a thing could have happened, and was absolutely furious when he discovered that he hadn't been guilty of unintentional plagiarism after all.

Going Out in Style

When he was dying, the nineteenth-century writer Jippensha Ikku handed several parcels to his followers, together with the request that they put them, unopened, on his funeral pyre.

After the solemn prayers had been said, the parcels were duly placed around Ikku's corpse and the bonfire was lit. Within moments, the mourners were running for cover. The parcels were filled with firecrackers.

Maupassant Passes an Uneasy Night

The French short story writer Guy de Maupassant was extremely fond of practical joking. Eventually, it had got to the stage where he had carried out jokes on all his acquaintances and even Maupassant recognised that they were getting a little sick of it.

He was on the lookout for some retaliatory hoaxing when he went to stay with some friends for a weekend's hunting at their retreat in Picardy. Some sixth sense told him that something was afoot and that they had been planning some great hoax with him as the intended victim. Well, they would have to get up early in the morning to catch him out.

Maupassant examined his food very closely during the evening meal, eating much less than he would normally do. He also took great care that whatever was in his glass was served to others too.

When nothing happened, he surmised that the practical joke, in whatever form it would take, must have been arranged in his bedroom. He examined the room closely, but could find no indication of what his friends might have planned for him. He put a chair up against the door and prepared to retire.

That was when it all became clear to him. If nothing else in the room was sabotaged, then it must surely be the bed. Despite minute examination, he could find nothing wrong with it, but he wasn't going to be caught out that easily. He took the bedclothes off the bed and settled down for the night on the floor.

A most uncomfortable night it was too. The floor was hard and with Maupassant expecting something startling to happen at any moment he got little sleep. He was woken by a terrible crash and found himself soaked by scalding hot water. The servant bringing him his morning tea had obviously not expected to find the guest lying on the floor and had tripped over him.

His hosts had not planned a practical joke at all. It was simply Maupassant's fear of them revenging themselves upon him that led to such a rude awakening.

Happy Days

The American critic and satirist H.L. Mencken was, despite his highbrow reputation, rather fond of the odd bit of leg-pulling. A whole chapter in his autobiography *Happy Days* is devoted to practical joking. He inherited his keenness for it from his father who, together with his brother, invented a fictitious third brother Fred, who was a clergyman. Fred was considered to be a disgrace to the family, because their father was a devout atheist.

The brothers took care to warn visitors that they mustn't mention Fred in the company of their father, who was terribly sensitive about the black sheep of the family. Fred became an ongoing joke with an increasingly successful career, as the brothers recounted how he had become chaplain of the American Senate; how he had converted thousands of unbelievers in just one week when he visited Chicago; and how he had subsequently been elevated to become a bishop. Mencken claimed that fifty years later, he was sometimes still asked by people what had become of his Uncle Fred.

On another occasion Mencken's father bought a summer home in Mount Washington and convinced the local residents that he planned on turning the place into a hog-breeding farm. He even went as far as drawing up blueprints to show the protesting residents.

The Bathtub's Birthday

Mencken was less devoted to the cause than his father. His most famous hoax horrified him when he discovered that it was not only taken seriously, but that it was impossible to convince people that it was actually a joke, despite numerous attempts to do so.

It was back in 1917 that Mencken wrote an article in the *New York Evening Mail* headed 'A Neglected Anniversary', bemoaning the fact that no-one was celebrating the 75th anniversary of the introduction of the bathtub into the United States. 'Not a plumber fired a salute or hung out a flag,' lamented Mencken. 'Not a governor proclaimed a day of prayer. Not a newspaper called attention to the day.'

According to Mencken, one Adam Thompson, a wealthy merchant, had installed the first tub, made of mahogany and lined with sheet lead, in his home in Cincinnati in December 1842 after he took to the idea when on holiday in England. Thompson refined it so that it could be filled through pipes emanating from a tank, rather than needing the help of a servant. He held a launch party, inviting some of his friends round to try it.

Like any new invention, it met with hostility from many quarters, with some doctors believing it to be a health hazard and other critics labelling it, 'An obnoxious toy from England, designed to corrupt the democratic simplicity.'

Although many states tried to suppress bathtubs, said Mencken, by imposing taxes on the owners of the infernal machines – with Boston actually making their use illegal for a time – once President Millard Filmore installed one in the White House in 1851 it achieved respectability. Eight years later, the medical profession abandoned its earlier opposition when the American Medical Association reported that 55 per cent of its members regarded bathing in a tub as harmless, from a medical point of view, with 20 per cent of the more enlightened members actually believing it to be beneficial.

To Mencken's horror, what seemed to him to be a perfectly obvious spoof intended to provide a bit of cheer in the midst of the war, was taken seriously in many quarters. So contrite were people at neglecting such a pivotal event in American history that Mencken's facts were soon being repeated verbatim in newspapers, magazines and even encyclopaedias.

Nine years later, Mencken admitted to the hoax in his newspaper column, which was syndicated throughout the United States. When Mencken saw that the bathtub story was *still* being treated as true in some quarters, he tried again. Yet even though the *Boston Herald* ran the second confession, only three weeks later it reprinted his original article as gospel on the matter of bathtubs.

Nothing Mencken did could curb the bathtub hoax being treated as fact. In 1933 a book on 750 great American inventions repeated the whole tale. In 1935, the *New York Times* included Mencken's information in a piece and the *New Yorker* referred to it. So did the *New Statesman*, the *Military Review* and the *Herald Tribune* and many, many others. In 1952 President Truman referred to the 'facts' in a speech in Philadelphia as an illustration of the great progress made in public health in America, while *CBS News* mentioned them in 1976. It is said that, even now, the information crops up regularly in different publications.

Mencken claimed that his reason for writing the original article was, 'simply to have some harmless fun in war days. It never occurred to me that it would be taken seriously.' In the end, he realised that he would never convince some people that what he had written was not true so he gave up trying.

The Cruise of the Kawa

In the wake of World War I, the American reading public's tastes understandably tended towards escapism. The publisher George Palmer Putnam, however, became increasingly irritated by the enormous success of books, usually appallingly written and often frequently unbelievable, about adventures in the South Seas.

Putnam was a dab hand at publicity stunts, as he was to show later when he helped promote the career of his wife, flyer Amelia Earhart. Together with humorist George S. Chappell, in 1921 the two concocted a book to test what they felt was the enormous gullibility of book buyers. Ostensibly written by the explorer Walter E. Traprock, it was called *The Cruise of the Kawa* and, like any good publisher, Putnam arranged for a series of articles to appear in newspapers in advance of publication. These told of Traprock discovering a new group of Polynesian Islands and whetted the public's appetite for the book itself.

Putnam himself wrote an introduction: 'Uninfluenced by professional self-interest, unshaken by our genuine admiration for its predecessors, and despite our inherent inclination toward modest conservatism, we unhesitatingly record the conviction that *The Cruise of the Kawa* stands pre-eminent in the literature of modern exploration – a supreme, superlative epic of the South Seas.'

Although some reviewers clearly recognised that the book was a spoof, many others did not, despite its quite outrageous content. It told of an expedition of five explorers who were blown by a tropical storm to unknown islands, which they christened The Filbert Islands, after the great number of filbert nut trees there. So luxuriant was their growth that the islanders were in danger of being struck by falling nuts, and had developed umbrella-like devices, called 'naa-naas' or 'taa-taas', out of panjandrus leaves to protect themselves from the nut showers.

The explorers 'went native', with four of them marrying half-clad Filbertine maidens, only to discover that they had brought disease with them to the islands. In the name of decency all but one decided to return home, the other remaining to wave goodbye to his colleagues as they returned to America.

Even the most outlandish details seemed not to tip many people off to the nature of the hoax. They appeared to swallow even such ludicrous things as a photograph of a nest, which showed four dice nestling inside, the dots perfectly visible. The caption read: 'This is without

question the most extraordinary picture which has ever been taken of any natural history subject. It corroborates in most convincing manner the author's claim to the discovery of the wonderful fatu-liva bird with its unique feat of laying square eggs. Here we see the eggs themselves in all the beauty of their cubical form and quaint marking. Sceptics have said that it would be impossible to lay a square egg. To which the author is justly entitled to say: "The camera never lies!" Other examples of wildlife included crabs big enough to pull boats and the gentle ooza snake which lived off coconut milk.

On page 147, Traprock's other books were listed. They included such titles as *Through Borneo on a Bicycle, Around Russia on Roller Skates, How to Explore, and What*, and *Curry-Dishes for Moderate Incomes*. Only the last was said to be still in print and it cost $200. There was also an advertisement calling for people who wanted to sign up with Traprock for his next cruise: 'See the cute cannibals. Excursion rates for round trip with stops at all important islands. Everybody's doing it. Don't be a back number.' Twelve people wanted to sign on.

The book was an enormous success. The Chamber of Commerce in Derby, where Dr Traprock was reportedly from, asked him to speak, as did the editorial board of *The National Geographic Magazine*.

Putnam was delighted with the outcome. Not only had he amply demonstrated the gullibility of the American public, but he had also managed to kill the genre of South Sea books that he hated so much almost stone dead.

The Greatest Liar of All Time

It was by no means the first time that a book had been published telling whopping tales of adventure and exploration. Back in 1371 Sir John Mandeville earned himself the title of 'The Greatest Liar of All Time' when he published his book *Travels*. Largely plagiarised from a seventh-century friar, Mandeville wasn't above making up some stuff himself.

In the Andaman Islands, according to him, '. . . there are ugly folk without heads, who have eyes in each shoulder; their mouths are round, like a horseshoe, in the middle of their chest . . . In another isle there are ugly fellows whose upper lip is so big that when they sleep in the sun they cover all their faces with it.'

Not Woman's Hour's Day

In 1925, *The Diary of a Young Lady of Fashion in 1764/5* was published. It was a spirited journal of Cleone Knox, an eighteenth-century Irish society girl. The book received favourable reviews and was extremely popular. Lord Darling, a prominent judge, said that it would rank with Pepys as one of the classic diaries in English literature.

That must have been very gratifying to Magdalen King-Hall, the novelist whose works include *The Wicked Lady*, for she had written it. Only in 1967, when it was republished, did she pen an introduction saying how, when bored at the age of eighteen, she had scribbled a few research notes on eighteenth-century Irish society on the back of an envelope while in a public library before writing what turned out to be a bestseller.

In the early eighties, the book was adapted for broadcast on Radio Four, the BBC apparently unaware that it was not genuine. They must have short memories at Radio Four for in 1994 it turned up again, being serialised on *Woman's Hour*. This time, the actress Caroline Harris introduced it as a major literary find. She had come across it in a London bookshop, she said, and was convinced by the intricate period detail and the many footnotes that it was genuine.

Sadly for *Woman's Hour*, many of their listeners were only too well aware of the book's history and wasted no time in ringing the BBC to put the record straight.

Jeeves and the Practical Joke

The young men (and several of the young women) who grace the pages of P.G. Wodehouse's remarkable novels adore practical jokes although they are, in the main, relatively unsophisticated evergreens such as the apple-pie bed and the hot foot.

There is, for instance, the time when The Drones Club *en masse* took revenge on a chap they didn't like by substituting a slightly larger but otherwise identical top hat for the original specimen, then replacing it with a slightly smaller one, and then alternating the three headpieces until its owner consulted his doctor about the way in which his head appeared to be expanding and contracting. It's a tale which was tried out for real on many occasions on the Stock Exchange floor in those days when hats were an essential part of the city uniform.

In *Jeeves and the Yule-Tide Spirit*, Bertie Wooster tells Jeeves of the terrible time that Tuppy Glossop bet him that he couldn't swing himself across the swimming-bath of the Drones Club after dinner by the ropes and rings. 'I took him on and was buzzing along in great style until I came to the last ring,' said Wooster. 'And then I found that this fiend in human shape had looped it back against the rail.' This left poor Bertie '. . . hanging in the void with no means of getting ashore to my home and loved ones. There was nothing for it but to drop into the water.'

Like so many other victims, Bertie makes the mistake of thinking that he is bright enough to get back at his tormentor while staying at the same country house as Tuppy Glossop. He is 'aided' by Bobbie Wickham, something of a veteran practical joker, and with whom Bertie is smitten. She tells him that at her school they used to put a darning-needle on the end of a long stick and use it to puncture the hot-water bottles of sleeping girls. Despite Jeeves's clucking, Bertie tries it on the sleeping form that he believes to be Tuppy Glossop, only to find it is instead Tuppy's uncle, Sir Roderick Glossop, a man who already believes Wooster to be a lunatic. The lovelight dies in Bertie's eyes when he hears that Bobbie Wickham put Tuppy up to carrying out the same hot-water bottle trick on Bertie that very same night.

While many of Wodehouse's stories are justifiably well known, what is less well known is that many of the tales in Wodehouse's books are based on real events that took place among the gay blades of London society around the turn of the century, principally at the Pelican Club. I am assured by Wodehouse historian N.T.P. Murphy, who has made a particular study of the way in which Wodehouse weaved factual tales into his works of fiction, that the story about Bertie dangling from the ropes above the Drones Club swimming-pool took place at the Bath Club in Dover Street, bombed out of existence in 1941.

Joe the Joker

There are many practical jokers in the pages of Damon Runyon, whose stories of Broadway and its lower strata citizens have delighted readers for years and led to such spin-offs as *Guys and Dolls*. However, the sense of humour is often somewhat vicious.

Joe the Joker 'has the most wonderful sense of humour of anybody in this town' according to the storyteller. In fact, Joe's idea of fun is to have a piece of Mindy's Limburger cheese in his palm when he shakes hands or to give someone a hot foot. A hot foot, perhaps more of an American than a British prank, involves sneaking up 'behind some guy who is standing around thinking of not much, and stick a paper match in his shoe between the sole and the upper along about where his little toe ought to be, and then light the match. By and by the guy will feel a terrible pain in his foot, and will start stamping around, and hollering, and carrying on generally, and it is always a most comical sight and a wonderful laugh to one and all to see him suffer.'

Such shenanigans require stealth on the part of the hot footer, which Joe the Joker has, as well as the capability of taking care of himself should the victim turn out to be substantially built. He still makes a mistake in giving a hot foot to Frankie Ferocious, though, a man with no discernible sense of humour. As a result Frankie renews an old acquaintanceship with Joe's wife Rosa. Before long, she has left Joe and soon business partners of both Joe the

Joker and Frankie Ferocious are ending up strangled in sacks and mown down by machine-guns.

When Rosa discusses divorce, Joe the Joker plans to get his own back on Frankie and tells the storyteller how he has arranged to be delivered to him in a sack, a mode of transport unwillingly employed by many people visiting Frankie. But instead of the dead meat Frankie will be expecting, Joe will be very much alive and will have two guns with him.

Tipped off beforehand about the plan, Frankie doesn't open the sack. Instead he pops it full of lead.

Inside is Rosa.

The Incomparable Joker Max

The caricaturist, dandy and writer Max Beerbohm, best known for his delightful novel *Zuleika Dobson*, was a great proponent of pranks, carrying out the making of apple-pie beds well into his twilight years.

He took great pleasure in altering and faking books. Even though he put much effort into this, he sometimes showed the amended works to nobody but was content to leave them in his own library. One of his most painstaking efforts was when he got hold of a book of poems by Herbert Trench, a poet Beerbohm found incredibly dull. Among the poems was a discussion between Apollo and a mariner which Beerbohm decided to change. He obliterated the 'H' at the beginning of every word in the passage, replacing it with an apostrophe. With the poem sounding as if it was Cockney, he sent it to the horrified Trench, claiming to have come across the hitherto undiscovered edition in his travels.

He once found a set of photographs of George Bernard Shaw in his younger years and amended each of them carefully, making a nose bigger here, a mouth more ridiculous there, and adding some interesting squints to the eyes. He distributed them among friends, asking them to forward the photographs to Shaw as if they had come from fans who wanted autographs.

According to Beerbohm's biographer Lord David Cecil, he once changed all the labels on the roses in a lady's garden. As she was showing them off proudly to some people, she was horrified to see that all her prized flowers were now named after famous criminals such as Crippen.

The Sex Life of the Polyp

The great American humorist Robert Benchley was probably the keenest japester around the famed Algonquin Round Table. It was he who sent a cable to the editor of the *New Yorker* magazine, Harold Ross, from Venice reading: 'STREETS FLOODED. PLEASE ADVISE.'

He was for some time the magazine's drama critic. One particularly dull Broadway first night was enlivened by Benchley when the telephone rang on the stage. 'I think that's for me,' Benchley said loudly, making good his escape.

A Chip Off the Old Benchley

After one particularly boozy session with his fellow wits at the Algonquin, he ordered the uniformed man outside the front door to get him a taxi. 'Now see here,' said the man haughtily, 'I happen to be a Rear Admiral in the United States Navy.' 'In that case,' replied Benchley without a pause, 'get me a battleship.'

A Case of High Spirits

On one occasion, Benchley invited the long-suffering manager of the Algonquin, Frank Case, to dinner at his home. Case was horrified to discover that all Benchley's towels, soap, cutlery, plates, napkins and so on carried the name of the Algonquin. Conspiring with Case's staff, Benchley had had a vanload of the stuff transferred to his house while the manager was occupied elsewhere.

Where's the Davenport?

Like so many others, Benchley first got a taste for hoaxes while at college. He attended Harvard and was walking one day with a fellow student through Louisburg Square, one of Boston's most elegant areas, when inspiration hit him.

Benchley knocked on the door of one of the houses in the square and told the maid that they had come to fetch the davenport. Although having no instructions about it, the flustered maid, faced with Benchley's determined attitude, let the pair into the house. They picked up the nearest davenport and marched straight across the square with it to another house. Knocking on the door there, they told the surprised maid, 'We've brought the davenport. Where shall we put it?' She showed them to the living-room, where they left the davenport and departed.

Quiet as the Tomb

In later years, Benchley stopped one night beside the tomb of Ulysses S. Grant in New York. As it was so late, the tomb was closed. Benchley found an envelope in his pocket, scribbled something on it and jammed it under the door.

'Please leave 2 quarts Grade A and 1 pint whipping cream. U.S.G.'

Just What the Doctor Ordered

When Benchley was being treated for mild pneumonia, he took against his doctor's bedside manner. Cutting open a pillow, he slapped paste on his bottom and stuck the feathers on.

When the doctor arrived for his daily visit and enquired how the patient was, Benchley claimed to be feeling rather peculiar. He rolled onto his front and pulled down the bedclothes, displaying the feathers in all their finery.

Thurber and Ross

With many of America's funniest writers regularly contributing to the magazine, the *New Yorker* was frequently the scene of high jinks. James Thurber was one of editor Harold Ross's main thorns in his side. He once rolled a water cooler bottle along the corridor outside Ross's office. Ross screamed out to someone, 'Go and find out what the hell is happening. But don't tell me.'

The ordinary chaos was compounded by almost perpetual building work. The noise of hammering and drilling infuriated the writers working there. Thurber was discovered one day hanging a sign outside the lift that read: 'ALTERATIONS GOING ON AS USUAL DURING BUSINESS.'

Discovering once that the ever present workmen had left a telephone booth lying on the floor, Thurber stretched out full length inside it as if he were in a coffin, his arms folded on his chest.

In the midst of an editorial conference, Ross was disturbed by Thurber who rushed in to tell him that somebody had stolen his jacket. Ross assured him that it was probably only mislaid and that it would soon turn up. Moments later Thurber was back. This time he was naked to the waist: 'Somebody stole my shirt, too,' he moaned.

The *New Yorker* was graced on its front cover by a drawing of a dandy about town known as Eustace Tilley. Ross had him listed in the Manhattan telephone directory and was overjoyed when this fictitious character was once sent a tax demand.

How Greene Was My Entry

The novelist Graham Greene was extremely partial to practical jokes. Greene once wrote to *The New Statesman* saying how delighted he was that Mr John Smith had won second prize in a contest in the magazine the week earlier for the best parody of Graham Greene's writing. He expressed regret, though, that two of the other entrants, a

Mr Joe Doakes and Mr William Jones, had not received prizes as well. Greene owned up to sending in all three entries himself, using prose from some of his unpublished works.

Greene Grow the Pranks Oh

Greene's friend Michael Meyer, the translator of many classic Strindberg and Ibsen plays, recalls that Greene was much more mischievious than the popular perception of him would have it. A poor Scrabble player, he cheerfully cheated by inventing words, although it did little to help him win.

But he could not be held back when it came to practical joking. He was fond of a game which involved opening the telephone directory at around midnight, picking a name at random and then ringing the number. The winner of the game was the person who kept their victim talking for the longest time. It was always Greene who won.

He told Meyer that he had once found another Graham Greene who lived in Golders Green. Greene rang him, demanding to know: 'Are you Graham Greene?'

'That is my name, but . . .'

'Are you the man who writes these filthy novels?'

'No, I am a retired solicior.'

'I'm not surprised you're ashamed to confess you're the author of this muck.'

'No, I assure you . . .'

'If I'd written them I'd at least have the guts to admit it.'

According to Meyer, Greene made several calls to the man, assuming a different voice on each occasion, until the chap eventually sought out the haven of an ex-directory number.

Greene was also a hoarder of other people's visiting cards, which he would later use in various ways. One of his favourites was to send a cryptic or sometimes obscene invitation via a waiter to a friend of his in a restaurant who had not yet spotted him.

Playwright Joe Orton was also something of a practical joker, although his pranks tended to be of a less innocent nature. Indeed, he actually spent six months in prison for it. He later claimed that it was that time in jail that had given his writing detachment and caused everything to click into place.

Shortly after Orton and his companion Kenneth Halliwell moved to Islington in 1959, the local libraries began to find their books being doctored. There were collages pasted on top of the dust jackets, jacket blurbs were amended and became slightly obscene and some books acquired new illustrations. For two years, the pair carried on undetected. But after comparing the new jacket blurbs with something they had managed to get hold of written on Orton's typewriter, the police swooped. They found over 70 library books in Orton and Halliwell's flat, as well as 1653 illustration plates while another 2000 taken from art books were pasted on the wall.

It was in the days before Orton was published or staged. 'I was really occupying myself with these library books,' he said in an interview almost ten years later. 'It used to be a full-time job. I would stagger home from libraries with books which I'd borrowed and also stolen . . . I used to stand in corners after I'd smuggled the doctored books back into the library and then watch people read them. It was very funny.'

It was a view held by Jim Connell, the librarian in charge of Islington Central Library at the time. 'I had officially to be appalled. As a private individual I was highly amused. They were only mildly obscene. If I had been younger I might have done them myself.'

Fortunately, the Islington Central Library kept a few examples of the books 'mutilated' by Orton and Halliwell. So many of them vanished over time as Orton's reputation grew that visitors can now only view photographs of the remaining 44 collage dust jackets and the one rude jacket blurb. Even the photographs are kept in a locked room and can be viewed only by making an appointment.

Love from Edna

Orton and Halliwell also invented Edna Wellthorpe, a woman who wrote a succession of preposterous letters of complaint. When Crosse and Blackwell heard from her that a tin of blackberry pie filling had almost poisoned her Aunt Lydia, they not only apologised but sent back a case of blackberry pie filling cans.

The Ritz Hotel received a letter from a distraught Edna, claiming that she had left her moroccan leather handbag in the lounge: 'The bag contained a Boots folder of snaps of Mrs Sullivan and me in risqué poses. You will naturally appreciate that neither of us wish such things to fall into the wrong hands.' The Ritz replied that they were saddened to report that no such handbag could be found.

Crossed Lines

Canadian novelist Mordecai Richler was another who loved playing pranks on the phone. Returning recently to Britain, where he had earlier spent twenty years of his life, he was dismayed to find the phone system much improved.

Back in the sixties he regularly sat back at the end of a day's work with a whisky and picked up the phone in the hope that there would be a crossed line. He once overheard a man calling from a pub ask a woman if she could get out that night. 'Not tonight,' she said. 'It's his birthday.'

'Just for a quick drink and a cuddle,' he pleaded, but was told that it wasn't possible.

At that point, Richler coughed.

'Was that you, luv?'

'I thought it was you.'

'Hang up immediately.'

Richler was once rung by his agent to say that a Canadian film producer was in town and wanted to know his home phone number. Richler, who knew the man, rang his hotel but a stranger answered the phone with the request: 'I want fried eggs, sausages and coffee.'

'I'm afraid there's been a misunderstanding,' said Richler.

'There's been no misunderstanding. When I wakes up, I wakes up hungry. I want two eggs, sausages, coffee and don't forget the toast.'

By now Richler was enjoying himself. 'You can't have it.'

'What's that?'

'You heard me.'

'I wish to speak to the manager at once.'

'I am the manager.'

'Then I'm coming right down to punch you in the nose.'

'I'll be waiting for you, you little prick,' said Richler, replacing the receiver contentedly.

More or Lessing

In 1981 the first novel of Jane Somer, *The Diary of a Good Neighbour*, made the rounds of the publishing houses. It was rejected by all but one. At Michael Joseph senior editor Phillippa Harrison thought that it had echoes of the young Doris Lessing.

Only when she contacted the author did she discover why. It actually *was* by Doris Lessing, writing under an assumed name. Yet only one of the publishers appeared to recognise her talent. Lessing's own publishers, Jonathan Cape and Granada, were among those that had turned it down.

Michael Joseph agreed to publish the book under the name of Jane Somer. They sent the book to a score of reviewers, puffing it as an example of promising new writing talent. Only two reviewed it favourably, despite the fact that several of those attacking it were avowed Doris Lessing fans.

Sadly for Michael Joseph the public didn't seem terribly interested in Jane Somer either. *The Diary of a Good Neighbour* sold far fewer copies than it would have done if Doris Lessing's name had been on the cover.

Only three years later did Lessing come clean about the hoax.

In 1975, the American journalist Chuck Ross sent to fourteen publishers and literary agents the first 21 pages of Jerzy Kosinski's book *Steps*, which had won the National Book Award and had sold 400,000 copies in paperback. Not only did they all turn it down but Random House, which actually published the book, sent out a standardised letter to do so.

In 1990, *Punch* magazine decided to see just how on the ball British publishers were. Copies were made of five different works and popped in the post.

Under the pseudonym of Thomas Jeremy, Adolf Hitler sent a detailed synopsis of *Mein Kampf* together with four closely-typed pages of the book itself. Titled *Nation and Race*, the letter from its author said: 'I have now finished my life's work. Finally, I am ready. Before, I did not dare show my work to prying eyes. You never know just where your enemies may lurk. Here you see but the tip of the ice-floe. Everywhere there are those who would spy and frustrate my aims. You will make money. Together we could change the world. Yours in the knowledge of final success.'

Sadly for Adolf, no-one seemed to recognise his genius, evil or not. 'The European inhabitant of the American continent,' he wrote, 'who has remained racially pure and unmixed, will remain the master as long as he doesn't fall a victim to the defilement of the blood.' Virago turned it down flat because he wasn't a woman. 'But good luck elsewhere,' they wished him. Grafton sent similar good wishes but, like Hodder & Stoughton, it was a most definite no.

Bizarrely, Hitler even got turned down by two vanity publishers. These are firms to which potential 'authors' pay money to have their books published. Usually the writers end up heavily out of pocket with little to show for it other than a loft full of unsold books. Both The Book Guild and Dorrance showed him the door. Fortunately for the great dictator, Adelphi Press, another vanity publisher, reckoned that his work '. . . shows a novel approach to what is basically a philosophical theme. The writing is good and the subject matter interesting.' Not only that, but he was told that, 'No man has the right to curse the darkness unless he is prepared to light a candle.'

The first ever Booker Prize winner, P.H. Newby, had his book *Something To Answer For* submitted under the pseudonym of R. Perkins. Sadly, few people remember Newby now and even fewer publishers were interested in his book, with Hutchinson, Virago, Futura and Hodder & Stoughton all rejecting it outright. Grafton asked to see the whole manuscript as did its original publishers, Faber & Faber, although they said that 'the chances of publication are probably quite small'. Vanity publishers Dorrance turned it down, but The Book Guild seemed more interested.

Sixties LSD guru Timothy Leary's bestselling *The Politics of Ecstasy* received absolutely no interest whatsoever from the regular publishers, with Penguin, Secker & Warburg, Hodder & Stoughton and Virago all giving it the thumbs down. Only a couple of the vanity publishers showed any sign of wanting it. One of them, New York-based Vantage wanted to add his book to their list, which included 'bestselling' titles like *Being a Fire Fighter isn't Just Squirting Water* and *Letters I Wish I'd Mailed to the Man Who Divorced Me to Marry a Waitress*.

Jewel of the Seven Stars was written by eight-year-old Daniel Silverton and he had already been turned down by a good many publishers, despite his novel being packed full of stuff about football, spies and aeroplanes. He had no more luck this time. Grafton regretted that 'the market for this type of fiction is very difficult at the moment' while Viking were sorry to inform him that their list was 'extremely full over the next couple of years'. Even the vanity publishers were a bust, although Gollancz sent a letter giving Peter guidance if he wanted to follow a career as a crime writer.

Samuel Beckett had no more luck with his book *Stirrings Still* despite the accompanying letter from R. White: 'As I heard I wrote. A single page appeared. Then more. I send them. Shall you publish them?' The answer was no. 'Not something for our list,' said Secker & Warburg, while Viking thought, 'Prose of this type is best appreciated in small, one-off pieces, but to read this over a long period of time proves difficult, as it can be quite hard to maintain the rhythm and the flow of thoughts.'

Not even the vanity publishers would touch Beckett. Hodder & Stoughton claimed to be considering it at one point but then said that they couldn't publish it 'successfully in book form. I found the writing very unusual and idiosyncratic. I found the sentences distracting and felt that they pulled the reader back.'

Alone among all the publishers who received manuscripts, John Calder, who actually published Beckett, recognised what they had been sent. They wrote back:

Even a page
Can plage
But plageing Beckett
Can only wreck it.

Let Them Eat Locks

The Sitwells once had as a guest the architect Sir Edwin Landseer Lutyens, the man responsible for the great line: 'This piece of cod passeth all understanding.' While staying with them, Lutyens pulled some horsehair out from a fraying sofa and wrapped it in a piece of paper before hiding it away in a desk drawer. It was many years before Osbert Sitwell discovered it. On the paper was written: 'A lock from Marie Antoinette's hair, cut from her head ten minutes after execution.'

Betjeman Plays Dead

John Betjeman was a lifelong practical joker. As a small boy, he used to lie beside the road pretending to be dead to see what people driving past in cars would do. Such japes weren't restricted to his childhood. At the end of the twenties, he was a teacher at Heddon Court, a preparatory school, where he was a particular favourite with the boys.

Faced with the problem of keeping the boys amused on Sunday afternoons, he would often take them to the nearby road where he would get them to hide in bushes while he lay down on the road as if he had been run over. When a bus or other vehicle came along, he would wait until people climbed out to rescue him, at which point he would jump up and run away into the bushes. The boys apparently enjoyed this not only for the spectacle, but also for the betting that went on, with peppermint creams changing hands as they wagered on whether the vehicles would stop or not.

The Conkering Poet

When he was in his mid-twenties, Betjeman went with his friend Alan Pryce-Jones to the Geological Museum, in those days located in Piccadilly. They were delighted by the sheer banality of some of the exhibits, such as a 'section of cast-iron pipe nearly choked with calcerous deposit from water derived from the Oolites and supplied to the City of Bath'.

Betjeman took advantage of an unlocked display case to add his own exhibit. Searching through his pockets, he found a conker and placed it in the case, together with a card beside it that read: 'Mount Prospect Bequest. Horse chestnut found at Mount Prospect and presented by Viscount Mount Prospect, 1892.'

Pryce-Jones wrote to Betjeman some seven months later to tell him that the conker was still there. As it was somewhat dusty, he had taken out his handkerchief and cleaned it. It is reckoned that the horse chestnut remained there for years until the building was demolished to make way for Simpson's department store.

Later in life, Betjeman took to hiding a stuffed crocodile in the long grass in his garden to frighten unwary guests.

Christopher Who?

Mark Twain loved practical jokes (*see* Chapter 9). In print, many were carried out in his books by Huck Finn, but Twain also loved them in real life.

When on a tour of Europe, later recounted in his book *The Innocents Abroad*, he delighted in making life a misery for the stream of guides that he felt dogged his every step. In Genoa, his party was shown a letter of Christopher Columbus's.

Twain and his companion drove their guide to distraction by claiming never to have heard of this chap Columbus. Did he take them for fools? They disparaged Columbus's handwriting, saying that there were fourteen-year-old kids back home who could write better than that. When told that Columbus was the man who discovered America they roared with laughter and said that whoever discovered America, it certainly wasn't him. Was the man still alive? Why didn't he use a decent fountain pen? Why hadn't the imposter been exposed before now?

Me Feet's Too Big

J.M. Barrie once called Peter Davies, the young son of a friend of his, into his study at night. Davies found him sitting in a darkened room in a despondent mood, complaining that there was something wrong with his feet.

'Glancing down,' said Davies, 'I saw to my horror that his feet were bare and swollen to four or five times their natural size. For several seconds I was deceived, and have never since forgotten the terror that filled me, until I realised that the feet were artificial, made of the waxed linen masks are made of, and that I had been most successfully hoaxed.'

Farrago at Virago

Virago, the publisher specialising in women's writings, received a collection of short stories called *Down the Road, Worlds Away* in 1987. They had already made an appeal for books from young writers and those from ethnic minorities, feeling that they were under-represented in the publishing world. So they were delighted with this book, penned by Rahila Khan, a British Indian teenager.

Without ever meeting Khan, whose work was sent to them by a intermediary because she was so shy, they printed up a staggering 10,000 copies of the book. Then they discovered that the stories had been written by Toby Forward, an Anglican vicar. Horrified to find a male – and a white, middle-class male what's more – sullying their catalogue, they withdrew all 10,000 copies of *Down the Road, Worlds Away*.

Naked Came a Stranger

Whether *Naked Came a Stranger* by Penelope Ashe is a work of literature is a matter of opinion, but it is certainly the most successful publishing hoax ever seen. Like Putnam before him, *Newsday* columnist Mike McGrady was horrified by the standard of writing in the bonkbusters that became popular in the sixties, with authors like Harold Robbins and Jacqueline Susann topping the best-seller lists.

As with so many other hoaxers, McGrady thought that he would be able to highlight just how dreadful these books really were by spoofing the genre, writing a book in the style of such authors but taking it so far over the top that publishers would recoil from such novels for ever more. Despite being a journalist on a popular newspaper, McGrady sadly misjudged the tastes both of American publishers and of the American reading public at large.

His idea was that he and 23 of his fellow *Newsday* journalists should each write a chapter of a bonkbuster concerning a sex-mad radio talk-show hostess who sets out to revenge herself on her adulterous husband by bedding all the married men in her town. Although their number even included a Pulitzer Prize-winning reporter, Gene Goltz, the authors were told that, 'Fine writing would be *ruthlessly* expurgated' with 'true excellence in writing . . . blue-pencilled into oblivion.' Each chapter had to have at least two sex scenes, which should be as kinky as possible. The initial writing of the book took just a fortnight.

McGrady got his sister-in-law, Billie Young, to pass herself off as the author, Penelope Ashe. In only a few weeks she had sold the book to publisher Lyle Stuart, who apparently took it at its face value. For McGrady, the hoax had succeeded, so he confessed all to Stuart.

To his surprise, Stuart told him that it was every bit as 'good' as others in the field and so he wanted to publish it anyway. What's more, he was so convinced that McGrady had been right in his original opinion that he went somewhat over the top in promoting the book, spending an amazing $50,000 on plugging it. He arranged for what was, by the standards of the time, an incredibly saucy dust jacket featuring a nude woman.

Mrs Young, a well-endowed woman, appeared on chat shows as Penelope Ashe sporting a deep décolletage. Her pronouncements were well in line with the spirit of the book, perhaps her deepest insight into modern problems being that 'the trouble in America is that most men and women can't communicate on a mattress'.

The book was taken seriously. Some reviewers damned it, but others praised it to the skies. The journalists at *Newsday* were delighted when a rival, the *Long Island Press*, said, 'This scorching novel makes *Portnoy's Complaint* and *Valley of the Dolls* read like *Rebecca of Sunnybrook Farm.*'

Hollywood wanted in on the act and Stuart received at least twenty offers for the film rights. With so much publicity, the book could hardly fail to sell. 20,000 copies were bought within a month of publication and the book went into a third printing.

Naturally, with almost 30 people in on the hoax, it was bound to leak out before too long. When McGrady was rung by a journalist chasing the story, he confessed all. But instead of that being the end of *Naked Came the Stranger*, news of the truth behind the book actually boosted sales. With *Life* magazine carrying a large-scale story about the hoax, the public's appetite for it quickly propelled the novel into the bestseller lists. Over 100,000 copies of the book were sold in hardback, with over a dozen foreign language versions appearing.

Initially McGrady seems to have been mightily embarrassed by the whole thing. Although the hoax had been initiated out of sheer mischief, each of the 'authors' received around $5000. As proof that he had not been in it for the money, McGrady turned down a massive half a million dollars advance for a sequel.

He did write another book, though. *Stranger Than Naked, or How to Write Dirty Books for Fun & Profit*, is a hilarious account of the writing of *Naked Came the Stranger*. In it, McGrady reveals that he received a letter from a Joseph G. Doughterty: 'Dear Sirs, May I congratulate you and your co-authors on your charming little hoax. It is unfortunate, however, that it is not original. You see, a few years ago, 32 of my friends (including twelve plumbers, four used car dealers, a number of illiterate migrant farm workers, a homosexual tree surgeon, and a defrocked priest) and myself combined our talents to 'write' a sex novel of no intrinsic value. We called our book *Valley of the Dolls . . .*'

McGrady concludes *Stranger Than Naked*: 'It was too easy; it all went too smoothly. America. You sit there, you plump beauty, still buying neckties from sidewalk sharpies, still guessing which walnut shell contains the pea, still praying along with Elmer Gantry. America, sometimes I worry about you.'

Despite the exposure of the hoax, it is splendid to see that not everyone is aware that it was a spoof. As recently as November 1994, *The Daily Telegraph* mentioned it in passing as a 'third-rate erotic novel'.

Tigers Eating Lemons

With some forms of poetry, it is often hard to tell when weirdness ends and hoaxing begins. There have been several spoofs worth mentioning. In 1916, poet Witter Bynner got involved in a conversation with another poet, Arthur Ficke, about the staggering number of new poetry 'schools' that were mushrooming in America, among them the Chorists, the Futurists, the Vorticists and the Imagists.

Much of the new poetry by people like Ezra Pound and Amy Lowell, they felt, was nothing more than pretentious tosh which was swallowed up by ignorant critics and gullible readers.

The pair invented the Spectric school of poetry, supposedly hailing from Pittsburgh. Their method of composition involved consuming a considerable amount of whisky and then writing virtually any random thought that came into their heads. Bynner said later that they '... let all reins go, to give the idea or the phrase complete head, to take whatever road or field or fence it chose. In other words, it was a sort of runaway poetry, the poet seated in the wagon but the reins flung aside.'

Leading lights in the Spectric movement were to be Emanuel Morgan and Anne Knish (named after a recipe in a Jewish cookbook). Part of one of their more readable poems contained the lines:

Cream is better than lemon
In tea at breakfast.
I think of tigers as eating lemons.
Thank God this tea comes from the green grocer
Not from Ceylon.

When their own publishers accepted the collected works of Morgan and Knish on their own merits, the pair came clean. But the publisher decided to go along with the spoof to see what happened. *Spectra: A Book of Poetic Experiments* duly appeared and it was taken completely at face value by everybody. Although some were more enthusiastic than others, no critics were openly hostile to the new school.

The public went for the book in a big way, with the volume more popular than most other books of poetry at the time. Its popularity ensured that there was plenty of demand for more Spectric poetry which Bynner and Ficke tried their best to keep up with. Before long, though, they had to recruit another poet, Marjorie Allen Seiffert, to help them. She adopted the name of Elijah Hay.

The most extraordinary aspect of the whole thing was still to come, for in 1917 a group of Wisconsin poets produced a parody of the Spectric school of poetry, inventing an obviously tongue-in-cheek Ultra-Violet school of poetry penned principally by Nanne Pish and Manual Organ.

The mystery surrounding Morgan, Knish and Hay, who never appeared in public unlike other publicity-hungry poets, probably goes some way towards explaining the popularity of the Spectric school. Bynner and Ficke started rumours circulating about Anne Knish's gorgeous looks and the passionate tangled triangle of love that tortured the three great poets.

But after two years, in the middle of a speech in Detroit, Bynner found himself being taunted by a member of the audience about the Spectrics and he readily confessed that the whole thing had been a prank. 'Our intent in publishing the book,' he later wrote, 'was not to question the use of free verse and not to bait the pubic, but to satirise fussy pretence.'

The backlash was understandably severe, with relatively few people in literary circles taking it in good humour. Some professed that the Spectric poetry was actually better than the stuff Bynner and Ficke wrote in their own names.

If you ever come across a copy of *Spectra*, grab it. It has become a highly-regarded satire on the pretentiousness of the poetry world and is worth a considerable sum of money.

Bet You It Won't

I think it's safe to say that if you know any experienced practical jokers, it is never sensible to enter into a bet with them. Hugh Troy's sister should have known that while it might have been all right to rubbish her teenage brother's faltering attempts at poetry, actually betting him that they would never be published was downright foolish. Troy told her that one would be published within the month and, of course, he was right.

He wrote to the literary editor of the *New York Times:* 'Dear Sirs, I am anxious to find a piece of poetry by an American, I believe, with some particularly moving stanzas about a gypsy maiden abandoned on the trail by her tribe.'

He signed it 'Titus Grisby'. Once the initial letter was published, Troy was able to send a reply from 'G. Claude Fletcher' of Ithaca: 'Dear Sir, Titus Grisby must be referring to the beautiful "Curse of the Gypsy" written in 1870 by the celebrated Poet Laureate of Syracuse, New York; Hugh Troy.

> So we leave her,
> So we leave her,
> Far from where her swarthy kindred roam.
> In the scarlet fever,
> In the scarlet fever,
> In the scarlet fever convalescent home.'

Angry Penguins

The most famous Australian hoax concerns the poet Ern Malley. Previously unknown, some of his work was sent to the country's top poetry magazine, *Angry Penguins*, in 1944. The editor, Max Harris, was very taken with his style and wrote back, asking for more.

Harris received a reply from Malley's sister, saying that her brother, a garage mechanic, had sadly died the year earlier. Harris devoted a whole issue, called 'The Darkening Ecliptic', to Malley's poems, many of which later reappeared in several books of poetry and became very popular in the United States.

In fact Malley never existed, but was the invention of a pair of Australian poets who were in the Army – Lt James McAuley and Corporal Harold Stewart. Like Bynner and Ficke, they found much of the modern poetry that was being lapped up pretentious claptrap, particularly the stuff printed by avowedly avant-garde publications like *Angry Penguins*.

So they set out to see how poems that were deliberately contrived to be nonsensical would be received. It is said that their poems were largely derived from three works: the *Oxford Dictionary of Quotations*, an encyclopaedia and a Government Report on the drainage of swamps to prevent them being used as breeding grounds for mosquitoes. The pair said that they were trying to imitate 'the whole literary fashion as we knew it from the works of Dylan Thomas and others'. What's more, they claimed that they had written Malley's entire output, sixteen poems, in just one afternoon.

As far as McAuley and Stewart were concerned, Malley had succeeded beyond their wildest dreams. Unfortunately for Harris, the poems were labelled obscene by the authorities. He was convicted of publishing obscenity and fined £5. Despite testimony from T.S. Eliot and others to the poems' quality and morality, it was felt that lines like 'The swung torch scatters seeds/ In the unbelliferous dark' were obviously depraved.

Let us leave the last word to Malley himself:

> In the twenty-fifth year of my age
> I find myself to be a dromedary
> That has run short of water between
> One oasis and the next mirage.

3

The Arts

Stupefied Naval Ladies

The French nineteenth-century writer Alphonse Allais once organised an exhibition of work by a group of artists called *Salon Des Incoherents*. Although abstract art has since become respectable, this early instance of the school was actually intended to be a spoof. For Allais had, as his artists, got together a group of friends who were completely incompetent at painting.

Allais's own picture in the exhibition was a work of genius. Called 'Negroes Fighting in a Cave at Night', it was an entirely black canvas. It proved to be very popular, enabling Allais to continue the series. They included a red canvas titled 'Apoplectic Cardinals Harvesting Tomatoes by the Red Sea', a blue one named 'Stupefied Naval Cadets Seeing the Mediterranean for the First Time', and one which was all white called, understandably, 'Anaemic Young Girls Going to their First Communion through a Blizzard'.

Taking Your Hat Off To Hat

In 1980 Christie's sold a painting titled 'Pears in a Bowl' by the artist Bruno Hat, dating from 1929. It was bought for the princely sum of £500, which wasn't bad for something that had been knocked up as a joke in the first place.

It was actually painted by artist John Banting who, together with his friends Brian Howard, Tom Mitford and Evelyn Waugh, had put together an exhibition 51 years earlier which was intended to expose the ridiculous pretentiousness of modern art. As well as surrealistic and cubist art spoofs, there were others made up of hunks of wool and bits of cork stuck on canvas. Many of the pictures were framed in unusual materials, such as rope. The ludicrous nonsense in the catalogue was written by Evelyn Waugh.

The great Bruno Hat (actually Mitford) was present at his exhibition, sitting in a wheelchair in dark glasses, sporting a long moustache and a near impenetrable German accent. Lytton Strachey bought one of the pictures, while Lady Diane Mosley was heard to say that the paintings were 'lovely'.

'Pardon?' Said Van Gogh

When in 1935 the Museum of Modern Art in New York had an exhibition of Van Gogh, it drew immense crowds. Hugh Troy, an artist himself as well as one of the great practical jokers of all time, was convinced that many so-called art lovers were really just ghouls, drawn to the exhibition by the story of Van Gogh's tortured life and in particular the tale of his severed ear, which had featured prominently in newspaper reports of the show. Troy was annoyed that it was so difficult for true art lovers like himself to see the paintings because of the immense crowds.

To test his theory, Troy modelled an ear from corned beef and mounted it on blue velvet in a handsome presentation box, together with a card which read: 'This is the ear which Vincent Van Gogh cut off and sent to his mistress, a French prostitute, Dec 24 1888.'

After placing it on a table close by the Van Gogh paintings, Troy was delighted to see that it was not long before the visitors turned their back on the pictures as they crowded to have a look at the infamous ear.

One September Morn

One of the earliest press agents, Harry Reichenbach, was also something of a hoaxer. An acquaintance of his ran a small art shop in New York and was dispirited in 1905 because he had bought a couple of thousand copies of a lithograph done by a rather poor French artist, Paul Chabas, showing a nude girl standing by the edge of the sea. He hadn't been able to sell one.

Reichenbach soon put that right. He rang Anthony Comstock, head of the New York Anti-Vice League, the city's equivalent of Mary Whitehouse, about the outrageous display of an immoral painting in full view of small children. When Comstock paid him no attention, Reichenbach paid 50 street kids to hang around the window making suggestive noises, then went round in person to scream at Comstock and tell him that something must be done before the morals of New York's youth were completely undermined.

Comstock had the dealer arrested and prosecuted and the matter was taken up by the newspapers. Whereas the original copies hadn't shifted at an asking price of ten cents each, 'September Morn' went on to sell over seven million copies at a dollar a time. The original – worthless just a short while before – was bought by an oil magnate for $70,000 many years later. Reichenbach's fee for the thing was a mere $45.

It's a Steal

The *pièce de résistance* of Brian G. Hughes, one of the most active practical jokers in America in the early years of the century was the occasion when he got together the tools of the burglar's trade – jemmy, pliers, glass-cutter, a rope ladder and so on – and made his way to the Metropolitan Museum of Art one night. There he left the tools, together with half a dozen ornate but empty picture frames, lying around on the ground outside the museum. There was pandemonium the following day while the curators tried, unsuccessfully of course, to work out what had been stolen.

I Think, Therefore I'm a Banana

The novelist and literary critic of the *Los Angeles Times*, Paul Jordan Smith, was fed up with what he saw as the often ludicrous burgeoning 'schools' of art in the twenties such as Dadaism. He had a particular loathing for Picasso and the way people fawned over him. Like Witter Bynner and Arthur Ficke with their Spectric school of poetry, he decided to invent a new school of art, which he called the Disumbrationist school.

Although he had never painted before, he managed to brush up a nude woman with a crown of flowers holding aloft a peeled banana. He called it 'Exaltation' and claimed it was painted by a Russian artist, Pavel Jerdanovitch.

Smith entered it in a French exhibition in 1925. The French art magazine *Revue du Vrai et du Beau* wrote to Smith, as Jerdanovitch, and asked to see more of his work. The artist claimed to be too poor to be able to afford to photograph his paintings but he sent back details of his life, including his flight from Russia where he was a dissident, to Chicago, from where he had to journey to the South Seas because of steadily worsening tuberculosis.

As Jerdanovitch's known work increased, so did the praise with which it was received. Even Havelock Ellis was among the artist's fans. One critic said that his work combined 'Gauguin, pop art and Negro minstrelsy'. Another said that Jerdanovitch '. . . uses his brush to symbolize the sentiments: he explores the heights and does not hesitate to peer into the abysses.'

Having proved that the art world would praise any old rubbish, Smith got bored of the whole thing and in 1927 told his story to a writer on his own paper, the *Los Angeles Times*.

I Think, Therefore I Eat Bananas

The artist Pierre Brassau was very highly thought of by the artistic community in Sweden when he burst on to the scene in 1964. It was the era of pop art and Brassau was admired as a master of the medium and exhibited prominently in a leading gallery. According to one critic: 'Brassau paints with powerful strokes, but also with clear determination . . . He is an artist who performs with the delicacy of a ballet dancer.'

Pierre Brasssu was only four years old and what's more, a West African chimpanzee called Peter, who lived in Sweden's Boras Zoo in Göteborg.

The stunt was conjured up by reporters on the *Göteborgs-Tidningen* newspaper to show how ridiculous the enthusiasm for modern art was. They had bribed the chimpanzee's keeper to give Peter some paints, canvas and brushes. Although he initially ate some of the paint, it wasn't long before he was imbued with the artistic muse and daubed a few masterpieces.

The journalists were delighted when Pierre Brassau achieved the ultimate accolade; a handful of red 'sold' stickers on some of his pictures hanging in the gallery.

I Paint, Therefore I Make Monkeys of the Experts

In 1993, the Manchester Academy of Fine Arts annual show saw the public debut of a new artist; one Carly Johnson. Her painting 'Rhythm of the Trees' was one of just 150 accepted for display in the Manchester City Art Gallery out of over 1000 pictures submitted to the panel. The panel, composed of seven experts, felt that it displayed 'a certain quality of colour balance, composition and technical skill'.

It is unlikely that Carly would have agreed. She said of her work: 'It's just a little pattern.' But then she was only four and as far as her mother was concerned her pictures were nothing more than 'shapeless blobs'. It was Mrs Johnson, a freelance artist, who entered Carly's work: 'I thought I'd just have a go and pull the wool over the eyes of the experts by sending it in, and they fell for it. Either Carly is a great artist or the judges are easily fooled.'

Glenys Latham, president of the Manchester Academy of Fine Arts, was quoted as saying: 'The art of children often has a very uncluttered quality which adults often strive to gain, so I don't feel in the least embarrassed about it. Technical skill can get in the way of instinctive response.'

On sale for £295, it wasn't long before the picture was snapped up, by an Irish gallery owner. 'The picture is sheer, innocent poetry,' he said.

Beaten By a Nose

Mozart once bet Haydn that he could write a piece of music that he could play and Haydn couldn't. Not surprisingly, Haydn was unwilling to believe that his pupil could play a piece more competently than his teacher. However, when he came to look at the music, he confessed that he found it unplayable, as it involved chords at either end of the piano and a single note somewhere in between. Mozart then showed Papa Haydn how it should be done. He sat at the keyboard and, with his hands occupied at the ends of the keyboard, he dipped his head and played the note in the middle with his nose!

Some say, scurrilously, that knowing Mozart's reputation for coarseness, it probably wasn't his nose that he used.

Early on in the career of the world-famous violinist Fritz Kreisler, a German critic reviewing his playing said: 'He played beautifully, but naturally his temperament lacks the strength and maturity to reach the heights of the Pugnani music.'

He was unaware, as was everyone else, that the piece was not by Pugnani at all but by Kreisler himself. When he was starting out in the 1890s, Kreisler felt handicapped by the small number of virtuoso pieces available for unaccompanied violin. As an unknown, he had few chances to play with an orchestra, so he decided to write himself the sort of showy music he wanted to display his extraordinary talents to the full.

Aware that no-one would take seriously an unheard-of violinist writing his own compositions, he claimed that he had discovered pieces by the likes of Vivaldi and lesser-known composers like Francoeur, Porpora and Pugnani in music libraries while touring Europe. The music aroused considerable interest among critics as well as among other violinists, who were as keen as Kreisler to find new music to play. But Kreisler was attacked by a critic in the *Berliner Tageblatt* when he included a piece of his own with some waltzes by 'Joseph Lanner'. The critic said that the waltzes were worthy of Schubert and was furious that Kreisler dared to include his own pathetic piece, 'Caprice Viennois', in the same programme.

It was only in 1935, when he was 60, that Kreisler confessed what he had done to the music critic of the *New York Times*. By then, many of his compositions were a standard part of the violinist's repertoire.

A Little Something By Chrysler

A Japanese car firm once spent a small fortune promoting a new model in the United States. A substantial part of the cost went on a concert held at Carnegie Hall at which some very prestigious names played, among them Cleo

Laine and John Dankworth as well as the world-famous violinist Itzhak Perlman.

The Japanese hosts were not best pleased when Perlman mischievously announced that his first piece would be by Kreisler.

Warlock's Invitation

Like many of us, classical composer Peter Warlock – best known for his Capriol Suite – liked having train compartments to himself. In those days, when each pair of facing seats had its own door, he found the perfect way of ensuring that this was always the case.

He would lean out of the window and, as soon as anybody showed any sign that they might want to enter his compartment, he would beam broadly and beckon them in. For some reason, people rarely took him up on his offer, but found they would prefer to sit somewhere else instead.

The Dummy Audience

The TV quiz show about classical music, *Face the Music*, had a 'dummy keyboard'. Contestants had to guess what piece was being played on it by the presenter Joseph Cooper.

It wasn't a new idea. Back in 1961, a whole concert was actually given on such a dummy keyboard, when a Cambridge antique dealer decided to show up the slavish regard some people had for what he considered hideous modern classical music. Passing himself off as the Hungarian pianist Tomas Blod, 'musician of silence', he played his way through an 'Evening of Surrealism in Music' on a piano which had had the keys disconnected from the strings.

Instead of throwing things and demanding their money back, the audience at the Wigmore Hall, one of London's main chamber music venues, applauded Blod.

The above is what I *had* written, based on a newspaper report of the event. However, just as the book was due to be published, I discovered the truth about Blod, quite by chance. Somebody lent me a rare recording of some of ABC-TV's early *Candid Camera* spoofs and it seems that Blod was in fact the creation of the extraordinary Jonathan Routh (of whom, more later).

On the record, in halting Eastern European-accented English, we can hear 'Blod' announce, 'Fourth prelude. A . . . uh . . . minor, which is short and . . . uh . . . you know very well,' as he sits at the keyboard to a round of applause.

After the usual coughing and shuffling around that you hear at every concert, you can hear Blod hammering away at the keys. One or two people in the audience begin giggling and are immediately shushed by the more serious concertgoers, eager to experience the full joy of this 'musician of silence'. Strange to say, the earlier report I had read of the concert seems to be true. After a minute or two of Blod running through a piece of music that I'm ashamed to say I didn't recognise, he finishes with a flourish and receives an extremely generous round of applause.

The Magic Grand

The fifties property developer Felix Fenston was told by a friend of his that he would love to have a grand piano in his place. Unfortunately, he lamented, he only lived in a small flat in Belgravia so it simply wasn't possible.

When the chap went away for a while, Fenston arranged access to the flat. He had a whole wall removed in order that a full-sized concert grand could be lifted into place. Then the wall was reinstalled and redecorated exactly the way it had been before, with the pictures hung in the same position, all neatly awaiting the return of the astonished resident.

4

The Sciences

Pull the Other Leg

The eighteenth-century botanist John Hill was rather more certain of his own abilities than were others. When the King of Sweden sent him the Order of Vasa for a botanical treatise he had written, he switched to calling himself Sir John and claimed to be a doctor.

Unsurprisingly, the Royal Society showed him the door when he asked to become a member. Hill got his own back by sending a letter to the Society from Portsmouth detailing a case in which a sailor had broken his leg when falling from a ship's rigging. The leg was promptly treated, however, with bandages and tarwater and, within just three days, was as good as new.

The letter was taken seriously by the Society and was the subject of much discussion until the second letter arrived from Hill, apologising: he had forgotten to mention that the sailor's leg was a wooden one.

The Vegetarian Devil

The French zoologist Baron George Léopold Cuvier was a pioneer in reconstructing the skeletons of animals from fossils. His dry, logical approach to everything infuriated his students who wanted to see if they could put the fear of God into Cuvier.

They crept into his bedroom one night, led by one who was dressed in the traditional outfit of the devil with horns, hooves and a tail. 'Cuvier,' moaned the apparition, 'I have come to eat you.'

Cuvier was roused from his sleep by the noise but, to the dismay of the students, instead of panicking, he examined the devil then said: 'All animals with horns and hooves are herbivorous. You won't eat me.'

Then he put his head back on the pillow and returned to his slumbers.

I Could Eat a Horse

Although the British in the nineteenth century have a reputation for – by modern-day standards – being gluttons, the geologist and palaeontologist Professor William Buckland had an appetite second to none. It wasn't how much he ate that set him apart so much as what he ate. For he was extremely curious, gastronomically speaking.

His one time student, John Ruskin, claimed that he had once been offered a toasted mouse by Buckland. The professor claimed that the most unpleasant thing he ever tasted was a mole, although he later changed his mind and said that even a mole didn't match the nastiness of eating bluebottles.

On one occasion, possibly apocryphal, someone showed him a snuff box, inside which was supposedly the heart of King Louis XIV of France. 'I have eaten some strange things,' said the professor, 'but never the heart of a king.' So saying, he swallowed it.

Alligatawny

Dinner parties with Buckland could be fraught occasions. After serving a particularly delicious soup, he challenged his guests to see if they could identify the main ingredient. Although he went right round the table, not one of them was correct. When Buckland told them that it was what was left of an alligator that he had dissected earlier, several of them stumbled from the room in some haste.

'See what imagination is,' mused Buckland to those with stronger stomachs. 'If I told them it was turtle, or terrapin, or bird's-nest soup, they would have pronounced it excellent and their digestion would have been none of the worse.' In fact, said Buckland, when asked if it really had been alligator that they had eaten, it was 'as good a calf's head as ever wore a coronet'.

Giving His Students the Finger

It is thought that the Edinburgh doctor Joseph Bell was the model for Sherlock Holmes. Arthur Conan Doyle studied medicine under him and no doubt found inspiration in his obsession with, as the *Dictionary of National Biography* puts it, 'The value in diagnosis of close observation of facts and the intelligent interpretation of them.'

Every set of students that passed through Bell's hands underwent the same test, to see just how good at observing and interpreting they really were. He showed them a sample of urine into which he dipped his finger. He then put his finger in his mouth and tasted it. He asked his students to follow suit, before demanding to know what they could learn from the experiment.

The students, still reeling from the unpleasantness of what they had just done, offered various suggestions about what could be deduced fom the smell, the taste, the colour and the density of the urine.

Bell snorted with derision. They had all missed the really important thing: while he had dipped his index finger into the urine, it was his middle finger that he had put in his mouth.

Oil on Troubled Waters

Benjamin Franklin was once taking a stroll with friends by the side of a stream which the wind was whipping up into small waves. Franklin boasted that he had the power to make stormy waters calm.

Not unnaturally, his friends scoffed at this fanciful idea. Franklin, tutting at their lack of belief in his abilities, waved his walking stick over the waters. To the astonishment of his companions, the stream in the vicinity of the walking stick did indeed suddenly become as smooth as glass. The stick was made of bamboo and Franklin, it turned out, had hidden some drops of oil inside it before setting out.

Two Close Shaves

The Swiss physicist Auguste Piccard had a twin brother, Jean Felix. They were once in a town they'd never been to before and found themselves in need of a shave. Auguste went into a barber's shop on his own and, as he got into the chair, he said that he wanted a particularly close shave. 'My beard grows so rapidly that two hours after I've had a shave, I need another.'

The barber laughed out loud and told Piccard that, 'If your beard grows in two hours, I'll give you another shave free.' Piccard congratulated the barber on a good shave and left the shop contented.

Just a little under two hours later Jean Felix opened the door to the shop and took his place in the barber's chair. 'Now do you believe me?' he asked the barber, who was mystified to see how much stubble had grown back on his recent customer's chin.

Crazy Computer

Hungarian-American mathematician John von Neumann worked in the States during the Second World War on the construction of an 'electronic brain', an early version of a computer.

When he delivered it, he told the Government that it was called a Mathematical Analyser, Numerical Integrater and Computer. It was several days before those working with the machine realised that its acronym was MANIAC.

It's All Bosch

During the Second World War, one of our top boffins was Professor R.V. Jones, a prime mover in Ultra, the operation at Bletchley Park that cracked the secrets of the German code machine known as Enigma, with enormous benefits to the Allied cause.

Before the war, Jones' active mind wasn't always directed towards scientific endeavours. In his book on the role science played in intelligence during World War II, *Most Secret War*, Jones has a section in the index: 'practical joking as exercise.' When at Cambridge's Clarendon Laboratory in the pre-war years, he became friendly with the German physicist Carl Bosch. A few years later, they were to be working against each other but for the time being they were the closest of friends, sharing a great interest in practical jokes, particularly those involving the telephone.

Bosch told Jones that a laboratory he once worked in had clear sight of vision into a block of flats opposite, one of which was occupied by a journalist. Bosch noticed that the reporter's telephone was visible from where he worked and he decided to telephone the man pretending to be his own professor. He was very excited, he said, because he had just invented a device that could be attached to any telephone and which would enable the user to see what was happening at the other end.

As this was in the early thirties, when talk of 'television' was in the air, such a thing sounded feasible. Even so, the reporter was sceptical and demanded to be given some proof. So Bosch told him to leave the telephone pointing towards the middle of the room and to do some sort of exercise in front of it.

When the reporter picked up the phone again, Bosch, who could see him clearly through the window, was able to describe exactly what contortions he had gone through. The reporter was convinced and wrote a long piece praising the professor and his amazing invention which appeared in the newspaper the following morning.

There's a Phone in My Bucket

Jones and Bosch spent much time discussing what sort of pranks were possible with a telephone, with Jones eventually boasting that he could use it to persuade somebody to put a telephone into a bucket of water. They decided to put this to the test by ringing the digs where several research students lived.

Jones rang several times, ringing off each time before anybody could answer so that the impression would be created that something was wrong with the phone. When he let it ring uninterrupted, he recognised the person answering as a chemistry research student, a very bright chap who had won the Senior Scholarship in Chemistry in the whole university that year.

Resorting to the Cockney of his youth, Jones explained that he was an engineer following up a complaint from someone who was having problems getting through. He believed from the symptoms described that it might be either a question of the dial going too quickly or a leak to earth at the receiving end. It was possible that the fault could be cleared up at the exchange if the chap would be willing to help with a few tests.

'I realised,' said Jones, 'that he was so firmly 'hooked' that I could even afford to clown, and I persuaded him to sing loudly into the telephone on the pretext that its carbon granules had seized up. By this time, of course, all the residents of the household had now been alerted, and watched with some amazement the rest of his performance.'

Telling his victim that the microphone had been cleared, Jones asked for help in tracing the leak to earth and made him hold the telephone receiver in a variety of peculiar positions before asking him to fetch a bucket of water. The chap was about to follow Jones' instructions and lower the receiver into the water when he was stopped by Gerald Touch, a physicist who was in on the joke. When Touch tried to explain that the victim might damage the telephone by putting it in water Jones told the chap, 'Oh, a physicist is he, sir? We know his kind – they think they know everything about electricity. They're always trying to put telephones right by themselves and wrecking them. Don't you worry about him, sir, it's all in my book here.'

To Jones' delight, he heard the chemist repeating all this to Touch and telling him that he was going to follow what the engineer told him to do. However, at this point, Touch couldn't control himself any longer and, convulsed with laughter, explained that it was Jones on the other end.

The Invisible Battleship

Jones and Bosch managed to get the scientist Leo Szilard to go to the *Daily Express* offices because of a hoax call, supposedly from the editor, asking Szilard about a radioactive death ray that he had invented. Szilard was very agitated when he got the call and Jones only discovered after the war that the scientist had only just taken out a patent which he had assigned to the Admiralty concerning the possibility of a uranium chain reaction.

When one of Jones' wartime colleagues was probing a little too closely into his work, Jones sent him off in the wrong direction by claiming that he was working on developing a battleship that was both invisible and transparent. Although they had only managed to make enough material for a torpedo boat so far, Jones intimated that they were also being handicapped by the fact that they had not yet discovered a means of concealing the ship's wake nor, indeed, of making the crew invisible.

Jones moved away from practical practical jokes to theoretical practical jokes. He decided that it was all too easy to hoax people and that it was particularly unfair to anyone who didn't know who their tormentor was and were thus unable to retaliate. Instead he was content merely to conjure them up in his mind, believing that if he ever chose to carry them out the victims would respond just as he expected.

When Jones was asked once by a colleague about his delight in practical jokes, 'My reply was that an academic life gave us no exercise in quick thinking, and that I had a hunch that the practice that jokes gave in quick thinking would one day come in useful.'

In his book, Jones mentions R.W. Wood, the Professor of Physics at John Hopkins University in Baltimore, who much enjoyed practical jokes. One of his favourites was to conceal a large spinning gyroscope inside a suitcase which he would place on a station platform. Asking someone to carry it for him, he would derive considerable amusement from watching what happened when they tried to turn a corner, only to find the suitcase wanting to continue in the same direction.

Jones claims that when Wood worked in Paris he noticed that the lady in the flat underneath him kept a small tortoise in a windowbox. He bought a quantity of similar-looking tortoises in assorted sizes and by means of a piece of wire at the end of a broomstick handle Wood was able to capture the original tortoise and replace it with one that was a little larger. He then replaced that one with one that was larger still, then another that was even larger and so on. The woman was soon convinced that her tortoise was growing at an extraordinary rate.

To Wood's delight, she chose to consult him about her astonishing pet because of his scientific bent. When he suggested that she write to a paper about it, the tortoise became a *cause célèbre*. Wood was able to keep the gag going by reversing the process, substituting steadily smaller tortoises until he had returned the original pet to the woman.

As with so many other great hoaxes, the story is told as having been carried out by others such as, for instance, artist and poet Waldo Peirce. The fact that both versions place it firmly in Paris give one hope for believing that one or the other – or even both – really did happen.

Nobel Prize-Winning Nickel Hoax

Richard P. Feynman was one of the world's greatest theoretical physicists. One of the team working during the Second World War on the Manhattan Project that developed the atomic bomb, he won the Nobel Prize for Physics in 1965. One of the reasons Feynman was so popular with the students he taught was that he had an irrepressible sense of fun and a love of practical jokes.

When he worked at MIT (The Massachusetts Institute of Technology) in Boston, Feynman regularly ate at a particular restaurant and became well known to the staff. Realising one day that they were invariably so busy that they did things without thinking about them, Feynman left the tip for his waitress Sue, two nickels, under two glasses. He filled each glass to the top with water, dropped the nickel in and, using a card, turned each over so that it was standing upside down on the table. Withdrawing the card, the water stayed in the glass.

Feynman deliberately used two glasses. If he had only used one, then the waitress would have got wet but just shrugged it off. This way, he knew she would have to stop and think about how to get the nickel out of the second glass. On the way out, he even warned her that something was amiss: 'There's something funny about the glasses you gave me – they're filled in on the top, and there's a hole on the bottom!'

The next day Sue refused to serve him. His new waitress said that Sue was furious with him because, after getting wet picking up the first glass, she had then got wet again when neither she nor the boss could work out another way to get the money out.

Feynman explained that if it had been him, he'd have got something like a soup plate to catch the water and then slid the glass to the edge, waiting for all the water to run out before taking the nickel out of the glass.

That evening he left his tip under an upside down coffee cup, knowing that the waitress would go and get a soup plate and slide it to the edge of the table. There was, however, no water in it, an omission she complained about when he returned the following day.

At Los Alamos in New Mexico, where the atomic bomb was being developed, secrecy was supposedly held by the authorities to be of prime importance. But Feynman became irritated that all the ostensibly secret documents were kept in wooden filing cabinets secured with pathetic padlocks, particularly after he discovered that by tilting the cabinets you could easily pull all the papers out.

Feynman taught himself how to pick locks, just to show how easy it was to open the cabinets. In an effort to prove how lamentable the security was on the world's most secret project, Feynman simply took things he needed when the owners were not around. Yet nothing he did seemed to convince people how lax they were being.

Even when filing cabinets with combination locks arrived, Feynman quickly worked out how to open them, achieving a reputation on the project as being something of a safe-cracker.

After the war, the Army was thinking of declassifying some of the documents relating to the Manhattan Project. Feynman's friend Frederic de Hoffman was in the Declassification Section and thus had a copy of every single document involved in nine filing cabinets in his office. They were highly secret, detailing as they did how to make the atomic bomb.

When Feynman was in de Hoffman's office one day, he whiled away the time by experimenting with the locks. He started by trying out various mathematical constants. Pi, his first choice, didn't work. So Feynman tried the second most important constant in mathematics, the base of natural logarithms, 2.71828. The combination 27-18-28 opened the lock immediately. He wasn't surprised that all the other locks had the same combination.

Feynman began to contemplate writing the ultimate safe-cracker's confessional. Not for him the paltry rewards of gold bullion. 'I would tell how I opened safes whose contents were bigger and more valuable than any safe-cracker anywhere had opened . . . compared to furs or gold bullion, I have them all beat: I opened the safes which contained all the secrets to the atomic bomb: the schedules for the production of the plutonium, the purification procedures, how much material is needed, how the bomb works, how the neutrons are generated, what the design is, the dimensions – the entire information that was known at Los Alamos: *the whole schmeer!'*

Feynman took out a document from the filing cabinet he had opened and scribbled on a piece of paper: 'I borrowed document no. LA4312 – Feynman the safe-cracker.' He dropped it on top of the papers in the filing cabinet and shut it. Opening another two, he left messages inside that read, 'This one was no harder to open than the other one – Wise Guy' and 'When the combinations are all the same, one is no harder to open than another – Same Guy.' Then he scarpered.

That evening, he ate in the cafeteria with Freddy de Hoffman. When de Hoffman said he was going to his office to do some work, Feynman decided it might be fun to go with him. It wasn't long before de Hoffman had to open one of the filing cabinets. Unfortunately, it was not the first that Feynman had opened, but the final one. Feynman watched de Hoffman's face as he saw the yellow paper with the message scribbled on it in red crayon. 'I had read in books that when somebody is afraid, his face gets sallow, but I had never seen it before. Well, it's absolutely true. His face turned a grey, yellow green – it was really frightening to see. He picked up the paper, and his hand was shaking. "L-l-look at this!" he said, trembling.'

The note he was holding was the one that said: 'When the combinations are all the same, one is no harder to open than another – Same Guy.' Feynman feigned ignorance, asking what it meant. When de Hoffman confessed that all his safe combinations were the same, Feynman gently pointed out that that wasn't such a bright idea.

Feynman suggested they look through the other cabinets, trying to guide de Hoffman to the cabinet from which he had taken the document. But the second cabinet Feynman had opened came before that, inside which was the note: 'This one was no harder to open than the other one – Wise Guy.'

Eventually, Feynman got him to try the cabinet in which he had put the confession: 'I borrowed document no. LA4312 – Feynman the safe-cracker.' As de Hoffman spun the combination, Feynman legged it down the hall, believing that he might be in some danger.

Within moments Freddy de Hoffman came running after him but, instead of being angry, he turned out to be incredibly relieved that the secrets of the atom bomb hadn't been stolen and that it was only Feynman up to his old tricks.

Buy This Book – Buy This Book

There are strict rules about the use of subliminal messages in TV advertising. Quite right too, you may think, except that there has never been any proof that subliminal advertising has any effect whatsoever.

The authorities' fear of it is based on research carried out by James Vicary in the late 1950s when he said that flashing messages in a cinema saying 'Drink Coke' and 'Eat Popcorn' led to queues for both products. Yet there was no scientific proof of this and Vicary never satisfactorily reproduced his experiment.

When the Canadian Broadcasting Corporation flashed the message 'Phone Now' onto its screens during a popular TV show, not one person called the station. That was despite the message being flashed up 352 times. The station also asked its viewers to guess what the message might be. Of 500 replies, not one guessed it correctly.

The same apparently goes for any 'subliminal learning' tools such as tapes designed to be played while you're asleep to improve memory, word power, concentration or to teach you languages or stop you smoking.

Everlasting Mice

In 1993, the scientific journal *Nature* published an article by Professor Robin Weiss of the Institute of Cancer Research in London, saying that he had discovered the secret of longevity in laboratory mice.

Scientists around the world were fascinated by Weiss's assertion that 'newly generated transgenic mice' could grow indefinitely without any sign of ageing. Although Weiss felt that he had given plenty of hints that he had his tongue in his cheek, he was received perfectly seriously in most quarters, perhaps because *Nature* was not as a rule given to devoting space to hoaxes.

An American film producer contacted Weiss to see if they could capture his work on film, Professor Francis Crick – who won a Nobel prize for his work in the structure of DNA – fell for it, and students at Oviedo University in Spain asked to be allowed to research the subject.

Best of all was Peter Starling of Cologne University, who was extremely miffed at having been fooled. He admitted that in being German he came from a 'non-British country with a less developed sense of humour . . . at the negative end of the fun spectrum.'

Weiss himself was delighted: 'The article is deliberately written in a deadpan way and is a bit pretentious. Not only should you read my article sceptically, you should read every article in *Nature* sceptically.'

The Missing Link

The Piltdown man is hardly one of the most amusing of pranks, but ought to be included as it is probably the best known of all hoaxes. After many years in which important fossil finds were uncovered with regularity throughout continental Europe, in 1912 it was announced with a degree of patriotic pride that the much sought after Missing Link – proof that man was descended from apes – had been discovered in England. It was what the scientific community had been looking for ever since Charles Darwin published *The Origin of Species* in 1859.

In fact, the whole thing was a hoax. Although the details are still a little uncertain, it seems that solicitor and amateur palaeontologist Charles Dawson spent several years salting a gravel pit near Piltdown in Kent with fragments of 'aged' human fossils, the prize pieces being a skull and jawbone. He made them appear much older than they were, filing down the teeth on an ape's jawbone to show the correct signs of wear and staining assorted fossilised bones with potassium dichromate to make them look suitably ancient.

Arthur Smith Woodward, head of the Geology Department at the South Kensington Museum and a friend of Dawson, appears to have been taken in completely. He was so enthusiastic about what was uncovered there over the space of three or four years that he went public before the Geological Society in December 1912 with the news that the skull of an ancestor of man, perhaps the missing link between *Homo sapiens* and the apes, had been discovered. It was, said Woodward, possibly 500,000 years old, dating from the early Ice Age. Piltdown man was classified as *Eoanthropus Dawsoni*.

There were some dissenting voices who cast doubt on the discovery, claiming that it didn't fit into the pattern established by other anthropological finds over recent years. But the dissenters were stilled when a tooth was discovered a year later and a similar skull and jawbone were found close to the Piltdown site in 1915. The Piltdown man was exhibited proudly in the British Museum.

It wasn't until 1953 that anthropologist Joseph Weiner of Oxford University exposed the Piltdown man as a hoax, although various discoveries in the intervening years had already led many to be sceptical. Using scientific techniques unavailable in 1912, such as X-rays, spectrographs and Geiger counters, Weiner demonstrated that far from being an ancient ancestor of man, the skull was actually part orangutan and part an old, but not old enough, human skull.

Although it is now generally accepted that Dawson was the main culprit, for some time Arthur Conan Doyle was a suspect, as it was known that he had visited the site several times in 1912 before the Piltdown man was discovered. However, it seems likely that, as with the Cottingley Fairies, Doyle was a victim rather than a perpetrator of the hoax.

The Cardiff Giant

Visitors to the Farmer's Museum in Cooperstown, New York, can see The Cardiff Giant, a ten-foot-high stone figure, probably America's most famous hoax.

It came about when a cigar maker, George Hull, got involved in the 1860s in an argument with a small-minded hell-and-damnation evangelical preacher, who claimed that Hull would be consigned to hell for his lack of faith. The preacher maintained that everything written in the Bible was true. No matter how much Hull baited him, he would not shift his position one jot, claiming that even the section in Genesis which says that 'there were giants in the earth in those days' was factually accurate.

The conversation lingered in the mind of the livid Hull, who decided to make his own 'giant' to expose such narrow-minded thinking. From a quarry in Iowa he bought a block of gypsum, with dark streaks running through it that looked like veins, and had it shipped to Chicago. It was a monumental task, for the gypsum block, twelve feet by four feet by two feet, weighed around three tons. With the nearest station over 40 miles away, the wagon and horses struggled under the load and Hull had to chip away some of the gypsum to reduce the weight.

Eventually it reached Chicago, where mason Edward Burghardt and two assistants set to work. Hull had ordered them to sculpt a giant, ten foot high, who looked as if he had died in agony. The giant was endowed with nails, pores and appropriately gigantic wedding tackle and then given the appearance of considerable age through applications of acid. Hull took care that there was no hair on the man because he knew that hair did not fossilise.

The giant, over ten feet tall and still weighing a ton and a half, was taken to a farm owned by Hull's cousin William Newell near Cardiff in New York State. There the pair buried the giant. Hull then departed, to bide his time.

It was an area already well known for fossil discoveries. Indeed, not long after they had hidden the giant, a local farmer was reported to have uncovered some fresh fossilised bones. In October 1869, after a year had elapsed, Hull felt that the time was right. Newell hired some men to make a well for him and professed as much surprise as them when, three feet down, they found what appeared to be a stone foot. After fevered digging, they uncovered a ten foot long giant nude man, who had obviously died in some pain.

As news of the discovery spread, people started flooding in to have a look at the giant. Newell erected a tent over the man and charged visitors 50 cents a time to view what he claimed to be the eighth wonder of the world. A stagecoach service was rapidly set up to transport people to the farm.

It was felt that the giant should be taken from Newell's farm to nearby Syracuse. A group of businessmen bought a three-quarters stake in the venture for $30,000, which Hull was only too ready to accept. Once installed in its new venue, the crowds swelled still further, with the New York Central Railroad even arranging a special stop so that passengers could get off to gawp at the giant.

Opinion was sharply divided over whether the giant was a fossil or not. Many believed that it was a statue, possibly made by early Jesuit missionaries. There were some, Hull was delighted to see, who felt it was proof of the very passage in Genesis that had impelled him to have the giant made in the first place.

Even some scientists were bamboozled, with two visiting Yale professors claiming that it was indeed a fossilised giant. Other experts went the statue route, but still believed it to be ancient in origin. There were some sceptics, with leading paleontologist Othniel Marsh reporting that, 'It is of very recent origin and a most decided humbug.' However, in the hubbub, their voices were barely noticed.

A reporter soon uncovered the link between Newell and Hull and it did not take too long before he found out the entire story and published it, together with Hull's explanation of why he had begun the hoax in the first place.

As with several other hoaxes, the exposure did not lessen the public's interest. Far from it. The giant was taken to New York City and exhibited at the Apollo Hall on Broadway. The American showman P.T. Barnum offered to rent it for $60,000, but he was turned down. Barnum was not a man to be beaten that easily. He had a copy made from plaster of Paris, offering a $1000 prize to anyone who could prove that his giant was any less genuine than the other. Thanks to Barnum's showmanship, his giant began to attract the greater number of visitors. An injunction against him failed, but by then public interest in the pair of giants was waning.

The Cardiff Giant was exhibited in Boston in 1870 and then taken around New England and Pennsylvania before being stored, reappearing at the Pan-American Exposition in Buffalo in 1901. It was later bought by a carnival owner who went bankrupt along with so many others in the 1930s and was then bought by an Iowan publisher who kept it in his house as a rather startling conversation piece. Eventually he sold it to the Farmer's Museum, where it is still on show.

Hull tried to pull the same trick again later, unearthing a fossilised man (made of clay and ape bones) in Colorado, but this time nobody was fooled.

They Called It Mellow Yellow

Those with long memories may recall the song by Donovan about 'mellow yellow' in the sixties. It was about a supposedly psychedelic mind-bending drug called Bananadine which, according to the newspapers, was made from bananas and was popular in San Francisco.

The drug was apparently made by baking the insides of banana peel, which was then rolled into a cigarette and smoked. Bananadine was apparently taken seriously by anti-drug agencies for a time and, given the popularity of the song, there must have been countless experimenters around the world trying to get high on bananas. In some 'scientific' experiments conducted by chemists from New

York University, 'highs' were indeed reported. Yet this was believed to be a psychological response to smoking the banana peel in a large group under psychedelic lighting.

In a rather more serious analysis undertaken by a team from the University of California, the scientists found that there was in fact no way of making a hallucinogenic drug from bananas. In *Science Digest* in February 1968, they reported that 'there are no known hallucinogens in bananadine'.

It transpired that a band of hippies in San Francisco had made the story up simply in order to irritate the authorities.

Corn Flakes

The mystery of corn circles has baffled people for getting on for almost twenty years. These strange, elaborate patterns in the midst of otherwise untouched wheat or other cereal fields began appearing in the late seventies and, before long, there were almost as many explanations for their creation as there were circles. Books appeared on the subject, with several 'experts' making their living out of writing and talking about the phenomenon. The circles were attributed to alien craft landing in the fields, to freak weather conditions, to electro-magnetic forces, to plasma fire and who knows what else.

Then, in 1991, two men in their sixties, Doug Bower and David Chorley, claimed that it was they who had started the corn circle bandwagon rolling, producing many of the most remarkable examples over the preceding thirteen years. *Today* newspaper put their claim to the test, getting them to make a corn circle near Sevenoaks in Kent. After jotting down their plan on paper, they used string, planks and a sighting device attached to a baseball cap to reproduce it.

The paper then brought in corn circle expert Patrick Delgado to pass judgement on it. Only after he said that 'no human could have done this' did the paper reveal how it had been made. Delgado took it remarkably well, saying: 'If everything you say is true, I'll look a fool. I admire your courage for coming forward. I find this quite hilarious really. It's quite a relief it is all over . . . You've done so much good in this world, you have brought millions of people together over this . . . It is a lesson to us all that we should look and listen to the beautiful and small things in life.'

It seems extremely unlikely, however, that even if the pair *did* originate corn circles, they could have been responsible for more than a small fraction of the corn circles that have appeared around the world. As someone pointed out, they would have had to produce 100 corn circles, scattered in different places, each week for that to be the case in Britain alone.

Some students from Southampton University, the Wessex Sceptics, have admitted responsibility for some of the other circles. Perhaps the corn circles in other countries around the world are the responsibility of other similar bands of sceptics?

Many of those who believe in the Loch Ness Monster do so because of what is known as the Surgeon's Photograph, a picture taken of 'Nessie' in April 1934. It shows the monster lifting its long neck out of the water and is responsible for sparking off the industry that has grown around the mysterious creature lurking in the depths of the Loch. Clearly, to those who were believers in the Loch Ness Monster, the Surgeon's Photograph shows that the creature is in some way related to the plesiosaur.

Sadly, what the experts and amateurs had been looking at for years was actually a toy submarine from Woolworth's, powered by clockwork, to which a head and neck made out of plastic wood had been attached.

In 1933, the *Daily Mail* sent film-maker and big game hunter Marmaduke Wetherell to Loch Ness to track down the monster. Just 48 hours later he claimed to have found the footprints of the Loch Ness Monster on one of the Loch's beaches. But these were quickly revealed by the Natural History Museum to have been made by a dried hippo foot, in all probability one that had been made into an umbrella stand.

Wetherell was not happy at being publicly humiliated. He got together with his son Ian, his stepson Christian Spurling, London insurance broker Maurice Chambers and Wilson to convince the world that there really was a monster.

Before his death at the age of 90 in November 1993 Spurling, the last of the hoaxers still alive, revealed to two Loch Ness investigators just how they had made the monster. Spurling, it appears, was an expert model-maker and built the creature in eight days out of materials provided by Wetherell. It was a foot high and about a foot and a half long and had a lead keel to give it stability. Modelled on the idea of a sea serpent after being tested on a pond, it was taken up to Scotland and launched into the waters of Loch Ness. Four photographs were taken and the plates were then handed over to Wilson.

Colonel Robert Wilson was a respected Harley Street gynaecologist and an unlikely participant in such a hoax. Although there were reports that Wilson knew Wetherell, it was not known that the two were friends. So when Wilson claimed to have seen 'something in the water' on 19 April 1934 and produced his photograph to back it up, there was no obvious reason to connect the two. When Wilson offered the *Daily Mail* a world exclusive on the photographs, they were delighted.

Wilson never claimed that the picture showed the Loch Ness Monster, only that he had seen 'something in the water'. He only ever gave one interview about the episode, in 1956, and tended to keep his head down because the medical establishment felt that the media attention he had brought upon himself was bringing the profession into disrepute.

It remains to be seen how the exposure of the Surgeon's Photograph as a hoax will affect the millions of pounds brought into the Loch Ness area each year by tourism.

Kidnapping Nessie

Before the discovery that the famous photo of Nessie was a hoax, arch prankster Alan Abel was planning his own Loch Ness Monster hoax. He had a monster built to his specifications out of chicken wire covered with material which was then painted by some artists. The idea was to set up a fake team of scientists who could do the 'discovering', have the monster kidnapped from them and then demand from The Natural History Museum a hefty ransom.

Unfortunately Maxwell Sackheim, the man who invented the concept of the book club when he founded The Book of the Month Club and the chap who had bankrolled Abel's hoaxes for years, died before this one could be carried out. However, the monster still exists in a barn somewhere and if Abel ever gets enough cash together, maybe Nessie will ride again.

Abel has also confessed that one of his ambitions is to

'. . . land a Martian; someday I'd like to have somebody dumped from a spaceship and discovered . . . who'll speak a language no-one will understand . . . We were going to do it a few years ago, but we couldn't quite get enough money to build the spaceship.'

Take Me To Your Leader

In 1989, a story emerged from Russia that an alien had been seen in Voronezh by a group of schoolchildren. The creature, so they said, was about nine feet tall and had three eyes.

The story was widely reported in the West, as well in Russia, with headlines like 'UFO LANDING IS FACT, NOT FANTASY, RUSSIANS INSIST' in the *New York Times*.

While it seems only too easy to believe that the alien was in reality an actor shrouded in aluminium foil, what is a little more far-fetched is that the whole thing was planned by Alan Abel. He claims that he got together the necessary props in America and had them shipped over to Russia. Unless there's an equivalent Alan Abelski, perhaps it is true. With Alan Abel, who can tell?

Bet You a Monkey Aliens Exist

In 1953, there was a spate of sightings of UFOs. When a Georgia barber, Edward Watters, made a $10 dollar bet with a friend that he could get his picture into the local papers within a fortnight, he used the UFO scares as his inspiration.

Buying a monkey for $50, he killed it, shaved it and removed its tail before driving out to a remote stretch of road near Austell with a couple of friends. Braking suddenly to produce skid marks on the road, Watters lay the monkey on the ground in front of the truck and waited.

A policeman happened across them, apparently in a state of shock and mumbling something about Martians and creatures from outer space. They talked of seeing lights in the sky and of creatures like men emerging from a spacecraft before they ran over one of them.

Although Watters' bet had been to get his photo into the local papers, the story travelled far wider than that. The national papers and TV stations sent reporters, while the Air Force and the FBI also sent investigators to the scene. It wasn't long, of course, before an autopsy confirmed that the animal was actually a Capuchin monkey and very definitely of this earth.

Watters readily confessed his hoax. Although he won his $10 dollar bet, the hoax had actually cost him far more.

Calling All Cars

In late 1993, police in South Yorkshire transmitted a message saying that a flying saucer had landed at Kearsley Lane in Doncaster. Several people turned up to have a look and were rather surprised by the nature of the Close Encounter. Instead of the expected Unidentified Flying Object, they were instead collared by the police.

Knowing that people, particularly those in the criminal fraternity, were prone to eavesdropping on their transmissions, the police had transmitted the message in an attempt to flush them out. Those who turned up in Kearsley Lane were charged.

Capricorn Two

In the summer of 1994 Ralph Rene wrote a book, *A Funny Thing Happened on the Way to the Moon*, claiming that the Apollo moon missions were a hoax of literally astronomical proportions. The book makes many claims to prove its thesis: the lunar landing module was so flimsy no-one really believes it could fly; in the photos of the landing site, not a speck of dust has been blown out of place by the landing's impact; you cannot slice a golf ball on the moon as we saw one of the astronauts do in the TV pictures; it is much too hot on the surface of the moon for the astronauts to walk on it for as long as they did; the image of Neil Armstrong on Buzz Aldrin's space mask was spray-painted on and so on. Quoting someone who says that they saw one of the landings being staged at a CBS studio, the book lambasts Congress for wasting $24 billion of taxpayers' money.

Although the substance of the book closely resembles the plot of the great 1978 film *Capricorn One*, its claims have yet to be generally accepted by the public.

5

Luvviedom

A Lotta Bottle

The Duke of Montague once claimed in an argument with the Earl of Chesterfield that people were so stupid that they would pay to see anything in a theatre, even if it was glaringly obvious to all but a fool that the attraction being advertised was clearly impossible. Not, replied the Earl of Chesterfield, if somebody was to say that they would jump into a quart bottle. The Duke wagered the Earl that they would even fall for that.

He arranged for an advert to appear saying that at 6.30 p.m. on the Monday of the following week, an extraordinary act would take place at the New Theatre in the Haymarket. Among other things, a person would climb into a wine bottle and then sing to the audience.

At the designated hour, the theatre was completely full. Not only that, but there were more people thronging outside trying to get in. When nothing happened, the crowd got ugly and began to throw things. A riot ensued, with the interior of the theatre being virtually destroyed. Seats, curtains, indeed anything the crowd could get their hands on, were taken into the street and burnt.

She Stoops to Conquer

Oliver Goldsmith's classic play *She Stoops to Conquer* was actually based on an incident in his youth. In Ardagh, he asked a fencing master named Kely for the best house in town. Although Goldsmith meant an inn, Kely mischievously misdirected him to the large, imposing home of Sir Ralph Featherstone, the local bigwig.

Although the play had the host being berated by his guest, who believes that the home of his betrothed is actually the village pub, in reality Sir Ralph apparently realised what was happening and went along with the gag. In any case, Goldsmith appears not to have thrown his weight around too pompously. He offered his host and his family the chance to partake of the supper he ordered and treated them to a couple of bottles of wine. Only in the morning, when Goldsmith called for his bill, did Sir Ralph reveal that he had been not at an inn, but at the home of one of the top families in the country.

On the subject of *She Stoops to Conquer*, according to theatre legend a conman in the American West approached the box-office of a small town theatre in the late nineteenth century and asked to be given complimentary seats as he was the author. They let him in.

The famous actor manager Beerbohm Tree once waltzed into a Post Office and asked the woman behind the counter if she sold stamps. On being told that she did, he demanded to be shown some.

She brought out a large sheet of stamps. Tree stuck out his finger and pointed at one right in the middle of the sheet. 'I'll have that one,' he said.

A Pawn Actor

In the 1850s the celebrated American tragedian, Mr Cooke, found that he was short of money while playing in Philadelphia. On the evening of one of his benefit nights, he was without any ready cash.

As he wandered around town, trying to think of a new wheeze to raise money, he came across the sign of the three golden balls. He entered the pawnbroker's shop and said: 'My name is Cooke. This is my benefit night. The manager can't do without me. I am up for Richard III. I want something to eat. I have no money. Now I propose to pledge myself for ten dollars, and you may lay me upon one of your shelves.'

So persuasive was he that the pawnbroker paid the $10 dollars and Cooke climbed on to a shelf. The theatre was crowded that evening, but there was no Cooke. At seven o'clock, the time the curtain should have gone up, the manager appeared before the audience and apologised, stating that with their permission, the evening would begin with a farce.

In the meantime, he sent scouts off all over town. But they couldn't locate Cooke in any of the usual places. Before long, a messenger found the manager and gave him a letter which Cooke had written in code. When finally translated, it read: 'My Dear Jones – I am pawned for ten dollars; send and redeem me, or it will be impossible for Richard to be himself tonight. Yours &c, W. Cooke.'

Heading for the pawnbroker's, the manager found

Cooke on the shelf eating a plate of biscuits and cheese. In his buttonhole was a piece of paper that said: 'No. 1473; pawned for $10.'

Paying the money, the manager redeemed Cooke and the pair headed back to the theatre. Cooke quickly dressed and strode on to the stage to declaim: 'Now is the winter of our discontent.'

It is said that he gave one of the best performances of his life.

Something Fishy

The actress Sarah Bernhardt was not only one of the greatest actresses of her generation, but also something of an eccentric, eating off a skull Victor Hugo had autographed and sleeping in her coffin, which travelled with her.

When Mrs Patrick Campbell acted with her in *Pelleas and Melisande*, she was told by somebody in the company, perhaps unwisely, that Bernhardt never indulged in the sort of tomfoolery other actors were prone to. She never played jokes or had them played on her on stage.

This was like a red rag to Campbell, who decided to have a little fun. Knowing that there was a point in the second act where Bernhardt stood by a fountain and pulled a fish out of it, she bought a tobacco pouch that was shaped and painted like a fish. Returning to the theatre, she attached it firmly to the bottom of the fountain.

The next evening, Bernhardt adopted her usual position and bent down to take the fish out. But she hadn't reckoned on it being tied down and nearly lost her balance. Although Bernhardt carried on as if nothing had happened, Campbell couldn't resist laughing and muffed her lines.

Bernhardt said nothing at the end of the performance, nor when Campbell and she had lunch the following day. At the matinée afterwards, in a scene where Bernhardt helped Campbell over some rocks, Bernhardt took hold of her hand only for Campbell to discover that there was a raw egg squashed in it.

'I did not smile,' records Campbell, 'but with calm dignity I went on with my part. I can see now the tears of laughter trickling down her cheeks, and her dear body shaking with merriment as I grew more and more dignified to the end of the scene. Her company told me afterwards, almost with awe, that Madame must love me very, very much.'

What a Knight

Although Sir Gerald du Maurier played terribly serious roles on stage like Bulldog Drummond and the gentleman burglar Raffles, when he was around it was said that nobody was safe from his practical jokes. His friend Alfred Hitchcock and he used to vie with each other to see who could fool the other (*see* Chapter 6). He would take infinite time and trouble over his practical jokes and, unlike some other hoaxers who took such things calmly, he would often laugh until the tears ran down his cheeks when telling how one of his pranks had turned out.

According to Daphne du Maurier, he would invent strange contraptions that he hid under the tablecloth. By pressing a bulb, he could make plates move around, to the discomfiture of those trying to eat off them. Collapsible knives and forks and glasses that melted when you poured liquid into them were very popular with du Maurier. He would fill bread rolls with cotton wool, produce bananas that were actually made of soap and apples that squeaked when you touched them. He was also a great fan of whoopee cushions.

He once staged a theatrical version of the Chinese water torture, going to great trouble to make sure that while one of his fellow performers was tied to a chair on stage for some time, a drop of water would fall on his forehead every so often, distracting him from his lines.

Eye, Eye

Richard Burton went in for some bizarre practical jokes when performing on stage. He was a member of the cast of

The Lady's Not for Burning by Christopher Fry, along with Esme Percy, whose career was not hindered by the fact that he had a glass eye.

According to Bryan Forbes, to whom Burton told the story, Burton bought up a collection of glass eyes which, along with a fellow actor, he hid all over the set. These kept turning up throughout the performance. 'Somebody proposed a toast and found an eye staring at them in magnified liquid fashion at the bottom of the glass. People trod on glass eyes, slipped on glass eyes, opened purses and were confronted with an abundance of glass eyes.'

It's for You

Once into a play, actors can understandably become bored with repeating the same words night after night. Many try to relieve the tedium by trying to get their fellow thespians to 'corpse' or break up laughing.

A.E. Matthews was a veteran of British stage and screen who worked until well on in years. He once said, 'I always wait for *The Times* each morning. I look at the obituary column, and if I'm not in it, I go to work.' He was known in the profession for being one of those actors who could not be thrown by anything, no matter how ridiculous or unexpected. The other members of the casts of the plays he was in would try their damnedest, though.

Matthews was once playing in a genteel comedy when the telephone on a table began to ring. This was not in the script but Matthews could see from the expression on the face of another actor on stage with him that he had been set up.

He went over to the phone. 'Hello there,' he boomed. 'Oh yes. I see.' Then he looked at the actor who was having trouble suppressing his giggling. 'It's for you,' he said, handing the phone over.

Other versions of the tale have it that the phone actually was for Matthews, but that the increasingly forgetful actor simply couldn't remember his lines. I prefer the story the first way. In the States, the story is also told about the great Eve Arden.

Britain's great farceur, Brian Rix, was in a smash Whitehall farce in 1962. The House Full signs were up and there were people standing at the back of the auditorium at every performance. The cast became a little complacent and, to relieve the monotony, they resorted to practical jokes and attempts to 'corpse' the other actors.

Rix recalls that during the play he took a strange drug which sent him off-stage barking like a dog while Terry Scott would yell out, 'Look at him – just look at him. 'Alfway up that lamppost.' All the cast on the stage would follow Terry's gaze while the audience laughed at the line and Rix used this as an opportunity to fool around off-stage while the other actors were looking at him.

On Terry Scott's last night, Rix went to rather more trouble than usual. As Scott looked off-stage, there was Rix's understudy Gerry Dawson, dressed in a dog suit, on all fours by an actual lamppost. His costume was equipped with a rather phallic tube and a soda siphon connected to it. As the actors stared, Dawson lifted his leg against the lamppost and sprayed away.

Rix spent about £5 on the joke '. . . but it cost a lot more in actual fact, for the cast were quite incapable of another word and it was some time before we won the audience back.'

The Two Musketeers

When working on Richard Lester's *The Three Musketeers*, Michael York and Oliver Reed found themselves staying at the same posh hotel.

According to York, the main feature of the hotel's lobby was a large ornamental pond, well stocked with waterlilies and fish. The temptation to outrage the other guests was too great for Reed to resist, so he got hold of some carrots and cut them so that they resembled goldfish.

Sitting on the edge of the pond, he scooped his hand into the water, pulled out what to all appearances was a large goldfish and, holding it above his open mouth, dropped it in, munching it loudly.

The hotel suddenly found that it had no room for Mr Reed.

The Laughing Cavalier

Although now largely forgotten, Sid Field was considered, in his day, to be one of the greatest stand-up comedians ever to tread the boards. Among those of his admirers in the cast at his benefit performance at the London Palladium in 1951 were Danny Kaye, Laurence Olivier, Orson Welles, Elizabeth Taylor, Judy Garland and Douglas Fairbanks Jr.

The year before his death, Field was filming the movie *Cardboard Cavalier* at Pinewood Studios. Eating lunch in the canteen one day he noticed another actor from the film using the payphone there. Field realised that there was something unusual about the call. The actor didn't appear to be talking to anyone. In fact, he was not concentrating on the call at all, instead giving the appearance that he did not even expect anyone to answer the phone. For five minutes he simply stood there with the phone to his ear, before replacing the receiver, pressing button B and taking back his coin.

This happened the following day, and the day after that. By the time Field had witnessed it for the fifth occasion, curiousity got the better of him and he approached the man, begging to be told the point of the phone calls.

'Oh, it's nothing mysterious,' said the actor. 'It's just that I've got a dog that needs a lot of exercise and I can't afford to have someone look after him for me while I'm filming. Luckily, he goes mad whenever he hears the phone. So I ring him once a day, knowing that when I do, he will go crazy, running round the flat until he's exhausted. This way, I go home in the evening knowing that he's had some decent exercise.'

Field was impressed with the man's ingenuity and couldn't get the thought of it out of his head. It wasn't long before he decided to check the story out for himself. He found out the man's address from the studios and excused himself well before the next lunch break, taking a taxi to the actor's block of flats. The caretaker was only too happy to let the great Sid Field in.

True to form, the actor put his money in the phone in the canteen at the usual time, unaware that this time everyone in the room was watching. As usual, he paid little attention to the ringing tones, but gazed around the canteen. Seconds later, the assembled company witnessed his startled expression as the call was answered by the noise of a heavily panting dog.

The actors in the canteen, who were in on the joke, dissolved with laughter at his discomfiture. Moments later, realising what must have happened, the actor joined them.

Author, Author

The outspoken theatre critic James Agate made many enemies over the years with his barbed comments on theatrical performances. When he worked on an adaptation of *Blessed are the Rich* at the Vaudeville Theatre, it was too good an opportunity for those with an axe to grind to miss.

As the curtain fell on a lacklustre first night, there was wild applause and a barrage of loud cheers. Such was the enthusiasm shown that Agate appeared on stage to take a bow, at which point the claque changed to booing and hissing, hurling abuse at the stage.

Just Like That!

Comedian Tommy Cooper charmed everyone he met. He was not one to be fazed by anybody, apparently once asking the Queen at a Royal Variety performance whether she liked football. 'Not particularly,' she replied. 'In that case,' said Cooper, 'can I have your Cup Final tickets?'

He had a reputation for being somewhat stingy. It is said that he often used to spend ages chatting to stage crew, doormen or cab drivers, keeping them in stitches and then, as he left, he'd shove something into their pocket, saying, 'Here, have a drink on me.'

When the recipient got round to seeing just how generous Cooper had been, they would dig their hand into the pocket and pull out a tea bag.

A Drop of What You Fancy

There's a tale that seems to be told by almost every actor, variety and music-hall star. Arthur Askey was only one of many who professed that it happened to a friend of his. Staying in the usual cold, depressing boarding-house with the usual cold, depressing landlady and her terrible food, the chap got himself a bottle of sherry to keep himself warm.

He became suspicious that somebody had discovered where he had stashed the bottle and that suspicion turned to certainty when he began marking the level of the liquid on the label. It could only be the landlady. But two could play at that game, so the artiste decided to replace the golden liquid with some of his own.

The level kept going down and he kept topping it up until the time came for the chap to leave. He gave the bottle of sherry to the landlady, saying that as she was in the habit of stealing it, she may as well have the rest of the bottle. The lady was horrified. On the contrary, she said. She had been using the sherry to spice up her guest's food for him!

This story has acquired the status of an urban legend. At the opposite end of the social scale, it is interesting to note that it appears in the book *Great Country House Disasters*. It is said that at Townend in the thirties, the Brownes, the last generation of the Lakeland farming family, held a family council to discuss what to do about Collines, their butler, who had been at the sherry. Childish though it was, those family members who suggested retaliating by adding some of their own fluid won the day.

Despite their best efforts, the decanter ran out in a week. Concerned that his health might be suffering, they summoned him and took him to task, only to be told that 'Madam had herself suggested that a couple of teaspoonsful per plate helps most soups along.' With growing alarm, they realised that as it was winter they had been having soup every day!

Excuse Moi, Monsewer

'Monsewer' Eddie Gray was one of the great practical jokers of the British variety scene. He enjoyed such japes as pretending, along with Crazy Gang old-timer Charlie Naughton, that they were both doddery old men. Crossing the road incredibly slowly with stooped backs, they would wait until the traffic had backed up some way before straightening up and dancing the rest of the way across.

Gray is another of those credited with the postbox gag, shouting into the slot, 'Well, how did you get in there, then?' As the crowd gathered, listening to his end of the conversation, he would tell them that a postman had fallen inside when he opened the door to collect the letters and that the door had slammed shut after him. While he went off to the nearest Post Office to see if he could get a key, he'd ask them to keep the chap's spirits up by talking to him.

Arthur English, who played the porter in *Are You Being Served?*, was in a show with him when he turned up at his digs in Birmingham.

He had been told that the landlady was deaf, so he shouted at her, 'MY NAME IS ENGLISH. ARTHUR ENGLISH.' She roared back at him that she was pleased to meet him and so the conversation continued, with both of them yelling at the tops of their voices until eventually the landlady said, 'There's no need to shout. *I'm* not deaf.'

'Neither am I,' said English. Eddie Gray had warned each of them in advance that the other was almost completely deaf.

Crazy is as Crazy Does

The Crazy Gang were every bit as mad off-stage as they were on. During World War II they had been booked to appear at a large RAF camp. In the first of the two cars were the famous duo Flanagan and Allen, but the RAF police examining the offered papers were for some reason doubtful that they were who they said they were.

Eddie Gray, in the second car, stuck his head out of the window and, giving the outstretched Nazi salute said, 'Ve haf cum for der plans of der Blenheim bomber.'

The senior policeman turned to his colleague and told him to let them through. 'It's all right. They're the Crazy Gang.'

Bringing the Roof Down

While the Crazy Gang were doing a run at the London Palladium in the war, a bomb hit the theatre. It didn't explode, but got stuck in the roof. The owner, George Black, strung a piece of canvas underneath and kept the place open.

The band weren't particularly keen on this idea but, with their eyes warily on the roof, they settled down to play on the next night. Within moments, stones began to fall on their heads. The band ran for their lives. When Black looked upwards, there was the grinning Charlie Naughton in the highest box, a bagful of gravel in his hand.

The Unique Postbox

The Victoria Palace was another venue that was home to the Crazy Gang for many years. One day Eddie Gray and Charlie Naughton noticed that some workmen were about to install a postbox near the theatre.

Baffling them with gobbledegook, the pair pretended to be from the Post Office, checking that the box was put in the right place. They said that while the workmen had got the right spot for the postbox they were putting it in the wrong way round.

For years afterwards, it was the only postbox in London where you actually had to go into the road in order to post a letter.

A Dainty Revenge

Rod Hull, together with his emu, once worked on a show visiting South Africa. Also on the bill was Billy Dainty. On the final night, while Dainty was on stage performing his act, Hull unpacked all his bags and restored the dressing-room to the way it had been when they first opened. Not surprisingly, Dainty missed his flight back to the UK that night.

Although they later worked in pantomime together, Dainty said nothing about the incident. There was a point in the panto where Hull was up in the flies with his bird, ready to descend to the stage in a hot-air balloon. He was up there one night when he saw Dainty giving away presents to the audience. It gradually dawned on him that the bottles of Scotch, wine, gin and even a case of champagne were his, the supply that he'd got in and which he'd intended should last him the whole season.

Please Fix It For Us

When the actors of the Royal Shakespeare Company became irritated by the increasing amount of time artistic director Trevor Nunn was spending on other projects, they wrote to Jimmy Saville, asking him if *Jim'll Fix It* could arrange for them to meet Nunn.

It's Not Unusual

In 1980 Bernie Clifton was compèring a variety show at the Theatre Royal in Nottingham in which Jimmy Tarbuck was appearing. At one point in the show Tarbuck impersonated Tom Jones, swinging not only his hips, but also the microphone around his head.

On the Friday night the mike came away from the lead and shot into the stalls. Luckily it was caught by an alert member of the audience before it could do anybody any damage. Tarbuck came off vowing that it was too dangerous ever to do the routine again.

By the time the curtain went up the next night, Jimmy Tarbuck was in a foul mood. He had been called to the telephone several times but there was never anybody on the other end.

His temper wasn't improved when the band went into 'It's Not Unusual' during his act, even though he had expressly told them the number was to be cut. Unfortunately, he couldn't attract the conductor's eye and so had to start the routine.

At the point where he began to swing the microphone around his head, the house lights came up. The audience and the band were wearing hard hats! Clifton and the company stage manager had borrowed them from building sites that day all over Nottingham. They had used the time bought by the fake phone calls to rehearse the audience.

Merry Monnier

I can't say that the actor Henry Monnier means very much to me, but he appears to have enjoyed a practical joke as much, if not more, than the next man. When an actor in an eighteenth-century costume drama was about to go on stage, playing a courtier being presented to the king, Monnier gingerly placed a hat on top of the chap's wig.

As he approached the king, the actor playing the sovereign tried to tip the poor man off as to what had happened. 'You fool, raise your hat,' he was told. But as the only hat he knew about was the one being flourished in his hand, he popped that one back on his head, right on top of the other one. The audience, as always at their happiest when things go wrong, were delighted.

On another occasion, Monnier stopped a young actor just about to go on stage for the first time in his first big part. The part demanded a costume moustache and Monnier told the horrified actor that the right half of his moustache had fallen off. With no time to waste, the actor decided that he had better take the left side off too and forget the moustache completely for that performance.

When he arrived on stage with only the right side of his moustache on his face, the audience dissolved into helpless laughter.

Hardee Annual

Malcolm Hardee is one of the grand old men of the alternative comedy circuit, launching many now famous names at a series of clubs including The Tunnel Club and the Comedy Empire. He is no mean performer himself, in the variety tradition. His 'Greatest Show on Legs' is very popular in Germany and Sweden, where the idea of three naked men protected from prying eyes by a handful of rapidly popping balloons has given him enormous cult status.

Hardee frequently ends up nude on stage displaying what he feels is his most distinguished feature – his large testicles. 'They didn't so much drop as abseil,' he boasts.

While performing at the Edinburgh Fringe in 1983 he became irritated by the loud music coming from the neighbouring show, featuring Eric Bogosian, most famous for starring in Oliver Stone's *Talk Radio*. Both shows were being held in tents in a field and when Bogosian refused to keep the noise down, Hardee took matters into his own hand.

He got a tractor and, stark-bollock-naked, drove it through Bogosian's tent. He was followed out the other side by the curious audience, numbering about 40, while Bogosian went ballistic.

Not one to let a good enemy go to waste, the next year Hardee bribed the staff at the Albany Empire to give him access to the loading bay when Bogosian was recording a show there. Sadly, although Hardee tried to drive a fork-lift truck in just as Bogosian was about to begin his act, the truck was slightly too tall to get through the door.

Slobovian Visitors

When half-term came round, the teenage Michael Bentine would head from Eton to London to meet his brother Tony, six years older, who was studying at the Royal College of Art. Both looked foreign and had endured years of being called bloody foreigners. Bentine had once come home crying, saying that he had been called a 'Dago' at school, only to be told by his mother that he should be proud of being a Dago.

Because the trip home to the South Coast from London was quite long and boring, they devised a way to liven things up. The news-stand at Charing Cross station stocked a wide variety of foreign newspapers and the Bentines would buy the most foreign-looking they could find. Not for them the only mildly alien journals like *Berline Zeitung* or *Le Monde*. They were after the truly exotic papers with weird and wonderful scripts, usually from Eastern Europe.

Initially the two would pretend to do the crossword, counting the numbers of letters on their fingers and mumbling various words in Slobovian, a nonsense language that the two had invented. 'Vizavinya Kokoya Barustikay,' they would muse, as they puzzled over another tricky clue before exclaiming with delight, 'Brusti, Brusti, ya, da da.'

They relied on the intrinsic politeness of the British, who would soon attempt to talk to them. The nation's lamentable language skills were even worse back then and the standard way of communicating with Johnny Foreigner was simply to talk in English, but more loudly and slowly than usual.

'DO YOU SPEAK ENGLISH?' they would ask.

'Yes, few words, thanking you,' Tony Bentine would reply haltingly, all the time translating into Slobovian ('Sputna davisma manya vodkayitya') for Michael, who apparently spoke no English at all.

'IS THIS YOUR FIRST VISIT TO BRITAIN?'

'Yes, this ees first visit, my leetle bruzzer Stevodyev and me. Thank you please.'

'ARE YOU ENJOYING IT?'

'Henjoy very much. Yes. What is "henjoy"?' and so on.

By the time they reached Shorncliff, on the outskirts of Folkestone, the other passengers in the carriage were getting pretty hoarse. Praying that no-one else was going to alight with them, it was as the train pulled into the station that the brothers would get off saying, 'Well, thank you very much for a most entertaining two hours. Goodbye!'

6

Cinema

The Dumb Waiter

The Dream Factory was more of a nightmare for those on the receiving end of the incessant practical jokes played by many of the denizens of Hollywood. David Niven, Carol Lombard, Douglas Fairbanks, Tallulah Bankhead and countless others occupied their idle hours with hoaxes and japes.

In the days before his scandalous departure from the pinnacle of success, silent film comedian Fatty Arbuckle was a great prankster, often planning them with his friend Buster Keaton.

Arbuckle celebrated signing a new contract with Paramount by inviting the head of the studio, Adolph Zukor, to a dinner in his honour. Sadly, one of the waiters didn't seem to be up to the work demanded of him. Arbuckle admonished him for serving the first course to the men before the women, only to find him taking the shrimps by hand off the men's plates and dropping them on the women's.

The soup plates were placed in front of each diner but when the waiter returned to the kitchen, there was a terrible noise of crockery breaking. The waiter returned, covered in soup, and took all the plates away again.

Arbuckle began to lose his temper, claiming that it was so difficult getting decent servants he'd half a mind to give up films altogether and leave Los Angeles. This shook Zukor, for Arbuckle was then one of the hottest stars in Hollywood.

Finally, after an interminable wait, the waiter carried in a giant turkey on a platter. He dropped his napkin and bent to pick it up, only to be sent flying when someone opened the kitchen door behind him. The turkey landed on the floor, but the waiter was not deterred by that and picked it up, scooping as much of the gravy as he could onto the platter. Noticing that the bird wasn't in quite as pristine condition as before, he dusted it down with his napkin.

Arbuckle hit the roof and chased the waiter onto the kitchen, vowing to kill the man. There were terrible sounds of fighting, with horrendous smashing and banging noises audible to the guests, all of whom very properly kept their place, pretending they could hear nothing.

When Arbuckle returned, he apologised to his guests, telling them that the man had been dismissed and that a second turkey was being prepared. He was called to the phone and returned to say that his good friend Buster Keaton had rung and had been invited to drop by.

It was only some time after Buster Keaton joined the dinner party that Zukor twigged why it was that the new arrival so closely resembled the waiter. It had been Keaton, still largely unknown, all along, with all the other guests apart from Zukor in on the secret from the beginning.

The Blazing Bushman

We've already encountered press agent Harry Reichenbach, a man who got his break as a showman exhibiting a bowl of water billed as containing 'The Only Living Brazilian Invisible Fish'. In later, slightly more respectable days, he was a friend of Francis X. Bushman, a silent film actor whose greatest role was as a villain in the original *Ben Hur*. Earlier in the twenties, when Bushman was virtually unknown, Reichenbach set to work building up his profile.

First he brought him to New York, arranging a meeting with Metro Pictures. As Bushman had only been getting $200 or so a week in Chicago, Reichenbach knew he had to do something to impress Metro. So he stuffed his pockets with one cent coins and dropped them on the ground as he walked with Bushman from the station to Metro's offices.

By the time they arrived, the pair were being followed by a crowd of children who were gathering up the money and a good many adults simply curious to see what was going on. Impressed at the public's reaction to Bushman, the Metro executives offered him $1000 a week.

Reichenbach became the first ever Hollywood PR man, numbering among his clients Charles Chaplin, Gloria Swanson and Rudolph Valentino. He is probably the one man who can lay claim to having invented the publicity stunt.

Al Spoof You Again

Another Hollywood publicist, Al Horwitz, used to send hopeful film actors telegrams that read: 'DISREGARD MY PREVIOUS TELEGRAM. ZANUCK.'

Darryl Zanuck was head of Twentieth Century-Fox and Horwitz loved to imagine the confusion and complications which the wires would cause.

Handcuffed by Hitch

Alfred Hitchcock was as keen on practical jokes as he was on making movies. They were often, however, rather sadistic in tone, many of them revolving around the lavatory.

In *The Thirty-Nine Steps*, Madeleine Carroll and Robert Donat had to spend part of the film handcuffed together. The first day they were to work together, Hitchcock went through the scene as he saw it, then snapped a pair of handcuffs on them and led them through the first rehearsal. He then arranged to be called away on some technical matter. When he returned, he pretended that he had lost the key. Disappearing off to find it, Hitch was gone for much of the day.

The pair hardly knew each other and were extremely angry, particularly when Donat later discovered that the key had been left in the keeping of the studio guard the whole time. For his part, it is said that Hitch was pruriently fascinated by what they would do when one of them needed to answer a call of nature.

The Master of Suspense

When a technician on one of his British movies suggested that the set didn't look scary enough, Hitchcock dared him to spend the night on it alone, in the dark.

The chap agreed and let himself be tied to a chair in the middle of the set. Just before he left him, Hitchcock offered the chap a glass of brandy to help him sleep, to which the technician readily agreed.

In the morning, the man was in a terrible state. Hitchcock had laced the drink with an extremely strong laxative.

Hitches in Time

It was Hitchcock who once arranged on the opening night of one of his actor friend Gerald du Maurier's plays to have in the dressing-room, not flowers or congratulatory telegrams, but a horse. On another occasion du Maurier turned up at one of Hitchcock's parties in a kilt and wearing heavy make-up, having been told by Hitch it was fancy dress, only to find everybody else in full evening dress (*see* Chapter 5).

Hitch took great delight at watching his friends trying, at a smart dinner party of his, to find out who the aristocratic elderly lady was at the end of the table. Hitch claimed not to know who she was. It was partly true. He had hired her from Central Casting for the evening, just to see how everyone would behave when confronted by a perfect stranger.

The Early Bird Catches the Bus

Hitchcock became increasingly irritated by the persistent lateness of a technician working on one of his British films. When he tackled him about it, the man claimed that he came in some way from the country and that, even though he got the first bus of the day, it still didn't get him there on time.

Hitchcock did a little digging round and told the man he had discovered that there was a bus at around four in the morning that would get him in in plenty of time. The chap protested that such a bus didn't exist but Hitchcock blew his top and said that he knew he was lying and that if he didn't catch the bus the following day he would be fired.

Terrified of losing his job, the technician turned up at the bus stop the next morning before four and was astonished to see a bus draw up. Hitchcock, of course, had arranged the whole thing, hiring not only the bus, but also a group of actors to play the other passengers. When the technician arrived on time, Hitch praised him highly, saying he expected to see him at that time every day.

On the morrow, the chap was at the stop before four. He was still there three hours later, waiting in the freezing rain, when the usual bus pulled up. Arriving at the studio, he was once more bawled out by Hitchcock who said that he now knew that there was no reasonable excuse for such tardiness.

Barrymore's Last Role

Practical joking was endemic in the school-like atmosphere of Hollywood in the days of the big studios. One of Hollywood's most famous japes happened during the making of *Casablanca*. John Barrymore, an alcoholic and a man who in earlier years had adored carrying out hoaxes himself, spent much of his last year at the home of one of his few remaining friends, Errol Flynn. Two of his drinking buddies were Humphrey Bogart and Peter Lorre. When, during the shooting of *Casablanca*, the pair heard that Barrymore had died they bribed the funeral director to let them borrow the body.

They arranged Barrymore in a chair in Flynn's living-room and hid, waiting for him to return. According to Lorre, Flynn entered the house, threw his hat and coat on a chair and walked past the dead Barrymore to the bar: 'He nodded at Barrymore and took about three steps, then froze. That moment was fantastic! There was a terrible silence, and then he said, "Oh my God!" and he hurried back and touched Barrymore, then jumped.

'I think in that second he realised what was happening, and he shouted, "All right, you bastards, come on out."'

In Like Flynn

Flynn could hardly have complained. He was one of Hollywood's biggest practical jokers himself. During the making of *The Private Lives of Elizabeth and Essex* in 1939, one of the more accommodating female stand-ins slept with most of the cast and crew.

One lunchtime, she disappeared with the director Michael Curtiz. When he returned, Flynn told him that the electrician had been taken ill while Curtiz was away. He had contracted a form of VD that struck without warning.

Curtiz said it served the man right for not being more careful. Then Flynn let slip the name of the woman in question. Curtiz turned ashen-faced and rushed off to the studio doctor as quickly as he could.

An Old Fan

While making the screwball comedy *Midnight* in 1939, Claudette Colbert was visited by an extremely old man who said, 'Miss Colbert, I've adored you ever since I was a little boy.'

Furious, Colbert deduced, correctly, that her co-star Don Ameche had set it up and she chased him all around the set.

Bogie's Gonzales

Bogart took Verita Peterson, his mistress, to Romanoff's and, on the spur of the moment, introduced her as Petée Gonzales, a Mexican actress. She played along, speaking in cod Spanish and broken English all evening.

Later, she admonished Bogie, saying that she didn't want to have to go through all that every time they ate there. Bogart had a solution. The following time they went to

Romanoff's, she was greeted by patron Mike Romanoff as Señorita Gonzales. Bogie went beserk, claiming that Romanoff must be getting senile. 'This is my executive secretary, Verita Peterson. Christ! Can't you tell one broad from another? This is really embarrassing!'

The Great Escape

David Niven tells of the moment that director John Huston was called up for military service. 'The word came by phone when he was in the middle of directing Bogie in a scene in which the Japanese enemy had surrounded the hero in a small building. His escape had been carefully rehearsed – who he shot, who he knifed and through which window he would jump, etc.

'Huston never said a word about the receipt of his "call-up", he just tripled the number of Japanese around the building, boarded it up with the hero inside and left for Europe. A hastily summoned take-over director found a note: "I'm in the Army – Bogie will know how to get out."'

Tracing Traven

In 1948, John Huston was to film *The Treasure of the Sierra Madre*. It was written by B. Traven, an author who was obsessive about secrecy, who shunned the limelight completely and who refused to be photographed. Huston corresponded with the writer and, when the film was set to start with Humphrey Bogart in the lead, he asked if he could come and visit him in Mexico.

Traven told Huston to go to a particular hotel in Mexico City, but once there, the mysterious author didn't show up. Just as Huston was about to leave, a grey-haired man approached him and presented him with a business card reading: 'H. Croves – Translator – Acapulco.' A letter from Traven said that, 'This man knows my work better than I do.'

Without Traven to help, Huston hired the chap as a technical adviser on the movie. During the months on location, the director noticed that while Croves was only too happy to cooperate in any aspect of filming, he wouldn't allow himself to be photographed. Huston's letters to Traven in Mexico went unanswered and, when he pointed this out to Croves, he got nowhere.

When they returned to the studio lot to do the interior scenes, Huston found an old picture of Traven. 'Recognise him?' he asked Bogart. 'Sure,' Bogie replied. 'That's old Croves. I'd know him anywhere.'

Goosey Goosey Fairbanks

One of the oldest American traditions is an activity known as goosing. This is, according to *The American Heritage Dictionary of the English Language*, 'To poke, prod, or pinch (a person) between or on the buttocks.' Goosing on Hollywood sets at one time grew to almost epidemic proportions, to the consternation of the bosses who became concerned at the cost involved, as so many scenes were having to be reshot.

Douglas Fairbanks was renowned as one of the chief goosers. After a time, people were so nervous of being near him that he took to hiding behind things and using a long fishing rod to carry out his gooses. In the end, he was firmly told by the studio heads that he had a choice between goosing and his career, at which point the fishing rod resorted to its original purpose.

There's Such Electricity Between Us

Douglas Fairbanks had a chair made up which would give a small electric shock to anyone sitting it. He took great delight in watching people as the juice was turned on. He was puzzled on one occasion when an attractive young woman seemed unconcerned. On enquiring if she hadn't felt something, she told Fairbanks that she had, but that she imagined it was exactly what you ought to feel when you met a famous movie star for the first time.

Hellzapoppin'

George Burns tells of going to a Hollywood party given by writer John P. Medbury in honour of the comedy duo Olsen and Johnson, a wacky vaudevillian team whose greatest screen success was the madcap *Hellzapoppin'*.

Medbury's house was in the Hollywood Hills, at the end of a long driveway. Burns and his wife Gracie Allen found that, unlike the usual film party, there were no attendants to park their car. Instead, there were four donkeys tied to a tree. So they parked the car themselves, walked around the animals and made their way towards the house.

On the way, they had to pass through a tent, in which a man was sitting on a lavatory reading a newspaper. Without glancing at them, he said, 'Keep walking, you're heading in the right direction.'

Slightly further on they saw a chap sitting in a tree. He had a rifle in his hands and yelled at them, 'This is private property. Don't pick any of the oranges!'

When they passed the garage, they noticed that the interior had been converted into a bedroom. There was a red light over the door and a woman underneath it touting for business.

When they arrived at the house, there was Medbury to greet them. He introduced them to a woman he claimed was his wife. As Burns passed her, she goosed him. As he says, in the thirties, this wasn't considered a socially acceptable gesture.

When they stepped inside, the butler asked if he could borrow some matches to light the candles. Burns later discovered that the man had asked all 200 guests if he could borrow their matches. There were plenty dotted around the place, so it didn't seem to be a problem. However, they were trick matches, which went out immediately they were lit. Everywhere you looked, somebody was trying desperately to get a cigarette lit.

Although the party was in July, the living-room was dominated by a Christmas tree, fully decorated in all its glory, with presents at the bottom. There was a big, jolly Santa Claus too. Whenever a guest tried to pick up one of the presents, Santa would whack them with a cane, saying 'Ho, Ho, Ho' as he did so,

At half-hourly intervals, a bellboy would walk through the party yelling out, 'It is now eight o'clock!' It remained eight o'clock all evening.

Medbury had bugged the ladies' loos, so that anything said in there was broadcast through the house. Among the comments heard was one from a woman saying, 'What a stupid party, when the hell do we eat?' It was answered immediately by Medbury saying, 'We'll eat when I'm damned good and ready!' Burns never knew whether Medbury was in the ladies' loo at the time or not.

At ten o'clock, Medbury introduced a man attired in full diplomatic rig with a red sash and a chestful of medals who got to his feet, spoke Russian for fifteen minutes and then left.

Dinner was eventually served at eleven o'clock and passed off without incident. At around 12.30 a.m., a twelve-piece orchestra came in, put up their music stands, put their music on them and tuned up. As a hush descended on the room, their leader picked up his baton. The orchestra played a loud fanfare, after which Medbury announced, 'Ladies and gentlemen, the party's over.'

The musicians folded their stands and put their instruments away and the guests began filing out. On the way back to their car, the same chap was still sitting on the lavatory, but he was now reading the morning newspaper.

The White Thread

Burns claims to have been one of the few people that could make deadpan comic Jack Benny laugh. At a party one night, the two men found themselves standing together at a bar in their dinner jackets. Burns noticed that there was a small piece of white thread on the lapel of Benny's jacket. 'Jack, that piece of thread you're wearing on your lapel tonight looks very smart. Do you mind if I borrow it?' Then he took the thread and transferred it to his own lapel. Although recognising that it wasn't particularly funny, Burns says that Benny simply could not stop laughing at the idea.

The following day, Burns sent a small box to Benny's house. Inside was the piece of white thread, together with a note: 'Jack, thanks for letting me wear this last night.' Benny's wife Mary rang to say that after an hour Benny was still laughing.

The Famous Match Trick

At another party, given by writer Norman Krasna, 30 or 40 guests were standing round having cocktails and swapping small talk when Burns noticed that Benny was taking a cigarette and match from a box on the mantelpiece.

Burns called out, 'Quiet, everybody!' As the room hushed, he continued: 'Jack Benny is now going to do his famous match bit!' Everyone turned to look at Benny who stood, bewildered, with a match in one hand and a cigarette in the other, not knowing what to do. When nothing else came to him, he simply put the cigarette in his mouth and lit it.

'Jack, that's much better,' yelled Burns to him across the room. 'I notice you've got a new finish!'

Telegram for You

When George Burns was playing at the Majestic Theatre in Chicago on one occasion, Jack Benny was at the Orpheum Theatre in Milwaukee. Benny decided that after the show ended on Saturday, he would go to Chicago and spend Sunday with Burns. He sent a telegram reading: 'AM ARRIVING CHICAGO 10.30 SUNDAY MORNING. MEET ME AT THE RAILROAD STATION.'

Burns sent a telegram to Benny: 'LOOKING FORWARD TO SEEING YOU. WHAT TIME ARE YOU ARRIVING? I'D LIKE TO MEET YOU.'

Benny replied: 'AM ARRIVING SUNDAY MORNING AT 10.30.'

Burns sent off another telegram: 'IF YOU DON'T WANT TO TELL ME WHAT TIME YOU'RE COMING IN, I'LL SEE YOU AT THE HOTEL.'

Benny's next wire read: 'STOP FOOLING AROUND. I'M ARRIVING 10:30 SUNDAY MORNING. MEET ME AT THE STATION.'

Despite the fact that Benny was obviously getting irritated, Burns replied: 'HOW COULD I MEET YOU? DIDN'T GET YOUR LAST WIRE.'

Then the telegrams began pouring in. Benny had contacted his friends across the country and told them all to send messages to Burns. There were telegrams from Sophie Tucker, Blossom Seeley, Benny Fields, Al Jolson, Eddie Cantor, George Jessel and so on. Burns recollects that there were about 25 of them altogether, all reading: 'JACK BENNY IS ARRIVING 10:30 SUNDAY MORNING. MEET HIM AT THE STATION.' Burns pinned each one up on the wall in his hotel room.

He didn't go to meet Jack Benny at the station. At about eleven o'clock, Benny turned up, wanting to know, 'George, why didn't you meet me?'

In the midst of all the telegrams, Burns said innocently, 'I didn't know what time you were coming in.'

Working at Home

Like many other famous American writers, William Faulkner had a spell as a Hollywood script writer. Writers did not find Warner Brothers the most sympathetic of studios, for Jack Warner insisted that they clock on like manual workers, toiling from 9.00 a.m. till 5.30 p.m. with only an hour for lunch. He even specified the length their pencils should be by the end of the day. Many was the writer criticised on a picture who said that they couldn't understand what could be wrong as they'd worn their pencils down to a stump.

Jack Warner was a little more considerate to Faulkner, promising him a big office and a couple of secretaries and reassuring him that he wouldn't have to punch in and out like lesser writers. After seeing the atmosphere of the studio and hearing how other writers were treated Faulkner said that, on balance, he thought he would prefer to work at home.

When Warner needed some emergency rewrites done on *The Big Sleep*, on which Faulkner was working, he asked his secretary to put a call in to him. Noticing that the line was poor, he asked the writer where he was.

'Oxford, Mississippi,' was the answer

Warner hit the roof. 'But you promised me that you would be working from home.'

'This *is* my home,' pointed out Faulkner patiently.

The Sax Playing Scientist

Tallulah Bankhead once attended a posh society party with a distinguished-looking black man who, she claimed, was the assistant of Albert Einstein at Princeton. Although such a party would usually be exclusively white, the guests fawned over Dr Bechet, who had to spend the evening fielding questions all evening about the atomic bomb, relativity and so on. As the party was drawing to a close, he took out a saxophone and let rip with some lively jazz. Dr Bechet was none other than the jazz musician Sidney Bechet.

Framing Gary Cooper

Gary Cooper discovered a surefire way of reducing his everyday expenditure. Lee Marvin was with him once when they stopped for petrol. When Cooper presented the attendant with a cheque for $10, the man was delighted, saying that he would frame it.

On being quizzed by Marvin, Cooper admitted that only about one in ten of his cheques were ever cashed.

The Rebel's Mother

During the making of *Rebel Without a Cause*, James Dean became quite close to Ann Doran, who played his mother in the movie. Dean begged her to let him take her for a ride on his new motorbike but she, knowing his penchant for fast driving, kept refusing.

Dean kept on at her until, finally, she agreed. She climbed on the pillion, all the while telling him that he mustn't go too fast. Unbeknown to her, Dean had spent a great deal of time reconnoitring the Warner Brothers lot carefully beforehand, noting exactly what stages had both their front and back doors open and which alleyways were clear of obstructions.

The moment Doran got on, Dean gunned the bike to full throttle, whizzing across soundstages and down narrow alleys at top speed while, behind him, Doran screamed fit to bust.

When he finally stopped, Doran crawled feebly away, a complete mess physically and mentally.

The Faith Healer

Marlon Brando's first movie was *The Men*, about World War II veterans who had lost their legs in battle. Ever the method actor, before filming he inisted on spending time in a wheelchair with some paraplegics in an army hospital to see exactly what it was like.

They went to a bar one day for a few drinks but were interrupted by a woman from the Salvation Army. 'Oh Lord,' she cried, when she saw them, 'grant that these men may be able to walk again!'

Perspiration breaking out on his brow, Brando struggled to his feet and shuffled over to her. Brando's new friends were helpless with laughter at the sight of her astonished face.

Get Me Henny Youngman

The comedian Alan King was unexpectedly hired by director Sidney Lumet to play the part of a tycoon in the film *Just Tell Me What You Want*. He was himself the producer of a movie in Mexico at the time on which there were quite a few problems. So during filming at Astoria Studios on Long Island he would often find himself having to make calls to Mexico during the breaks.

This drove Lumet into a furious temper. 'I'm warning you,' he would yell, 'I didn't hire you to be a producer, I hired you as an actor. I want you on the set on time, every time. For heaven's sake,' he would say turning to everyone else, 'can't you get me Henny Youngman?' referring to the well-known comic.

King was frequently late on set, sometimes because he'd just flown in from Mexico. But the latenesses were, he felt, relatively slight. Nonetheless, Lumet would scream with rage, 'I took a broken down Catskill comedian and made a movie star out of him and he can't be on the set on time. Get me Henny Youngman.'

One day when King was not needed on set until the afternoon, he was driving down Broadway when he saw Henny Youngman carrying his violin. He stopped him and begged him to come with him to the set. So Youngman was sneaked into Astoria studios and secreted in the closet of his co-star, Ali MacGraw. Lumet began screaming for King. 'Where is he?' he yelled. 'He's flying in,' he was told.

After five minutes had gone by, Lumet was apoplectic. 'For heaven's sake, get me Henny Youngman,' he yelled.

The door flew open and Henny stood there, his violin in his hand. 'Now take my wife,' he said, 'please.'

Sidney Lumet went into a catatonic fit and shut down the film for the rest of the day. King says that is the funniest thing he's ever been a part of.

Graham Greene, Movie Star

When, in the early 1970s, Francois Truffaut was filming the superb *Day for Night* or *La Nuit Americaine* in Nice, he needed an actor for a small part, that of an English insurance agent. Writer Michael Meyer was visiting the set and was considered by Truffaut for the role, before being rejected as too intellectual-looking.

When Meyer mentioned this to his friend Graham Greene, Greene suggested that he try for the part, asking to be introduced as Henry Graham, a former businessman now living in Antibes.

Truffaut thought him ideal for the role, although he became a little uneasy when Greene tried to rewrite the scene he was to appear in. With everyone around him wearing curious smiles and the odd one giggling, Truffaut soon guessed that some joke was being perpetrated. He quizzed Greene, saying that his face was terribly familiar and wondered where he might have seen him before.

Greene confessed all but, instead of blowing up as he was wont to do, Truffaut took it all in great spirits, believing the hoax to be splendidly funny. Indeed Greene is not only in the finished film, but is also in the credits under the name of Henry Graham.

Driving Mr Barry

In 1968, in the days before he hit it big over here, Barry Humphries introduced a new character into his show, *Just a Show*. He was a fey Australian avant-garde 'underground' movie-maker called Martin Agrippa, who had been experimenting with the revolutionary Blind Man's Cinema and whose film *The End* had won the acclaimed Bronze Scrotum in Helsinki. Humphries wanted the sketch to be illustrated with an example of Agrippa's cinematic work. Interludes in the form of short films gave him a chance to recharge his batteries and to change into another costume or don some make-up.

In London, before he returned to Australia for the show, he was introduced to a young Sydney film-maker who, he was told, showed considerable promise. His name was Bruce Beresford and he was then in charge of the production unit at the British Film Institute.

Humphries apparently took to him immediately, especially when Beresford pointed out that a great many people in Britain and Australia were able to get large grants to make the most pretentious piffle that the public had no interest in whatsoever. Together, the two created a parody of such films for *Just a Show*.

Beresford filmed it at his home in Brixton, using a Nigerian in place of an Aborigine and including a scene of a naked girl running through the Australian Bush, with a Highgate park substituting for the outback. It cost the grand sum of £200.

They had to rough it up a bit, scratching the film negative and making the editing as amateurish and jumpy as possible. As Beresford later said: 'The hard thing was making it bad enough.' Humphries' audiences loved it. Each night it was introduced by Agrippa: 'This isn't a pretty film. It's crude and rough and instinctual. As crude and rough and instinctual as the Australian landscape itself. It isn't a nice cosy motion picture made by those nice, cosy, sold-out professionals. But is the universe cosy? Is God a professional?' The show was a great success Down Under although not, sadly, in London.

But that wasn't the end of Agrippa's 'film' by any means. According to Humphries it was later shown at several international Festivals of Underground Cinema where it was acclaimed as a masterpiece. That might be pushing it a little, but it certainly was shown at at least one European Underground Film Festival where it was viewed with totally straight faces, not one festivalgoer getting the joke.

Beresford later went on to make quite a splash in the movie world with classics such as *The Adventures of Barry Mackenzie* and *Barry Mackenzie Holds his Own*, as well as lesser works such as *Driving Miss Daisy*.

Behind Closed Dors

In his autobiography, Bob Monkhouse relates how Diana Dors and her husband Denis Hamilton used to entertain lavishly and boisterously in the days when Dors was one of Britain's very few equivalents to the Hollywood superstar. Her parties were pretty much along the line of

Hugh Heffner's famous shindigs, with plenty of blue films for guests to enjoy and Hamilton making sure that there were obliging girls on hand so that no-one went lonely.

At one party, Monkhouse noticed that couples were disappearing from the room one by one, but that they weren't returning to see the non-stop movies that were keeping him and so many others at the party entertained. After a while, Hamilton told Monkhouse that there was somewhere he and his new friend, Anita, could go if they wanted to.

They were led to a room with a large bed without legs in the middle of a room 'draped about in scarlet and purple silks in the style of the Arabian Nights', brightly lit by spotlights. As Monkhouse remarks, 'Add the smell of camel dung and you'd have had a knocking shop in Marrakesh.'

Hamilton locked them in, telling them they'd only got a quarter of an hour. Although Monkhouse noticed a mirror on the ceiling, he thought nothing of it. While he stripped to his underpants, Anita took all her clothes off and got on the bed.

But although Monkhouse was riven by desire, perhaps it was his innate Englishness that saved him. First he tried to find a sheet for the bed to cover them. 'Don't be silly,' he was told, 'there are no sheets or blankets on this bed.' He noticed laughter from somewhere, but thought nothing of it.

Instead, after Anita had removed his underpants, he went searching around the wall for a light switch to plunge the room into darkness. Again he noticed a laugh coming from somewhere. It seemed to be somewhere above them. As Anita began to get cross and told him to come to bed at once, Monkhouse realised that she was showing off and performing for somebody and that it certainly wasn't him.

The penny suddenly dropped as he realised that, above them, there must be people watching them. Understandably embarrassed, he dragged his clothes on while, just as angrily, Anita tried dragging them back off again. 'Forget it,' he screamed, 'I'm no bloody peep-show.'

As he finished dressing, Diana Dors opened the door and ushered him out, claiming that his behaviour was 'a wicked, wicked, waste'. She led him upstairs, rather than back to where the blue movies were playing. The room there was full of amorous couples misbehaving in the dark, the only lighting coming from below. Underneath, through a one-way mirror, Monkhouse could see the room where he had very nearly made an exhibition of himself just a few minutes before.

After glimpsing a little of the show put on by another lady, apparently a favourite with Diana Dors' guests, Monkhouse made his excuses and left.

Carry On Underpaying

The mainstay members of the series of Carry On films were notoriously ill-paid. The producers believed that no one person was essential to the success of the films and usually responded to any request for a pay rise by showing the ungrateful performer the Exit sign.

There was therefore some resentment among the cast when Phil Silvers of *Bilko* fame was brought in to star in *Carry On Follow That Camel* in 1966 for a £30,000 fee and the services of a chauffeur-driven car. It was something like ten times the fee any of the others received.

As a result, the cast were prone to have a good deal of fun at Silvers' expense, particularly when they found out that he was somewhat stingy.

One evening, after Silvers had gone to bed, Jim Dale got hold of the headed notepaper of the hotel where they were all staying and had a fictitious account made up for a party held that night. The bill was for an enormous amount and the next morning, when Silvers came down to breakfast, the cast each made sure to thank him for the party he had thrown for them the previous evening.

Seeing Silvers' ashen expression when he saw the bill was, apparently, almost good enough to wipe out the resentment they felt at his favoured treatment.

Seeing Right Up Broadway

Working on a feature-length animated film can be a deathly boring task at times and it is not surprising that over the years animators have striven to liven things up by popping little jokes into the films. Usually it's a cheekily altered picture painted on to just one frame, the animators reckoning that something that passes by in 1/24th of a second will never be noticed.

Although nobody has ever found it, there have long been stories that somewhere in the original *Snow White and the Seven Dwarfs* the princess revealed rather more of herself than in the rest of the movie. But whereas ordinary members of the public may never notice such things, it is said that Walt Disney himself was amazingly quick at spotting where animators had sneaked visual graffiti into his movies.

It certainly happened several times with *Who Framed Roger Rabbit?* In the original version Betty Boop appeared briefly and, even more momentarily, flashed her boobs at the camera. Although this was cut out of the video version the animators had another surprise in store for the studio. When, near the opening of the film, the temperamental Baby Herman storms off the film set and through a woman's legs, those viewing it in slow motion will see rather more than the studio would have wished.

That wasn't the end of the matter, for the laserdisc version came after that and this, too, was subtly altered. Goodness knows who these people who watch such movies frame by frame are but there must have been somebody doing it, for there is a scene in which the lovely Jessica Rabbit is thrown out of the car driven by Bob Hoskins. The videodisc version was prepared shortly after *Basic Instinct* appeared and, as she takes a tumble, Jessica's legs very briefly fly apart enabling the freeze-frame viewer, as *Variety* so delicately put, 'to see right up Broadway'.

7

Academia

Comic Specimens

Britain's 'Mr Comedy', John Lloyd, the man behind shows like *Black Adder, Not The Nine O'Clock News* and *Spitting Image*, fondly remembers that at Trinity College, Cambridge, a note was posted welcoming all freshers to the college. 'Fines will be imposed', concluded the missive, 'on those new undergraduates who fail to deposit their urine samples outside the junior bursar's office by 8.30 a.m.'

The poor unsuspecting man arrived for work the following day at 9.30 a.m. to find the corridor full of specimen jars, milk bottles, jam jars, tupperware containers and any other receptacle the students could lay their hands on at such short notice, all full of pee.

Chamber Music

I suspect one of the nicest sounding of all college practical jokes is apocryphal but I'm not one to let such trifles stand in the way of me telling it again. It is said to have taken place at Gonville and Caius College in Cambridge, in the days when students still had need of chamber pots in their rooms.

One student, who lived above a crusty professor, lowered his china chamber pot out of his window on a piece of string and banged it against the window below. Because the college backed on to a busy street, there were bars on the window and, not unnaturally, the professor was irritated by the noise the pot was making. Fortunately for the teller of the tale, he didn't simply go upstairs to remonstrate with the miscreant, but made the mistake of opening the window and grapping the chamber pot in a temper.

The student immediately let go of the string and disappeared down to the street. The professor found himself in an impossible situation for he could not pull the chamber pot back into the room yet if he let go it would smash onto the pavement, thus drawing attention to himself.

Unfortunately, some of those passing by the window assumed that the professor was collecting for something and the man was mortified to find people dropping coins into the receptacle.

Have You Met the Master?

A tale told of Charles Stuart Calverley, the nineteenth-century writer, as well as of many others, has him as an undergraduate showing a group of visitors around Oxford University. 'That is Balliol College,' announced Calverley as they entered the college. 'That is the Master's house,' he said, showing them the building. Then he picked up a stone and threw it at the window in front of him, smashing it.

'And that,' he continued, as a furious voice bellowed down at him, 'is the Master.'

Oznot Waz Not

One perennial college favourite is the enrolment of a ficitious student. In 1964, out of 4908 applications, Princeton accepted 1165 to join the university. One of them was Joseph David Oznot, the figment of the imagination of four existing Princeton students.

They were intrigued to know what the admissions board would make of such an academically gifted young man who also had interests out of class; he was a good lacrosse player as well as being a concert pianist of no mean ability. One of the brightest students at Princeton sat the exam on Oznot's behalf but actually did *too* well. The Director of Admissions was so impressed that he asked to meet the brilliant young man. A friend from Columbia University agreed to pose as Oznot and when later told of the hoax, the Director confessed that he had been completely taken in.

Georgia's Oldest Student

The habit of enrolling fake students goes back rather further than that. In 1927 Ed Smith of Georgia Technological University combined the names of his cat Burdell with that of his old school principal, George P. Butler, to come up with George P. Burdell.

Not only did Burdell 'attend' Georgia Tech, but he did so for more than 40 years, as a succession of students kept his name alive. He became something of an institution within the institution. With the university authorities fully aware of Burdell and, indeed, encouraging his continued existence, students would subscribe to magazines in his name and supply information to local newspapers' society pages about Burdell's wonderful parties. Eventually the papers even reported Burdell's engagement to a woman astronomer.

Burdell has now graduated, although the year of his graduation is somewhat variable. Georgia Tech still regularly gets requests from companies for references for their potential new employee, George P. Burdell.

Three Cheers for the French Master

Eton School believes that the way for its pupils to speak French correctly is by having a teacher from France over for a couple of years at a time. In the mid sixties, one of these chaps achieved a remarkable degree of unpopularity.

He was somewhat surprised, therefore, to find on entering the class at the end of one term that all his pupils had risen to their feet and were applauding him wildly. He was told that he had been elected the most popular master at the school and that there was a hallowed tradition that the title holder be carried round the school yard on the boys' shoulders as they cheered him.

They took him out of the classroom and, yelling loudly, carried the chap round the yard. Soon the noise was such that the entire school came to a halt and the headmaster came down to see what was going on.

'I'm sorry, sir,' he was told by the ringleader, 'but *Monsieur* asked us to carry him round on our shoulders cheering. He said it was a tradition in French schools.'

The King and the Gentlemen

There is a large statue of King Alfred the Great in Winchester. Near it, at one time, were some public lavatories. One night a group of students, who presumably had nothing better to do with their time than carry out practical jokes, painted footsteps from the statue to the gents and back again.

Astonished Winchesterites the following morning were perplexed to see that even kings have to go to the lavatory from time to time.

Water By Phone

Richard Boston tells of fellow Cambridge student David Frost taking advantage of the severity of the cold war, at a time when everyone was concerned about civil defence, to play one of the oldest telephone pranks. Frost picked a phone number at random and told the woman who answered that the GPO was cooperating with the civil defence organisation in experiments to see if, in the event of an emergency, water could be delivered by telephone line instead of the usual pipes.

Frost asked her to hold the receiver over a bucket and then made sounds as if water was being poured into the other end. He was told by the woman that no water had emerged at her end and replied that there was too much telephone cable at his end. Could she please pull some of it through by tugging her line?

She did so and informed Frost that although there was still no water in the bucket, the receiver was getting damp.

Selhurst, the Old Alma Mater

Cambridge undergraduate Humphrey Berkeley, later an MP, got himself into hot water with a wonderful hoax that involved the invention of an English public school.

Selhurst was a brilliantly chosen name, for you are already half convinced not only that you've heard of it, but that you probably even know someone who went there. Berkeley had some stationery run up for the school, which he based in Petworth in Sussex, and conjured up a suitable sounding headmaster, H. Rochester Sneath.

He then began writing letters. The Master of Marlborough was told that Selhurst's 300th anniversary was coming up and could he provide some advice on hooking royalty for the occasion. 'Perhaps you would be kind enough to let me know how you managed to engineer a visit recently from the King and Queen?' The reply was far from warm and friendly.

The next letter the Master at Marlborough received was

a reply to an apparent request for a reference for one Robert Agincourt, a former French master at Selhurst who was now apparently applying for a position at Marlborough. Sneath pulled no punches in putting the record straight about the imaginary Agincourt, pointing out that five boys had to be removed from the school because of his 'Hunnish' practices, while three matrons had had nervous breakdowns.

Sneath corresponded with George Bernard Shaw about the possibility of him visiting the school, even though he was over 90 at the time, while Sir Adrian Boult and the heads of schools like Charterhouse, Ampleforth and Lancing College were the lucky recipients of other Sneath letters. Architect Sir Giles Gilbert Scott was invited to design a new House at Selhurst, but replied that he was too busy rebuilding the Houses of Parliament.

Shortly after Arthur Fforde was appointed as the new headmaster of Rugby, Sneath wrote that, 'As an old friend of your father's (I used to fag for him at school), I felt that he would wish me to give you some advice.' This included telling Fforde that he should 'not be taken in by the hysterical outcries against homosexuality which appear from time to time in the Press. I have found that most homosexuality amongst schoolboys is harmless, and you can afford to ignore what is in most cases a purely transitory phase. Do not quote me as saying this, because although I believe it to be true, you cannot say that kind of thing to parents.' When Fforde replied, it was with thanks to Sneath for a letter 'so closely packed with good and serviceable advice'.

Unfortunately for Berkeley, he went a little too far when he wrote to the *Daily Worker* in April 1948 about the objections parents were raising in opposition to his plans to introduce compulsory Russian lessons. As if that was not bad enough, the Board of Trade was collaborating by not issuing the permits necessary to import Russian textbooks. As Sneath pointed out: 'English is taught in every Russian school; ought we not to grasp this hand of friendship?'

After this letter appeared in the *Daily Worker*, correspondence was also published from the Board of Trade's Chief Information Officer and from the University of London's School of Slavonic and East European Studies. On the quest of an interesting story, journalists on another paper went routing around, only to discover the truth about H. Rochester Sneath.

Assorted prominent public school headmasters inundated Sir Montagu Butler, the Master of Pembroke College, with a torrent of letters of complaint. In less tolerant days than ours, Berkeley was sent down from his college for two years.

Hacking It in America

Although English universities are not devoid of practical jokes (the irregular turfing of Oxford college JCRs is one prank that springs to mind, while there is a story of a greased pig being let loose in Balliol in the thirties that I'd love to track down), such high jinks tend to be concentrated in rag weeks and are all, of course, in the best possible taste while at the same time being in aid of a good cause.

American universities, however, appear to compete with each other to see who can come up with the most innovative 'hacks', as they call them. Students are 'pennied' into their rooms with coins jammed under doors so that they can't be opened from the inside; coins are superglued to floors; dollar bills are stuck to the bottom of toilet bowls at parties and then filled with tell-tale dye; animals are escorted into lecture theatres; vehicles are driven into canteens; and rooms are filled with paper, foam, inflated condoms and goodness knows what else.

MIT's Hallowed Tradition

MIT, the Massachusetts Institute of Technology, has a long tradition of 'hacks', with the MIT museum even publishing books about them. It is at MIT that the now rather passé prank of dismantling a complicated piece of machinery such as a plough or a car and then reassembling it inside a student's room is said to have originated.

Over the years, the distinctive Great Dome that dominates the campus has come in for considerable mistreatment at the hand of MIT's students. On Halloween night in 1962, it was turned into the jack-o'-lantern that Linus of the Peanuts comic strip dreams about. At other times it, and its companion Small Dome, have been utilised for various mammary jokes, such as Mamma Maxima Scientiae, or the Great Breast of Knowledge, while the Small Dome was once turned into a curious looking giant called George peeping over at the campus, after being covered with black polythene sheeting on which were painted two eyes. The top of the Great Dome has seen a working telephone booth installed in 1972, a plastic cow in 1979 while a real life cow by the name of Maisie was discovered on the roof of a dormitory in 1929.

Technology naturally plays a considerable part in many of the hacks. Perhaps this is why the authorities at MIT are so indulgent of the students, although the fact that students discovered that the tenth president of MIT had been responsible in younger days for getting a car on to a campus roof may have left him on tricky ground when it came to waving an admonishing finger.

The Donut-Eating Panda

In recent years, two technologically-based pranks stand out. In May 1994, on the last day of term, what appeared to be a campus police car appeared on top of the Great Dome, complete with flashing lights. As the day dawned, the car attracted a big crowd, not just among students, but also among the locals, together with reporters and TV crews. By the time the campus authorities set to work getting the car down, there were even helicopters buzzing around the scene to get a closer look.

The car was not in fact the genuine article, but consisted of a wooden frame, on to which metal panels had been fastened. Inside was a dummy dressed as a police officer, together with a toy gun and even a box of doughnuts. The car sported furry dice and a sign in the back window saying: 'I break for donuts.'

The publicity the stunt received wasn't restricted to the States alone. There was a beautiful photograph of the car being examined by the police in the *Guardian*.

The Greasy Poles

Although it is probably apocryphal, MIT alumni like to tell of a variant on Hugh Troy's park bench prank that they claim was carried out in Boston. The story has it that some students bought a barber's pole, making sure that they had a receipt.

One evening, they wandered round downtown Boston with it, until they were inevitably approached by the police. After producing the receipt, they were left alone for a while until the same thing happened all over again, and again.

After the police had stopped them five or six times, the students were delighted to hear over the officer's radio that headquarters didn't want to hear any more about a blasted barber's pole. If any policeman saw a group of students wandering round Boston with a barber's pole, then they were the genuine owners and should be left alone.

This was what the MIT hackers had been waiting for. Every barber's pole in Boston was now theirs for the taking. So they took. And they took. And they took.

Legend has it that there exists a photo published in the local paper of the students lined up with their trophies.

The Boston Popometer

Boston is, of course, the home of the famed Boston Pops orchestra and one of the big events in the city's calendar is the annual 4 July concert. Most of the people who attend the concert take a picnic with them to eat on the banks of the Charles River, before settling back to listen to the music and watch the fireworks.

In 1993, MIT students turned one of the Institute's buildings, just across the river from the concert, into the biggest sound meter the world has ever seen. Consisting of nine 6 foot by 4 foot square light panels, it was over 200 times the size of the pathetic little sound meter you probably have on your hi-fi, with an output of 5000 watts.

Sadly, despite their scientific studies, the students had made one miscalculation. They linked the sound meter to the music being heard on the radio rather than to the sound travelling through the air. Sound in air, as they of all people should have realised, travels more slowly than radio waves. As a result, the meter was out of sync with the music.

Happily, they were able to adapt the meter and it was soon entertaining the crowds by simulating the computer game Tetris and tapping out, in morse code, the letters, IHTFP, short for The Institute for Hacks, Tomfoolery and Pranks, the body responsible for practical joking at MIT.

Caltech Hacks

The California Technological University, or Cal Tech, is one of MIT's main rivals when it comes to hoaxes. In one of the better known in a long line of pranks, freshman Chuck Connor took some time off from college to go to visit his girlfriend.

While he was away, his friends made him a 'non-person'. His room door was plastered over, his name removed from assorted directories, pigeon-holes, lockers and so on and, when Connor returned, everyone claimed that they had no idea who he was.

It isn't only the students who get involved though. In 1970, three members of the faculty, driven mad by an unpleasant college administrator, got back at him by causing his parking place to vanish. All the other parking bays were repainted so that they were slightly wider than before and the name plates were all moved, except the victim's, which disappeared.

Smarter than the Average Bear

Two college students were working one summer in Yellowstone Park and got on the wrong side of one of the rangers, an officious man who took every opportunity he could to make their lives a misery.

One of the ranger's duties was to escort tourists to the site of the famous geysers, where he explained to them the extraordinary phenomenon which saw hot water spurt hundreds of feet up into the air.

One of the geysers, however, was more regular than the others and, out of sight of the ranger, the two students positioned themselves with a car steering wheel on a stick. At the moment when they knew the geyser was getting ready to spout, they turned the wheel, in full view of the tourists, who presumably went home believing that the whole thing was one big con.

8

Television and Radio

Hoaxer in the Box

Many people are quite content to watch others carry out hoaxes rather than practise the art themselves. These days Jeremy Beadle is the undoubted king of the public practical jokers in the UK. But practical joking as mass entertainment goes back some time before Beadle.

The *War of the Worlds* broadcast in 1938, when Orson Welle's Mercury Theatre's dramatisation caused panic across America, probably doesn't count as Welles was after verisimilitude and had no intention of hoaxing the public. Pete Murray may have been the first hoaxing broadcaster, when he took part in Radio Luxembourg's *Candid Microphone*. This programme was later turned into *Candid Camera*, first in America and then over here.

Candid Camera

Candid Camera's originator was Allen Funt and, although there was an element of cruelty in many of the stunts carried out by *Candid Camera*, in the majority of cases people seemed so delighted that they'd been picked as the mark that any thought of how ridiculous they'd been made to appear seems not to have occurred to them.

One of the most famous of the gags carried out by the long-running American series took place in a car park. One of the programme's presenters kept the victim chatting in an open space while a car approached them at some speed. Just as the victim began to realise that they were about to be run over and the panic showed on their face, the car split in two with each half passing harmlessly on either side.

When *Candid Camera* parked a car on a $10 bill, one very smartly-dressed woman was shown trying rather delicately to get it out from underneath the car. When she failed, she walked away. Minutes later, she reappeared, using her own car to shunt the other one a few inches forward so that she could then pick up the $10 bill.

In a bowling alley, the programme arranged for all ten pins to fall down with every bowl sent down by some terrible bowlers. What was most wonderful about the prank was the expression on the other bowlers' faces. Initially they were delighted that someone who was so completely awful at the game could occasionally get a strike. Then, as the bad bowler's score mounted and exceeded their own, they become steadily more upset.

People Watching

Candid Camera should be a topic for study by Desmond Morris for it provides a fascinating look at human behaviour. Some people are unbelievably gullible, such as a postman who guided a walking, talking post-box to its designated site on a nearby street. Others are amazingly compliant, such as the men who let a woman hand them the lead on which she was leading around her husband; while she was away, the husband would plead to be let off the lead, but to no avail.

Other scams involved leaving people alone in a shop with a ringing phone, the handset of which was glued down; arranging typewriters so that the carriages flew off when secretaries moved to a new line; and rigging one of the windows in an automat. This was an establishment where customers paid their money and then opened a door to take their food. A piece of string was attached to a bread roll, so that it could be whipped off its plate and back behind the glass in an instant. It does the heart good to see the stolid persistence of most of the victims.

The bizarre balletic manoeuvres undertaken by those presented with a sign beside a chequered black and white tiled office floor saying 'Walk on White Squares Only' are extraordinary to behold.

Many now famous faces participated in *Candid Camera* in the early stage of their careers. Watching Woody Allen dictating a fake love letter to a temporary secretary, full of over the top language such as 'the world revolves around you' and then making her read it back to him, is surely even funnier to us now that everyone knows who Allen is than it was back then.

From the Horse's Mouth

The most gullible man on the whole programme must surely have been Judge Jim Blaine from Oakland in California. While visiting a stable, he was accosted by a talking horse which was keen to give him some racing tips, literally from the horse's mouth.

Other victims listened to the horse telling them to bet on himself, Pitpena, but the judge was the only one that engaged in an extended conversation. The horse asked him: 'Don't tell anybody where you got the tip,' and received the promise: 'I'll certainly never tell a soul.'

The horse was naturally curious to know if the judge, who readily told the animal his name, made a habit out of talking to horses. 'I've talked to them,' confessed the judge, 'but I've never had a horse talk to me before.'

The Car With No Engine

In Britain, the show – licensed from Funt – was under the inspired control of the inventive Jonathan Routh. Around 6400 hoaxes were set up over the seven years of its life. By far, the best-known stunt was The Car With No Engine, the telling of which has turned into something of an urban myth with people recalling it as being far longer and more involved than it was.

What actually happened was that a car which had no means of propulsion whatsoever was allowed to coast down a hill and on to a garage forecourt. The driver, Routh, asked the garage owner to fill it up with petrol and then claimed to be having trouble starting it up again.

In trying to locate the trouble, the garage proprietor lifted up the bonnet and quickly realised that the engine was missing. To the delight of audiences, this much-repeated clip showed the chap looking under the car, in the boot, even inside the car, while he talked.

'Look here, you've got no engine,' he very reasonably told Routh. Puzzled at Routh's protestations that he had just driven all the way from Davenport in the newly-bought car, the garage owner kept quizzing him. 'To me this is completely mad. You've come straight from Davenport here? You haven't got out of the car or anything?'

'You say there's a bit missing?' asks the bemused Routh.

'It isn't a bit. It's a damn great lump.'

'A little bit further back there was a nasty bump on the road. I wonder if anything fell out then?' wondered Routh.

'No. It couldn't have fallen out. It's been lifted out with a crane.'

Telling Routh that he ought to have strong words with the man who had just sold him the car, the garage man's parting words were, very reasonably under the circumstances, 'This is mad. Absolutely mad.'

Louie, Louie, Louie

One taxi driver was dismayed after transporting Routh to be told that the most famous member of his flea circus had escaped from his matchbox and was somewhere within the cab. While Routh searched desperately for 'Louie', the cab driver became steadily more exasperated.

'He comes when you call,' said Routh, persuading the cab driver to join him in calling him. 'I've never heard of a flea coming back once he's got away,' said the knowledgeable cabbie, in between calling out, 'Louie, Louie, Louie.' 'I don't want him anywhere round me or the cab or anywhere else. I don't like those sort of things.'

'I've got to find him. He's my living,' pleaded Routh.

'This don't make sense. I can't wait here all night looking for one of those sort of things,' said the cabbie.

'We'll have to have the seats out.'

'We definitely don't.'

Routh eventually found Louie, with the cabbie still muttering that the whole thing was barmy.

Other British Candid Camera Pranks

Other stunts included a phone box that rose in the air while someone was using it; a tulip in a restaurant that drank from a customer's glass; a woman seeking help with a heavy suitcase that was actually full of lead; a mirror that smashed as women tried on a hat; the old chestnut of a man trapped inside a post-box appealing for help; putting 'Ladies' and 'Gents' signs on phone boxes (people of the wrong sex would move to the other one, even if they had to queue and the other was empty); speeding up a conveyor belt in the packing department of a cake factory to the consternation of the workers; a 'Wipe Your Feet' notice at the entrance to a public park; arranging for a snooker ball to fly out of the TV set of someone watching the game; and paying taxi-drivers with wet money taken off a clothes-line while a printing press could be glimpsed nearby.

On one occasion, Routh posed as the new manager of an off-licence that had been taken over by The Brothers. When customers came in for their usual tipple, Brother Routh tried to dissuade them from buying alcohol. 'People should get the poisons out of their bodies and get on to milk,' he told customers.

One of the best programmes shows the time that Jonathan Routh and five others began to march in step behind an unsuspecting victim. After a while, an inkling that something odd is happening occurs to the mark. But every time he or she stops and looks round, the following marchers are doing something innocuous. Hard to describe, it is worth seeking out the *Candid Camera* highlights on video to catch a glimpse of one of the funniest things yet seen on television.

Backfiring Stunts

Not everything they tried worked. Bob Monkhouse, one-time presenter, tells in his autobiography of how he wanted to offer members of the public fivers in return for £4.10s., believing that people would be so suspicious that they wouldn't accept the offer.

'The only way I could persuade *Candid Camera* to try the idea was by offering to use my own money,' says Monkhouse. 'Unfortunately, I did a roaring trade. In half an hour I was sold out – and £50 out of pocket.'

Another stunt that backfired was when presenter Peter Dulay appeared to eat a goldfish in a tank in a dry-cleaning shop in front of the other customers. They were aghast, not knowing that it was actually a piece of carrot. So was a woman who rang the programme to say that her small son had gone into the next room after watching the show and eaten their goldfish.

According to Monkhouse, the show ran into problems because it was becoming increasingly popular with criminals, who were pretending to be members of the *Candid Camera* team as a cover for robberies. After one costly bank robbery took place while the cashiers looked on knowingly, believing that they would soon be watching themselves on *Candid Camera*, the show had to have all its location filming approved by the police.

Beedlebum

Britain's best-known practical joker Jeremy Beadle is frequently claimed to be the most hated man on British TV. But Jeremy Beadle first cut his hoaxing teeth on radio, when he was a superb late-night phone-in host on LBC.

He came up with some extraordinarily inventive spoofs in this time as 'Beedlebum'. Two in particular stick in the memory. There was the time when he convinced people that, as with eyesight and hands, people had a more prominent ear and that we were all, to a greater or lesser extent, left-eared or right-eared. Before long, listeners were ringing up to discuss what it meant if they were left-eared, but right-handed and right-footed.

Beadle's greatest triumph on radio was undoubtedly the night when he went mobile, going out in central London, giving listeners clues to his location and offering a free tracksuit to whoever could find him. Initially, he was in a car, but he then moved to the Underground, changing lines as often as he could to throw people off the scent. Scores of callers rang to say that they'd just missed him at a particular station.

The clues led to Hyde Park and before long, the police had called the station to say that 200 people were buzzing around Hyde Park Corner trying to find him, in cars, motorbikes, bicycles and even one on roller-skates. Could they please call the whole thing off because it was clogging up traffic throughout that part of the West End?

In fact Beadle had never left the studio. They had simply been playing sound effects in the background the whole time, after having sent an engineer out a few days' earlier to record hours of the noise of travelling by car and Underground.

Watch Out, Beadle's About

Beadle proudly boasts that his show *Beadle's About* is the longest running hidden camera show in the history of TV. The sort of stunts it carries out involve destroying much-loved cars; persuading a chap that his new employers believe him to be a hit-man for the Mafia and giving him a killing to do; digging up people's front drives and so on.

Although *Beadle's About* only plays stunts on people earmarked as victims by their relatives, friends or workmates and checks with their doctor whether there is any reason why they shouldn't play a prank on them, they can still backfire. One stunt involved a fake mortuary and was all about an experiment in which bodies were frozen in the hope that they could be revived when medical science had advanced further.

Unfortunately, when one of the 'corpses' sat up and asked for a pizza, the victim's reaction was to dive straight through the nearest window. He escaped with only minor cuts.

The Two-Way One-Way System

A friend of a friend – despite the opening sounding as if it is an urban legend, I'm assured it *is* true – rang a radio station in Dublin claiming to be from the gas board and informing the station that, as a result of work on the one-way system in the centre of Dublin, traffic should ignore the signs and go round the other way.

The station broadcast the message, causing chaos when those who heard it tried to obey while the rest of the motorists behaved as normal.

Victor Lewis-Smith peppered his radio shows with hoaxes, ringing up London Weekend Television reception, for instance, to ask them if they'll give Haile Selaissie the message that he's going to be late for his meeting; calling the Vatican to offer himself as a DJ on Vatican Radio and playing them samples of his jingles while boasting of his success as a DJ in Top Shop; offering the news editor of ITN the whereabouts of Salman Rushdie's hideaway in return for £1000 and a young boy to help around the house.

Lewis-Smith's hoaxes are often extremely embarrassing to listen to, so thick is his skin. He becomes ever ruder and more obnoxious in the face of quite extraordinary charm and politeness on the other end of the phone. Listeners to the programme heard a BBC receptionist asking loudly if there was a Benito Mussolini waiting while another tried to see if Marcel Proust was there, only to be told by Lewis-Smith that he couldn't be, now that he thought about it, as he had died in 1922.

The Sailor's Hornpipe in Three Seconds

Victor Lewis-Smith's hoaxes are usually very clever but if you're like me, you find yourself frequently sympathising more with the victim than the perpetrator. Lewis-Smith even managed the extraordinary feat of making many of his audiences feel sorry for the people on *That's Life* after he rang up pretending to be a paraplegic who could play 'The Sailor's Hornpipe' on a trombone in three seconds flat while his dog jumped between the spokes of his wheelchair – a prospect that had Adrian Mills audibly salivating. Came the 'Hornpipe', then an explosion and a crash, followed by Lewis-Smith feebly saying that he had fallen out of his wheelchair and needed help, to the obvious consternation of those at the BBC who were powerless to help.

Lewis-Smith once got Arthur Mullard to phone philosopher A.J. Ayer and ask him what his favourite colour was. After five minutes of prevarication, Ayer eventually opted for: 'Blue . . . but not in a political sense.'

Clint Rees-Bunce

Lewis-Smith created the character Clint Luciano Rees-Bunce in order to carry out many of his hoaxes, although Reece-Bunce's sex, title and even religion could change at whim. It was as the Reverend Rees-Bunce that he told a newspaper in York that he had invented a device to stop bikes being stolen. It essentially consisted of a spring-loaded dagger underneath the seat. Not only did the paper carry the story, but several potential manufacturers expressed an interest in making the things.

Lewis-Smith is presumably a man with no sense of fear. He complained to a soup company, in the persona of a Wee Free preacher, that his son had found a condom in a tin of their French onion soup. Not only was the production line halted, but the CID were called in, turning up at a dinner party to have a word with 'Bunce'. That didn't stop Bunce subsequently writing to a condom maker to say that he had come across a tin of soup in one of their rubbers at a most inconvenient moment.

On Pattie Coldwell's first day as a radio phone-in host, the programme was given over to the subject of debt. A distraught Rees-Bunce was put through, claiming to have run up a bill of £200,000 on his credit card. In the middle of the call, the man suddenly screamed as sounds of breaking glass and shouts were heard. 'The loan sharks are coming through my window in an HGV,' he yelled before the line went dead.

One local radio gardening show got a call from him, supposedly on his car phone, asking for advice about the cactus plants growing on the dashboard of his Ford Capri. During the call, there was a squeal of brakes and a terrible crash. Just in case that wasn't enough to put the gardening expert off his stroke, there was then a phone call from the hospital claiming that the car phone belonging to the dead person who had just been brought in had last dialled the programme's number.

Lewis-Smith appeared on Tyne Tees Television's *Friday Live* programme as gynaecologist Dr Rees-Bunce, dressed in the Batman outfit in which he professed to perform his exploratories in an effort to make the whole business a bit jollier. Hidden in his trunks was an inner tube connected to a compressed-air cylinder so that when he asked the poor presenter if she'd like to examine his bat erector, he was able to demonstrate its power in a remarkably short time.

Together with a group of friends in Arab robes, Sheikh Al-Rees-Bunce ran up a bill of £2000 at the Whitehouse Hotel at the expense of Thames TV. He had booked the disparate group (including a rabbi and an airline pilot) to play some of the music they were to perform at the forthcoming wedding of the Sultan of Oman's daughter. It was terrible music but it made for exciting live television.

He's in the Book

When the Belgian publishers of the *European Biographical Directory* invited Rees-Bunce, a 'highly regarded, leading European figure', to submit an entry, Lewis-Smith could not resist it. There, just above William Rees-Mogg, is the massive entry for the Rt Hon. Sir Clint Lucioni Rees-Bunce, British, grandson of the inventor of nylon, married to Katrina Wackerbath, with children including 'Lee Wibble', 'Wendy Clack' and 'Bobo Tampax-Turdy'.

Rees-Bunce lists his published works, including *'Ramming it Right Up – Biography of a Pope (1981)'*, *'Which One of You Maoris Farted? (1982)'*, *'A Knee Trembler with Mrs Thatcher (1983)'*, and *'3rd Edition and You've Still Not Sussed! (1985)'*. His club membership was equally varied. Many people list Whites as one of their clubs, but fewer belong to the Arthur Mullard Club for Donkey-Poking.

Captain Pugwash

It is Lewis-Smith, together with his writing partner Paul Sparks, who claim to have made up one of the great urban myths of modern time, namely that the sixties children's cartoon TV series, *Captain Pugwash*, had among its roster of pirates, characters by the name of Seaman Staines, Master Bates and Roger the Cabin Boy. Picked up and repeated by the *Guardian*, this was widely believed to be true, even among those of us who watched Captain Pugwash every week.

Hoaxing the Hoaxers

Lewis-Smith claims that he once rang *Beadle's About* with an idea for a stunt based around American prisoners on Death Row. They could adapt the old game played at fêtes where someone had to move a metal loop along a bendy copper wire. At fêtes, it was arranged so that a buzzer would sound if the metal was touched. In this instance, the principle could be adapted so that it sent 20,000 volts through wires attached to the prisoner's frontal lobes. According to Lewis-Smith, the idea was turned down, not on grounds of taste but because 'our budget doesn't extend to foreign trips'.

Lewis-Smith has been on the receiving end of a hoax when his agent got someone sounding like Janet Street-Porter to ring him the day after he had mounted an attack on her.

'I was completely conned,' he told an interviewer. 'I went white as a sheet. I was going, "I'm terribly sorry, Janet, I think *Style Trial* is an excellent show." When I discovered it was a wind-up, it was like the captor-captive relationship. I thought the person doing it to me was a genius; I just wanted to hug her with relief.'

Heseltine Dies Prematurely

Chris Morris, best known for hosting *The Day Today*, a spoof of the *Newsnight* style programme, got into hot water with one of his radio hoaxes. It was on his Radio Show in 1994 that Morris announced that Michael Heseltine, the President of the Board of Trade, had died.

He even persuaded MP Jerry Hayes to comment on the death during the programme.

Considering that Heseltine was still recovering from a heart attack, it was felt that the spoof announcement was not perhaps in the best possible taste. It did, however, receive immense publicity and increase Morris's profile.

Taking a Rise Out of the Sun

One of Morris's earlier, rather more pleasing, hoaxes for the radio series *On the Hour* took place just before the last general election when Morris, pretending to be a northern businessman, rang the *Sun* to tell them that he had a tape of Labour leader Neil Kinnock that he had recorded in the Manchester Holiday Inn. On the tape, which he played down the phone, Kinnock could be heard drunkenly demanding to be served drinks and using language unbecoming to the leader of Her Majesty's Opposition.

The voice of Kinnock was actually that of comedian Steve Coogan, now better known as Alan Partridge. But the *Sun* didn't know that and they promptly sent round a minicab with a note promising payment of £2500 for the tape, while four of their reporters were despatched to the hotel.

Another seemingly ludicrous *On the Hour* hoax involved Liverpool Street tube station becoming unbolted from the system and slipping as far as Holborn. Yet it was lambasted by a *Daily Express* columnist as 'grossly irresponsible'. He had cancelled his journey in to work as a result of hearing the story.

Morris claims that he liked recording family arguments when he was young, setting the machine going and then helping to provoke and escalate whatever controversy was going on at the time. While working at Radio Bristol, he once filled the studio with helium so that the newsreader would be broadcasting the news in a silly, high voice. Unfortunately, for Morris, that evening there was a horrendous pile-up on the motorway and the gag got him sacked.

The Wind-Up Man

One of Manchester's Piccadilly Key 103FM most popular DJs is Steve Penk, another man with an obviously thick skin. A large part of his morning programme is devoted to assorted practical jokes.

Sometimes he applies for jobs to which he is particularly unsuited, using names that never seem to tip off the recipient of the call, even when they're as silly as Hans Datdoodishes, Ewan Meebabe, Sam Enchantedevening or Ken Woodchef.

When he rang up about a carpet-fitting job, he refused to be fobbed off by his prospective employer's belief that a motorcycle and sidecar wasn't the ideal vehicle for the job. The poor man on the other end became steadily more terrified at the idea so that when the idiot on the phone said repeatedly, 'I'll see you on Monday, then,' he really did believe that he'd been hired.

The extreme charm and reasonableness of the lady answering the phone at NASA in the face of Penk begging to be allowed to travel on the next space shuttle so that he could get away from some gangsters, is almost painful to listen to.

Penk's most popular pranks are wind-ups initiated by partners wanting him to get their mates worked up into a fury or by children wanting to steam up their parents. So Penk will arrange for wives to find out that their husband has bought them the very car they said they would never be seen dead in, for instance, or claim to be from the council complaining about them making too much noise when it's the neighbours who are the noisy ones. People about to go on holiday lose their rag completely on being told that the hotel they have chosen is fully booked and that they may end up sleeping on the beach or that a wall they had put up in their flat without planning permission will cost them £500 for the council to put right.

Quite why people should derive such glee from hearing their partners, parents or children worked up in to such a fury that the bleep machine is working non-stop is a mystery to me, but there's no denying that many of the wind-ups are extremely funny and hugely popular with radio listeners in the Manchester area.

The Dreadful Michael Barrymore Impersonator

LBC's late-night phone-in programmes (and those of London Newstalk, the new station in its place) have provided a splendid forum for hoaxers in London over the years. Michael Barrymore was listening one night to Clive Bull's show on LBC on the way back from an engagement, when a talent competition was announced. Barrymore decided to enter, reckoning that as he only had 90 seconds in which to impress, he would do a variety of impressions.

Parking on an industrial estate, he rang on his mobile phone, got on-air under an assumed name and started his 'act' with Danny La Rue before segueing into Lloyd Grossman, Tommy Cooper and David Frost. His *pièce de résistance*, so he reckoned, would be the impersonation of himself.

One of the panel of 'experts' the station had put together to judge the contest hated Barrymore's act and derided his impressions, particularly that of Michael Barrymore which, she said, sounded nothing like him.

He came seventh out of ten.

Fishy Sven

The longest running hoaxer on Clive Bull's programme was undoubtedly Sven, the lugubrious Norwegian fisherman who kept listeners entertained with tales of his romantic liaisons and the importance of fish in the Norwegian way of life.

Bull cottoned on after a while that Sven was in reality the late comedian Peter Cook. Cook had been watching a documentary about the Norwegian fishing industry and felt the sudden urge to expound on the subject, enlightening listeners about the way in which a man in Norway is judged by the fish he catches. It is fish that are

161

the way to a woman's heart, said Sven, who poured out his heart after his girlfriend Jutta left him, subsequently ringing up from various parts of the world as he tried to get her back.

Sven sent Bull postcards from all over the world and Cook was particularly tickled when listeners began to offer Sven advice on his love-life. On one occasion, a temporary switchboard operator refused to put Sven through, believing he was the usual sort of nutter. Bull had to issue a general order saying that anyone who sounded as if they were from Norway should be put on-air, come what may.

Mice Wanted

Monty Python once did a sketch about people who wanted to be mice. At the end, it gave a phone number to call if your ambition, too, was to be a mouse.

It was the home phone number of David Frost. After days of calls from people squeaking at him to show just how mouse-like they were, Frost changed the number.

There'll Be Heavy Precipitation

In Fresno, California, television viewers receive their weather forecasts while in the background there is live coverage of the scene at Fresno's air terminal. In March 1992, just as people were being updated on the latest barometric pressure, they were startled to see a body fall from the catwalk of the control tower, plunging to the tarmac below.

The TV station was inundated with calls but the 'body' was soon discovered to be just a dummy, thrown to the ground by a bored employee of the Federal Aviation Administration as a lark.

Free T-Shirt and Fine

In America a cable company was fed up that so many people were illegally watching their programmes by buying unofficial decoder boxes. Their boffins had tried time and again to change the nature of the signal so that only those with the proper decoders could receive the signal, but they were repeatedly beaten by the pirates.

Someone in the engineering department happened to mention that the station could actually broadcast material that would *only* be received by those watching the company's programmes illegally. So such a message was transmitted, claiming that anyone wanting a free T-shirt was to ring a particular number. At the other end, the company gleefully took down their details. Every single one was watching its programmes illegally and were supplying the company with the necessary details to prosecute them.

People of Earth . . .

In 1977 TV viewers in the Newbury and Reading areas were alarmed when the sound of the evening news programme coming from Southern Television tailed off and was replaced by a message from 'Ashtar Galactic Command'. A voice, calling itself Vrillon, told them that, 'We come to warn you of the destiny of your race and your world,' and informed them that they should lay down their nuclear weapons and turn their backs on false prophets.

In fact, the hijacking of the audio signal was carried out by a group of electronics-orientated students. They drove a van to the IBA's transmitter at Hannington in Berkshire and jammed the signal being sent to Hannington from the Isle of Wight.

Their own broadcast, in which the deep voice of the alien was pre-recorded on tape with the aid of a cheap electronic synthesiser, was transmitted towards the mast at Hannington with the aid of nothing more sophisticated than a car battery and a domestic television aerial. Their original intention had been to announce the coming of the revolution and to call for 'all dissidents to report to the nearest police station on

Monday morning'. In the end, they decided they'd get into less trouble if they stuck to the alien hoax.

It was not the first time this particular group had pirated the airwaves. In 1976, on April Fools' Day, they had intercepted the Radio One signal from the Towbridge transmitter and broadcast a selection of records banned by the BBC.

The following year they commandeered both Radio Two and Three for a total of three hours, broadcasting music that purported to be coming from a radio station, KSAT, orbiting the earth in space.

The Rake's Progress

American radio host Jean Shepard had a show that went out in the early hours of the morning, listened to by shift workers and insomniacs. He once rhetorically asked his listeners what they thought would happen if he invented the name of a book. The idea took root with his audience and they concocted a fantasy about a book called *I, Libertine*, the tale of an eighteenth-century rake by Frederick R. Ewing. They even made up a life for Ewing, reckoning that he was an ex-officer of the British Royal Navy with a penchant for collecting erotica.

Shepard suggested that his listeners inundate bookshops with requests for *I, Libertine* to see what happened. A buzz grew up around the book, with word of the immense demand for it reaching the *New York Times*, which included it in a list of forthcoming titles.

Intrigued by such interest in a book that didn't even exist, publishers Ballantine contacted Shepard and asked him, together with sci-fi author Theodore Sturgeon, to dash off a quick cash-in paperback with that title. It did so well that the publishers later brought out a hardback version as well.

Such a hoax probably couldn't work in this day and age when bookshops have such difficulty in tracking down genuine titles, let alone spoof ones.

In 1991, Channel Four ran a five-part series called *Art is Dead, Long Live TV*. It was a little too highbrow and oddball for many people. One programme dealt with Kenneth Hutcheson, who sculpted rotting flesh, human faeces and vomit and who had exhibited in Düsseldorf and Edinburgh. Another was about Richard Bradley-Hudd, a commercial director turned art film-maker giving his fridge's eye view of New York. The third featured Hannah Patrizzio, a conceptualist architect who designed biodegradable houses in the forests of Bavaria, and the last concerned Laura Mason, a new writing talent from Scotland whose book *Bingham's Pond* was a 'radical redefinition of the novel'.

Each programme looked in detail at the artist's work, with various critics and other artists discussing its merits or otherwise. In the fifth programme, the four artists gathered in the studio with host Muriel Gray to comment on how they felt about the four films. The conversation became somewhat heated and ended with Kenneth Hutcheson calling Gray 'nothing but a failed artist and a failed TV presenter' before throwing a glass of red wine over her.

The critics lapped it up and lauded the programme, to Gray's amusement, some even claiming to have heard of the artist before. But at the end of the final programme, it was revealed that the whole thing was a hoax from beginning to end. Perhaps people might have cottoned on sooner if the film-makers had stuck to their original intention of calling the programme *ENC*, short for *Emperor's New Clothes*.

Although they had initially thought of using actors, they instead brought in friends as the 'artists'. Kenneth Hutcheson was a computer salesman, Bradley-Hudd was an architect, Hannah Patrizzio an antiques dealer called Marione Schnell and novelist Laura Mason was actually Carole Wilson, a beautician. Gray had set it up 'to show that, whether it's real or not, as soon as it is on telly it's elevated. TV programmes falsify truth and information all the time. To me, art is so important that, without it, we could cop it. I don't like to see it undervalued or devalued by the duplicity of programme-makers.'

When word of the truth got out, the papers went for it in a big way, with even the *Sun* splashing out on the story. 'I've never seen so much press coverage,' said Gray. 'I wish they'd get a grip. It's not as if we've shot the Pope; it's only an arts programme . . . we fooled the Press and they just can't bear that.'

Advertising agency Saatchi and Saatchi were so impressed with the commercial that Richard Bradley-Hudd had made that they got in touch, asking to see a show reel. Even when they found out that the whole thing was a hoax, they persisted, saying that they wanted to see more work from whoever put together the spoof because it was so good.

It's a Square-Eyed World

In the sixties, one-time Goon and eccentric genius Michael Bentine held TV audiences spellbound with his madcap programme *It's a Square World*, which took the documentary style of programme and turned it into slapstick with the help of its resident team of Dick Emery, Clive Dunn, Frank Thornton and, of course, Bentine.

The show, which ran for four years, used some wonderfully inventive and intricate models to recreate great events in history like 'The Battle of Waterloo', 'The Roman Invasion of Britain', 'Climbing the Smutterhorn' and 'The Flea Olympic Games', the last of which I still recollect with fondness to this day.

Each programme ended with a wild event that took place outside the studio, a style of humour that was later to be an obvious influence on Monty Python. Bentine mounted such extravaganzas as 'The Great Escape from the BBC by Tunnel' and 'The Search for the Source of the Thames'. A giant man-eating orchid chomped happily on BBC personnel, a band of Apache Indians set fire to TV Centre with blazing arrows and Clive Dunn once set off a giant rocket in the studio and blasted TV Centre into outer space.

'The Russian Expedition to Climb Woolwich Rubbish Dump' had the intrepid band of explorers disembarking from Captain Scott's ship, *The Discovery*, and proceeding along The Embankment on skis (with ball-bearings underneath) before, roped together, they tackled the zebra crossing and disappeared down the escalator of the Underground station. Michael Bentine says that he was always mystified by the way in which the great British public refused steadfastly to stare at them or regard them as behaving in any way oddly, whatever lunacy they might be up to.

This proved to be the case even with the most outrageous of all their stunts, 'Sinking the Houses of Parliament with a Chinese War-Junk'. After locating a life-size model of a real Chinese junk, they sailed it down the Thames to the Palace of Westminster and spent two hours bombarding the place with polystyrene cannon balls. 'Yet during that time,' recalls Bentine, 'nobody walking over Westminster and Lambeth bridges, at either end of this scene, took a blind bit of notice.'

On TV, it ended with the House of Commons sinking beneath the water, with the caption over: 'You have been watching a party political broadcast on behalf of the British people.'

One day a gang of stocking-masked crooks drove up to the BBC Accounts Department at TV Centre. They stormed inside, knocked out the cashiers and ran off with the staff payroll, amounting to some £10,000. According to popular legend at the BBC, the security guards not only did nothing to intervene, but actually asked the gangsters, as they squealed off in their stolen Jag: 'When is the programme going to be on, Mr Bentine?'

The Glass-Eyed Pilot

Bentine was in the RAF and claims that in the early days of contact lenses, an acquaintance of his, one of the RAF's top night-fighting pilots, was fitted with these revolutionary optical devices, then made of moulded glass. In the early, experimental stage, they were hideously uncomfortable but the chap persevered with them, even when he wasn't flying his de Havilland Mosquito fighter.

His navigator used to get most of his drinks free by telling people in bars that his pilot had a glass eye. As contact lenses were unknown to most people, they would ridicule the idea of a pilot having a glass eye. Before long, a bet would be set up, with the flyers entitled to a pair of double whiskies if they could prove their preposterous story.

The pilot would hold one of his eyelids wide open and, taking a coin, he would knock it against the surface of the contact lens. When people heard it tapping on the glass, they made their way to the bar to buy the won whiskies.

Invariably, so the story goes, they would ask, 'But doesn't the glass eye make flying difficult?'

The pilot would then get hold of the coin and tap it against the contact lens on the other eye, saying; 'Not half as much as this one does.'

Radioactive Peanut Butter

Just because they are not being filmed or recorded is no reason for inveterate practical jokers to cease their activities. Around 1950, Michael Bentine and the other Goons were in Jimmy Grafton's pub in Victoria when someone noticed that a briefcase had been left behind.

There had been a spate of atomic scientists leaving top secret papers in cabs, which gave Bentine food for thought. He set to work and, with his scientific background, was able to mock up some very impressive-looking documents, full of transcendental physics and formulae topped off with a great deal of German, French and Spanish annotations. He took delight in filling the pages with the sort of drawings that scientists like, giving the parts labels like 'Combustion chamber of rocket' and insisting that 'This venturi must not be too tight' and 'Tolerance must be 3 Angstroms'.

While he was at work, the others were making use of Jimmy Grafton's son's chemistry set, inventively mixing together not only the chemicals but also any other ingredients that were to hand. Their favourite was peanut butter, which they decided had rather an evil look to it when squashed into a test-tube and which Bentine felt closely resembled pitchblende, the primary source of uranium. The final touch was some scrapings of radium they scratched off a watch face, luminosity being a favourite gimmick with watch manufacturers in those days.

The briefcase was secreted in a phone box in Victoria Station in the tray where the telephone directories were kept and, tired from their hard work, the Goons headed off for breakfast.

Driving back just over an hour later, they were astonished to see that Victoria Station was cordoned off. Observing the staggering number of police around, they decided it would not be a good idea to own up to the prank.

They later heard that after the test-tube had registered on the Geiger counters, thanks to the watch scrapings, it was taken to the Harwell Nuclear Research Establishment, carried on the back of a motorbike by a man with asbestos gloves, while ahead of him rode other police bikes, sirens blaring to clear the way.

According to Bentine, the conclusion of the Harwell report was that the so-called dangerous substance was apparently 'radioactive peanut butter'.

9

The Printed Word

Fairy Tales

There was a time when, if there was no news interesting enough to put into newspapers, journalists would simply make it up. Some people would argue that that is still the case. Then it was often a case of necessity rather than sharp practice. Before the invention of the telephone it was often simply impossible for reporters to check on the veracity of facts in a story, particularly as people in the nineteenth century felt less compulsion to talk to people involved in such a lowly profession.

Even where the paper's own staff were conscientious, that was less often the case with 'stringers', who made their living supplying snippets to newspapers and who could not live unless they made sure that they always had some material that they could sell.

Never the Twain

Journalists were frequently hired, not just for their reporting talents, but also for their ability to come up with oddball stories to keep readers enthralled at the drop of the hat. Although now remembered largely for his novels, writer Mark Twain derived great enjoyment as a reporter from pulling the wool over other people's eyes, including his own editor. Some of this spirit found its way into some of his characters in his novels.

Writing as 'Josh', Twain (then Samuel Langhorne

Clemens) was a journalist on the *Virginia City Territorial Enterprise* in the 1860s. Among the stories penned by Twain was a report about a murderer who took refuge in a mine. With the posse afraid to go in after him, they instead blocked up the tunnel into the mine with rocks, only to find the following day that they had suffocated five Indians sleeping inside. There was not a shred of truth to the tale.

Nor was there anything to his report of a 100-year-old mummified man discovered in 1863. An inquest, according to Twain, came to the conclusion that the man had died of exposure. So severe was the petrification that even his wooden leg had turned to stone, while the body had become attached to the bedrock. Although the use of explosives to separate the body from the rock was mooted, the judge was adamant that he be left in peace.

On one occasion, the editor handed over to Twain while he took a few days' holiday. Even a few days was too much for the overworked Twain. Knowing that a simple entreaty to return would not work, Twain instead sent the poor man a copy of the newspaper. It libelled virtually every prominent citizen in Nevada, taking particular care to cast aspersions on the morals of many well-known women.

The editor dashed back the second he saw the paper, only to discover that Twain had printed just one issue of a special edition for his eyes only.

Massacre at Empire City

Twain's hoaxes sometimes had a more serious purpose. In 1863, he became outraged at the number of companies defrauding investors by inventing tales of forthcoming bumper dividends, waiting for the shares to rise, selling all they owned and then doing a runner.

He wrote a gruesome story headlined 'MASSACRE AT EMPIRE CITY' which told how one of the burnt investors in the real-life Spring Valley Water Company (which had conned its investors) was driven mad by the experience. The individual, according to Twain, had killed his wife and nine children with an axe, cut his own throat, and then ridden into Carson City holding his wife's red-haired scalp aloft before dropping dead himself.

Although the story was packed full of clues to give readers the nudge that it was a spoof, it was taken seriously across a wide area. The tale was taken up by many other newspapers and caused a panic. Twain later wrote that it had never occurred to him that '. . . anybody could ever take my massacre for a genuine occurrence . . . But I found out then, and never have forgotten since, that we never *read* the dull explanatory surroundings of marvellously exciting things . . . We skip all that, and hasten to revel in the bloodcurdling particular and be happy.'

Although Twain's editor had been happy until then to encourage him in his outlandish reports, he was alarmed at the reaction to the story of the massacre. A brief retraction appeared: 'I take it all back. Mark Twain.' It was the first time he had used his new pen name.

Dan De Quille

Twain wasn't the only reporter on the *Territorial Enterprise* with a talent for hoaxing. His colleague William Wright, writing under the *nom de plume* of Dan De Quille, could also be pretty imaginative. An ex-miner, his knowledge of the mining industry made him a highly-regarded source. However, like other journalists of the time, he was not averse to making things up on a quiet news day. His fake stories were often related to mining, as when he claimed that a perpetual motion mining machine was under construction, using a combination of windmill and turbines to extract sand and gravel in a non-stop operation.

His best hoax concerned 'solar armour'. This wonderful invention was made out of a sponge-like material, the brainchild of Dr Jonathan Newhouse, which enabled travellers to journey across deserts. The sponge was used to soak up water before the journey began and then, during the trip, a container full of water combined with ether could be squeezed to keep the suit wet. As the ether evaporated, it cooled the suit and protected the traveller from the effects of the sun.

Sadly, the suit worked far too well. According to De Quille's report, Newhouse had tested the suit by setting off across Death Valley. When nothing had been heard from him after three days, a search party was sent out after him. They discovered him, frozen to death in 120 degree heat, with his beard encrusted with frost. The story was widely held to be true, and was reprinted not only across America, but abroad too.

Among De Quille's other spoofs were The Travelling Stones of Pahranagat Valley. These were small stones largely composed, so De Quille hypothesised, of lodestone or magnetic ore, which moved together and apart in response to changes in the magnetic field in the valley. De Quille concocted a pseudo-scientific explanation about electrical attraction and repulsion which not only convinced many of his own readers, but also readers of other papers throughout the land.

A group of German scientists showed great interest in the stones, refusing to believe De Quille's protestation that the whole thing was a hoax. Showman extraordinaire P.T. Barnum offered De Quille $10,000 for the performing stones if the show could be repeated in his circus!

The Great Moon Hoax

It was a spoof that toppled *The Times* from its place as the bestselling newspaper in the world. Not only were journalists in America quite content to tell whoppers to their readers but, on occasion, so were their editors and owners, particularly if it led to an increase in circulation. There never had been such a circulation-booster as The Great Moon Hoax of 1835.

Richard Adams Locke was a writer on the relatively new newspaper, the *New York Sun*. With competition tough, the paper tried to win readers with snappy, sensationalist stories. Locke approached the paper's owner, Benjamin H. Day, with an idea for a spoof series which would cash in on the public's sudden interest in matters astronomical, with the return of Halley's Comet that year keenly anticipated.

For Locke, the purpose behind the articles seems to have been a wish to expose the public's extreme gullibility in scientific matters. To Day, it was a chance to boost circulation. The hoax began quietly enough, on 24 August, with an announcement that, 'We have just learnt from an eminent publisher . . . that Sir John Herschel, at the Cape of Good Hope, has made some astronomical discoveries of the most wonderful description, by means of an immense telescope of an entirely new principle.'

Herschel was an inspired choice as his work in South Africa meant that he would not be contactable to prove or disprove the story which, so the paper claimed, was being reprinted from reports in the *Edinburgh Journal of Science*. The hoax continued, four days later, with details of Herschel's new telescope, six and a half tons of it, with a power of magnification of 42,000 times. It enabled Herschel to sit in a chair and view the surface of the moon as if it seemed only 100 yards away instead of 40 miles, which would be the impression given by the most powerful telescope to date.

Over the ensuing days, the articles became more sensational in tone. Initially, Herschel described giant forests on the moon, lunar seas with beautiful beaches, deserts, volcanoes and poppy-like flowers growing on hillsides. Following that, as the newspaper's circulation soared day by day, he turned to the animal life that he had seen on the moon. There were multi-coloured birds, zebras, brown bison-like quadrapeds, reindeer, unicorns and even animals like beavers that walked on two feet and lived in huts.

Even before the most extraordinary revelations appeared, the *Sun* had become the most widely read newspaper in the world. On 28 August, when the fourth instalment appeared, the paper announced that it was

174

selling 19,360 copies, whereas *The London Times*, to date the most popular paper, was managing only 17,000.

It was that day's issue that carried the most startling news, that a race of 'man-bats', Vespertilio-homo, had been seen. They were, said Herschel, 'large winged creatures, wholly unlike any kind of birds . . . four feet in height [and] covered, except on the face, with short and glossy copper-colored hair and had wings composed of a thin membrane, without hair, lying snugly upon their backs from the top of the shoulders to the calves of the legs.' Their faces, 'of yellowish flesh color, are open and intelligent in their expression, having a great expansion of forehead.' These beings were clearly of some intelligence, for they were observed talking as well as bathing in lakes and flying. 'They are doubtless innocent and happy creatures,' Herschel was quoted as saying, 'notwithstanding that some of their amusements would but ill comport with our terrestrial notions of decorum.'

Nothing in the rest of the seven-part series could quite match the astonishment with which the man-bats were greeted, even though Herschel wrote that he had found a superior race of Vespertilio 'of infinitely greater personal beauty . . . scarcely less lovely than the general representations of angels by the more imaginative schools of painters.'

Not surprisingly, other newspapers were incredibly jealous and suspicious of the *Sun's* series. But even though the *New York Herald* pointed out that the *Edinburgh Journal of Science*, from which the articles were apparently taken, had not existed for several years, the public still chose to believe what they wrote in the *Sun*.

During the run of articles, the *Sun* was keeping the presses running for ten hours a day. Once it had finished its run, Day published it again in the form of an illustrated pamphlet which was then picked up by many newspapers in Europe, where readers were every bit as fascinated by the story as New Yorkers had been.

When Sir John Herschel was given a copy of the pamphlet, he took it in good humour even though, according to one report, he was later contacted by a women's club in Massachusetts that wanted to know how they could contact the man-bats, so that they could convert them to Christianity.

It was less than a month after the first article that the *Sun* came clean about the whole thing, although by then it was pretty universally known that the series had been a hoax. The *Sun* claimed credit for diverting 'the public mind, for a while, from that bitter apple of discord, the abolition of slavery.'

Poe-Faced

The paper was less happy nine years later when it was in turn conned into publishing a false story by Edgar Allan Poe. Despite the author's enormous success with horror stories such as 'The Fall of the House of Usher' and 'The Murders in the Rue Morgue', he was usually in pretty dire financial straits and perpetrated several literary hoaxes.

So he may have been motivated by the $50 he received, although he had reason to be irritated with the *Sun* in any case. A story of his, 'The Unparalleled Adventures of One Hans Pfaal', about a man travelling to the moon and living there among its inhabitants, was being serialised at the time that the *Sun* began the Great Moon Hoax. Its success was so great that Poe abandoned the serialisation.

Whatever his motives, Poe had little trouble convincing the owner of the paper that the Atlantic had been crossed by balloon. It was a time when ballooning was much in vogue and Poe invented an intrepid band of balloonists, Robert Holland and Misters Mason, Holland, Henson and Ainsworth (Mason and Holland were actually well-known balloonists) who had intended travelling from England to Paris in their balloon, *Victoria*, which had an envelope made of silk coated with rubber and was equipped with a propeller and rudder.

Unfortunately for the travellers, a high wind disabled the propeller and blew them out into the Atlantic. Seventy-five hours later and after difficulties posed by ice in mid-ocean, according to the article, the *Victoria* landed near Charleston in South Carolina. It caused a great stir, much as the first manned journey to the moon did, but the hoax did not survive for long.

Poe didn't seem particularly concerned to keep his prank secret. He actually stood on the steps of the *Sun* building telling people that that day's story was a hoax. When the owner of the paper discovered he had been had, he was livid and published a retraction of the story, to the delight of the *Sun*'s competitors who rubbed salt into the paper's wounds for several days afterwards.

Massacre in Central Park

As with Twain wanting to expose what he saw as financial misdemeanour among companies fleecing investors, so Thomas B. Connery later wanted to expose what he saw as wanton carelessness on the part of the Central Park Zoo in New York.

Connery, managing editor of the *New York Herald*, was walking through the zoo in 1874 – or so some reports have it – when a leopard that was being transported to an enclosure managed to escape. Although it was quickly surrounded and forced back into its cage, Connery was aghast to see just how many people had been nearby watching the procedure, among them children, who could have been savaged had the leopard got any further.

He determined to show up the laxness of the zoo's procedures (other accounts say that the whole thing was simply a fanciful attention-grabbing idea on Connery's part) and ordered one of his top writers to pen a satirical piece on the subject. With hindsight, Connery might have sought something a little less dramatic.

Rather than being tucked away somewhere discreet, it was front page news. It was headlined 'AWFUL CALAMITY', with sub-headings about 'Terrible Scenes of Mutilation'; 'Savage Brutes at Large'; 'A Shocking Sabbath Carnival' and 'Awful Combats Between the Beasts and Citizens'.

No punches were pulled as readers were told of a rhinoceros escaping and then battering down the bars of other animals' cages, allowing all the beasts to go on the rampage, killing other animals as well as people. According to the article a minimum of 27 people were savaged to death with 200 injured. Going into the sort of details that would have a modern tabloid editor reaching for the smelling salts, the report described 'a panther crouched over his body, gnawing horribly at his head' and an 'African lioness which saturated herself in the blood of eighteen victims; men, women and children.' Although many had been rounded up, the newspaper warned that about a dozen animals were still on the loose.

Although the piece admitted at the end to being a 'fabrication' from top to bottom, under the heading 'The Moral of the Whole', it was clear that most readers never got that far. New York was sent into a panic. While some people boarded themselves in their homes to protect themselves, a brave band of citizens took their weapons and searched the centre of town for animals to kill. Lest it be thought that people were unduly stupid for being taken in, one of those affected by it was the editor of the rival paper the *New Tork Times*, who ran into the street with a pair of pistols, turning up at the local police station to tear a strip off the officers for not keeping his paper informed.

The Spider Farm

Young journalist Ralph Delahaye Paine did not hold those who practised his own profession in terribly high regard. He particularly disliked the way in which, instead of investigating stories properly, journalists would simply lift pieces wholesale from other newspapers.

It was simple enough for Paine to devise an experiment to see if he was right, although it is unlikely he can have foreseen just how correct he was. In his own paper, the *Philadelphia Press*, he wrote a story about a spider farm near Philadelphia being run by Pierre Grantaire, an immigrant from France.

These were no ordinary spiders, but *Epeira vulgaris* and *Nephila plumipes*, which were being bred for one specific purpose. Their webs, it seemed, were particularly splendid and were much in demand by wine merchants, who could use them to give new wine bottles the appearance of great age.

The most magnificent spiders, according to Paine, were the queen spider, named Sarah Bernhardt, and her mate Emile Zola. Both of them were related to the 'bird-hunting spiders of Surinam' and were thus highly dangerous. The lesser spiders, costing $10 for 100, were sent out in small paper boxes by Grantaire who was doing a roaring business.

As he had anticipated, his paper's rivals lapped up the story and ran with it. But it didn't stop there. Newspapers across the country did so as well, often in the usually spoof-proof science sections. The Government was not immune. The bulletin of the US Department of Agriculture, Division of Entomology, mentioned the spider farm, as did several respectable scientific magazines.

Paine received hundreds of letters from people who wanted to invest in the spider farm industry and were after Grantaire's address, which they had been unable to find by other means. Over ten years after his death in 1925, reports about spider farms were still cropping up in publications.

The Ice Worms of Alaska

Not many hoaxes survive 100 years, but the ice worms of Alaska are still with us. They were the invention of E.J. 'Stroller' White, a journalist with a reputation for perpetrating hoaxes. He was hired at the time of the Alaskan gold rush by the *Klondike Nugget* specifically to pep up the paper with practical jokes of his own devising.

In his best-known spoof, White wrote of the ice worms that had been found to be living in the glaciers near to Dawson, Alaska. Because of a cold snap, they had 'come to the surface to bask in the unusual frigidity in such numbers that their chirping was seriously interfering with the slumbers of Dawson's inhabitants.'

Although a few locals did fall for the gag and go off looking for the worms, the rest of the town simply embraced the joke. Barmen were soon making Ice Worm Cocktails, using bits of spaghetti to dunk into customers' drinks.

Almost 100 years later there is still an annual Ice Worm Festival in Cordova in Alaska, with a giant multi-legged worm wending its way down the high street in a parade, while tourists can snap up postcards all over the area showing Klondike miners digging the worms out of glaciers.

No Moss on this Rolling Stone

Working for the *Evening Citizen* in Winsted, Connecticut in the 1890s was one Lou Stone, whose ambition it was to turn the town into the hoax capital of the United States. Over 35 years in journalism, from cub reporter to the paper's editor, he came up with some fairly extraordinary tales, the majority of which involved animals and weaved in the country equivalent of urban myths.

As with so many other hoaxes, other newspapers often picked up on Stone's stories and ran with them, as with his tale of a whale caught in a local pond that had 'Jonah' carved into its tail. Sadly, the creature disintegrated when removed from the water.

Other Stone reports included a tree that had baked apples on its branches, cows producing butter or ice-cream rather than milk, a river that ran uphill, a talking dog, a cat that whistled 'Yankee Doodle Dandy' (one for *That's Life*), a squirrel that brushed its owners shoes with its tail, a shy cow that would only let a woman milk her, another that produced hot milk after eating horseradish, a farmer that kept flies away by painting a picture of a spider on his bald head, another who plucked his hens with a vacuum-cleaner and a hen that laid red, white and blue eggs on the Fourth of July.

It was Stone who was responsible for the Winsted Wild Man in 1895, a hairy creature, naked, who appeared to take delight in scaring people. Once the story appeared, it was repeated in other newspapers and sightings began pouring in from people all over the area who claimed to have spotted the Wild Man.

The local inhabitants loved Stone's stories. He died in 1933 and, five years later, they put up a sign by Sucker Brook bridge that said: 'Winsted, founded in 1779, has been put on the map by the ingenious and queer stories that emanate from this town, and which are printed all over the country, thanks to L.T. Stone.'

The New York Times Hoaxer

Even the *New York Times* gave house-room to a hoaxing reporter, T. Walter Williams. Although his stories (best of which was a story about a monkey that learnt to play the ukelele) were less inspired than some others, it is the fact that they appeared in the *New York Times* at all that is remarkable, given that paper's highbrow tone and reputation.

The Sin Ship

In the midst of Prohibition, the *New York Herald Tribune* reported that a British ship operating as a speak-easy was moored outside the twelve-mile limit. 'New Yorkers Drink Sumptuously on 17,000-Ton Floating Cafe at Anchor 15 Miles Off Fire Island' ran the headline.

Ferried to the ship by small boats from Long Island, once on board the wealthy clientele were able to purchase drinks for the stiff price of a dollar, although presumably the presence of numerous 'unemployed chorus girls' helped reduce the pain to the wallet.

The piece actually included a map showing where the ship was anchored, prompting almost every thirsty New Yorker who knew someone with a boat to set out to find the Sin Ship. The customs and the coastguard were also keen to track it down, as were reporters for every rival newspaper. The following day the *Tribune* reported that the coastguard cutter *Seneca* was out looking for it. On the third day it reported that the search had been unsuccessful.

It was hardly surprising, as there was no Sin Ship or Booze Liner. It existed only in the imagination of reporter Sanford Jarrell. His bosses were not pleased to have such an inventive chap on the payroll. When they discovered that it had all been a hoax, he was fired.

Pigeon English

Horace Greeley, who founded the *New York Tribune* and edited it for 31 years, was renowned for his illegible handwriting. Indeed, there was only one compositor on the paper who was able to decipher it.

Two of Greeley's colleagues once caught a pair of pigeons while this chap was at lunch, put ink on the birds' feet, and let them run across a sheet of paper. This was then swapped for Greeley's real copy. The compositor did his best with the piece, but confessed to Greeley that there was one paragraph that he simply couldn't understand. Greeley looked at it and snarled: 'What's the matter with you? Do you expect me to print it myself? Here, I'll rewrite the whole page.'

Beachcomber

J.B. Morton, who wrote the Beachcomber column in the *Express* for some 50 years, was a keen practical joker. His persona was captured in *The Innocent Moon*, a novel by Henry Williamson in which he apparently appears, disguised as Rowley Meek, a writer for the *Daily Crusader*. In the book, Meek spent the course of a taxi ride raising his hat and bowing to pedestrians that he passed. When one chap started to run after the cab, Meek beckoned him on while telling the cab driver to drive more quickly.

Later he carried out a perennial favourite with practical jokers when he stopped beside a post-box, 'ear pressed to the red cylinder as he pretended to be listening intently . . . A crowd collected. Rowley then moved away and got back into the taxi, which drove off as a policeman walked across the road to find the reason why various puzzled people were listening and peering at the letter-box.'

According to one of Morton's friends, Gerald Barry, something very similar happened when he was walking through Guildford with Morton. Morton suddenly stopped at a letter-box and began talking into it, pretending that a small boy was stuck inside and telling him not to worry, that they'd soon get him out of there. When one of the growing crowd called for the fire brigade, Morton and Barry made good their exit.

The Country House Weekend

Another autobiographical novel which included a portrait of Morton was A.G. Macdonnell's *England, Their*

England, best known for its hilarious account of a village cricket match. The character Mr Huggins in the book is actually Morton, while Macdonnell called the character based on himself Donald Cameron.

There is one scene in the book where Cameron says that he is going away for a weekend to a country house. Huggins tells him that the only way to arrive is with a great deal of luggage: 'Take one suitcase: the butler sneers, the footman giggles, the under house parlourmaids have hysterics. Take fifty and they'll treat you like the Duke of Westminster!' Huggins then picks up a quantity of cheap, second-hand suitcases and, stuffing them full of anything heavy, he puts labels on them like 'Beagling Kit', 'Despatches: Secret' and 'Amateur Theatricals'.

By the time Cameron arrives, Huggins has been busy on the phone. 'The Secretary of the French Foreign Ministry rang up, sir,' the butler confides to Cameron, 'and Budapest has also been on the line. Budapest is to telephone again, sir.' On being presented to his hostess, he is surprised to hear her tell him, 'The Duke of Devonshire has been on the telephone . . . You are on no account to telephone him, but you are to go to Chatsworth in time for luncheon on Monday, and to say nothing to anyone.'

According to a close friend of Morton's, Hugh Mackintosh, this was based on a true incident, the hostess in question being Lady Houston, the quirky left-wing millionairess renowned for having trained over 600 parrots to screech 'Votes for Women' at the same time.

Morton seems to have had little of the diffidence that usually marks out an Englishman, once climbing on to the luggage rack of a train, screeching like a monkey and scratching himself, all to get back at a prim lady in the carriage who had taken against his ranting about something. At Harrow station one day, Morton leant out of the train window and yelled out to a group of schoolboys: 'Boys! I am Dr Smellcroft, your new headmaster!'

In its later years the magazine *Punch* was fond of performing practical jokes, with long-time contributor A.P. Herbert causing a stir when he wrote a cheque he objected to paying on the side of a cow.

It was at the end of the sixties that *Punch* really got into the swing of things, with humorist Alan Coren getting the ball rolling with his hilarious tale: Let Us Now Phone Famous Men.

International direct dialling had only recently become a fact of life for the British telephone user and Coren thought he ought to take advantage of the possibilities it offered. He recalled that, like so many other eight year olds, he and his friends had passed the time by ringing up Rickett Cockerell and having fourteen tons of coal delivered to one of their schoolmasters. Or there were those occasions when they would find people unfortunate enough to be called Dumm or Barmie and ring them up to enquire if they were.

Now the phone offered still greater possibilities. Why should Coren not simply pick up the handset and ring up a few world leaders? He started off by trying to find out Mao Tse-tung's phone number from the girl on International Directory Enquiries. She in turn got her supervisor, who told Coren that nobody ever phoned China. She gave him the number of the Chinese chargé d'affaires in London.

The voice which answered was not too keen on the idea of somebody ringing their beloved chairman. 'Not possible terrephone China! Not possible terrephone Chairman!' When Coren very reasonably asked how *they* spoke to China, he was told, 'GET OFF RINE! GET OFF RINE QUICK NOW!'

As Coren pointed out, 'The whole thing had taken 47 minutes. More than enough time for thermonuclear gee-gaws to have wiped both Asia and Europe off the map. I knew Harold didn't have a hotline to Mao, and it bothered me.'

Directory Inquiries didn't have Mr Kosygin's number, but they did have the number for the Kremlin and promised to ring back when they'd managed to get through. After thanking them, Coren asked for the Pope's number.

'Oooh, you are *awful!*' said the girl at Inquiries. 'You're not going to say nothing dirty to them, are you? You'd be surprised how many people ring up foreigners and swear at them.'

After promising to keep it clean, Coren was given the Pope's residential number. These were more innocent days and he could dial direct on 01039 6 6982. He got through but, sadly, his request to speak to the Pope directly was denied.

'The Bobe never gum to the delephone, *Signor.* Nod for you, nod for me, nod for Italians, nod for nobody. Is not bozzible, many regrets, 'Is 'Oliness never spig on delephone. You give me your name, I give mezzage to 'Is 'Oliness, 'e give you blezzing, okay?'

Coren was able to get the White House in three minutes flat, but a helpful secretary there told him that President Nixon himself was down in Florida. She was good enough to give him the number, telling him that somebody down there would speak to him. 'They did, and they were just as syrupy and sympathetic, and who knows but that I mightn't have got into the Great Ear if I hadn't played one card utterly wrong? What happened was, the call from the Kremlin, booked . . . an hour before, suddenly came through on my other phone, and I was mug enough, drunk with bogus enimence, to say to the American voice: "Sorry, can you hold on a sec, I've got Kosygin on the other line?" It was a nice moment, of course, but that's as long as it lasted. America hung up.'

Tickled when the Kremlin asked him, 'Is that Mr Coren?', Coren discovered that he was actually talking to Kosygin's private secretary. He asked for his good wishes to be presented to the Prime Minister and was promised that they would be passed on. 'I have not the slightest doubt that it was,' says Coren. 'It's a long way to Siberia, after all, and the cattle-trains leave every hour, on the hour.'

Although the leaders of Cuba and Egypt promised to ring back, at the time of writing Coren was still waiting.

Shaikh-ing It All About

At 10.43 a.m. on Monday, 14 January 1974, the London Stock Exchange ground to a halt. As *The Times* described it: 'An Arab shaikh appeared on the Stock Exchange visitors' gallery yesterday morning to see how Western capitalism operates. With his entourage of chauffeur and personal photographer, and in flowing Arab robes, he was soon recognised and a chorus of boos arose from the trading floor. He left hurriedly, but according to the Stock Exchange information service, calmly. Another £500m of foreign investment lost forever?'

The shaikh was Coren. In the midst of Britain's energy crisis, with the owners of oilfields holding the Western world to ransom and Britain suffering power cuts, he got hold of a costume from the BBC, adding a beard and a pair of dark glasses. Taking a cab, and suffering a lecture about the correctness of the Arabs dictating oil prices to the West in the process, his first stop was Cohen's Smoked Salmon Ltd in Golders Green. To his surprise, despite the presence of some 30 people in the shop, he walked out with his smoked salmon without much more than a raised eyebrow.

Even in the Duke of York pub in Finchley Road, he got little more than a 'Salaam, squire' from the barman as he ordered his orange juice. It was much the same as he went from Simpson's to Harrods, from a casino in Queensway to a strip joint in Soho. 'It has to be reported that the average Englishman,' wrote Coren, 'is a polite, generous, fairly incurious soul, whose worst excesses . . . are ignorance and a tendency to think in music-hall stereotypes and react with music-hall dialogue. He is also incredibly gullible.'

By now, Coren was ready for the big time. Borrowing a Rolls-Royce, a chauffeur and taking along a photographer, he bowled up to Downing Street. There were steel barricades across the end of the street in those days. But when the constable on duty peeped in the car, he was obviously happy with what he saw and saluted before letting the car through. The policeman guarding the door to Number Ten saluted too as the chauffeur opened the car door. Then, to Coren's surprise, one of the coppers pressed the doorbell. The door to the Prime Minister's residence opened and a footman appeared, ready to usher the visitor in.

At this point, says Coren, he felt enough was enough. As the Prime Minister of the day was Edward Heath, one can understand his reluctance at popping in for a chinwag. 'I wish merely for the souvenir photograph,' said the Arab-clad Coren. The photo was taken, and out they drove again. When Coren tackled another policeman later with the question of what would happen if he turned out to be a terrorist, he was told by the officer that an Arab terrorist would hardly dress as an Arab, would he?

Spurred on by such intriguing logic, Coren ended up by visiting the Stock Exchange visitors' gallery, where he was shown to a vantage point by one of the young women staffing the place. From there, he could peer down on the mass of brokers and jobbers doing business. His reception there was not as polite as elsewhere. 'One by one, these pecuniary paragons looked up; they nudged; they beckoned; they strode forward; they gathered. And, in a huge and univocal mob, they began to bay, 'Out! Out! Out! Oil! Oil! Oil!'

'Even if the action was promoted by a misguided sense of humour,' said Coren, 'there can, I promise, be no doubting the end result of its ugliness and its offensive puerility. Which was, staggeringly, capped by the young woman coming over to me and asking me to leave because I was "disturbing the members". They have a warm and winning way with guests, at the Exchange.'

As the *Evening News* put it: 'An Arab visitor appeared briefly in the visitors' gallery. The man, swathed in traditional burnous and djellaba, watched impassively as dealers cried, "Give us oil!" Who was he? "Just a casual visitor," says the Stock Exchange.'

The following year Coren and colleague Bill Hewison had business cards made up, showing them to be representatives of the Research Division of Anglo-Bahraini Oil Co. They travelled up to what Coren believed was the Scottish Klondike, the centre of Britain's new oil industry along the Moray Firth.

They kitted themselves out with a Land Rover, wellies, parkas and gloves and conjured up a brace of Heath Robinson-like equipment, including a metal detector and a poker welded to a trickle-charger with a set of headphones attached. Although they might not be able to explore the North Sea for oil, they saw no reason not to see how they got on on dry land, particularly as artist Hewison was able to knock up some very impressive surveying charts which implied that oil was just about everywhere, merely waiting for someone to stick their stiletto heel too heavily into the ground.

While failing to find scenes of excitement resembling California in 1849 or Alaska in 1890, they were the object of intense curiosity as they wielded their poker, marked their clipboards and spouted rubbish like: 'Deep pluvio-stratal echo-implosion soundings.' In the midst of beautiful countryside, residents would get terribly excited, telling the surveyors that they had heard the rumblings of oil underground and even smelt it on the air. They professed to have seen other men much like Coren and Hewison passing through on similar missions before and most tried getting a closer glimpse of the chart to see whether their homes were on top of a rich oil-bearing area.

Only one person seemed in the least concerned about the effect that oil exploration might have on the unspoilt landscape. He was the resident professional at Dornoch Golf Club who said, after they had wandered over his golf course: 'I hope to God you found nothing. They've played golf here for, oh, two hundred years. Would you dig all this up for a few barrels of oil?'

Under the editorship of David Thomas, *Punch* moved into overdrive on the hoaxing front, its inventive practical jokes being brought to an end by the magazine's sad demise.

With Saddam Hussein's Iraq being Britain's Public Enemy Number One in the early nineties, the magazine thought it would test just how patriotic the country's advertising chappies were. The ad-men were in the midst of a whopping recession, while Hussein was in desperate need of an image wash and brush up. Would they be willing to help?

Under the names Stephen Pearce and John Voland, *Punch*'s regular pranksters John Hind and Steven Mosco posed as media consultants who had been working in the Gulf for a number of years. They were back in England on a mission from the Iraqi Foreign Ministry to find an agency that would set up a 'balance redressing' publicity campaign. It would be a meaty contract, involving plenty of full-page ads in all the nationals.

The first contact, at Gold Greenlees Trott of 'Allo, Tosh. Got a Toshiba?' fame said: 'You are talking to the right person. Go no further. Let's start backwards. What sort of budget are we looking at?' But, after 'bouncing it off the chairman', the agency decided it was not interested at all.

Yellowhammer said that as they worked for the Central Office of Information, they thought the Government would probably take a dim view of them taking such an account. It was a similar story elsewhere. Bartle Bogle Hegarty turned it down because they never got involved in tobacco or politics. Saatchi and Saatchi simply told them to get lost, while J. Walter Thompson wouldn't handle it because of 'its highly charged political nature'. Young and Rubican also turned it down, while Collett Dickenson Pearce replied by fax: 'We have no interest in working on "Project K", whether you double, treble or quadruple our "usual commission". We would not work on it under any circumstances.'

Patriotic though the agencies were, the media caught a whiff of what was going on and lapped it up. After a story in the advertising bible *Campaign* and *The Financial Times*, headed 'PLAN FOR IRAQI ADVERTISING IN BRITAIN', the Press headed in force for Chelsea Harbour, where Iraq's representatives claimed to be. All the tabloids were there, along with BBC Television, which wanted to grab them for the evening news. As *Punch* editor David Thomas told the papers: 'The fact that British advertising agencies turn out to be patriotic after all is obviously a shocking revelation.'

Help Wanted for World Domination

Punch contributor Mike Conway wondered how the villains James Bond encountered got hold of all those disposable henchmen. Blofeld, Dr No, Auric Goldfinger, Sir Hugo Drax, Scaramanga and the rest were all able, with a click of their fingers, to summon hordes of black-clad cannon-fodder ready to lay down their lives in the struggle for world domination.

He prepared a series of ads:

MAJOR EXPANSION DRIVE: We require central command staff to work at Crab Key, our magnificent Caribbean headquarters just outside Kingston, Jamaica. Our military personnel structure combines the high standards and severe sanctions against personal failure you would expect with a more-than-generous salary. Benefits include free uniform, seven weeks annual holiday (subject to Crab Key's alert status) and the opportunity to work with one of the world's finest scientific minds. Definitely not a hands-on employer!

No experience necessary. Hurry, hurry, hurry. Interviews to take place as soon as possible. Apply to: Dr Julius No, Bauxite Mine, Crab Key, PO Box etc.

INTERNATIONAL APPOINTMENTS: When the boss disappears, would you work on or wimp out? The first is the kind of trainee we require at the Special Executive, a world-wide expert in breaking up and re-assembling old bonds. We are now involved in even bigger projects, and the successful candidates could work for such companies as Ernst Oil, Stavro Construction and Blofeld Engineering.

Most trainees enjoy privileged access to top executives. These may be tough in their methods, but if you survive, as we hope you do, the world will be your oyster. You may even meet the chief executive himself, as he travels from site to site in his corporate battle-sub.

If you have what it takes, send CV and covering letter to: Klebb Memorial Suite, Smersh, PO Box etc.

Sadly, getting the ads placed was a bit tricky. The *Glasgow Herald* rejected them out of hand, because they didn't take adverts for foreign work. *Ms London* was suspicious, as was the *Birmingham Post* and the *South London Press*. Conway tried putting cards in newsagents' windows, but got a lamentable response.

Fortunately, the *Manchester Evening News* ran the advert for Goldfinger. It ran just above an ad for a travel agent seeking employees:

BULLION DEALER seeks staff. Multi National Bullion Dealing Group require men and women to work in owner's personal cohort. Qualities necessary include loyalty, discretion and discipline. Generous salary and training. Staff problems personally and decisively dealt with by Managing Director. Based Kentucky and Switzerland. Expansion plans near Fort Knox. Apply: Auric Industries, 1 Austral St, London SE11.

Out of 200 replies, just four recognised that it had something to do with James Bond, with one saying that he had golf caddying experience and looked good in a bowler hat. Many were unsuitable, like the 20 stone fork-lift truck operator. But there were replies from a chauffeur to a lord, a former member of the Royal Corps of Signals with experience in Hong Kong of preventing the illegal entry of persons, together with a substantial number of ex-servicemen. The range of Army, Navy and Air Force veterans willing to sign up proved, to Conway's satisfaction at least, that 'a Blofeld or No need never be short of hired hands. All those who scoff at Ian Fleming's spy fantasies should think again. There are more Oddjobs than you think.'

Be My Valentine . . . Please

To mark Valentine's Day, *Punch*'s Hind and Mosco decided to place a series of lonely hearts advertisements on behalf of assorted celebrities.

Page Three girl Maria Whittaker got the most replies to the ad placed on her behalf in the *Sport*. 'Extremely busty, slightly plump, Maria Whittaker lookalike, early 20s, loves fast cars, photography, fun, fine food, seeks attractive, go-getting man, any age, for exciting conversation, poss more. Photo pse. Anywhere.' There were 59 replies, tempting her with sweet talk along the lines of, 'My big "turn-on" is to see a lady wearing sexy lingerie', 'Eating nice food is what I like, particularly steak, roast and seafood', 'I live in the Lake District and I'm single – if you saw the Cumbrian females, you'd know why', 'My dislikes are jumping out of an airplane without a chute and my likes are stockings and sussers' and 'I'm a quality assurance manager of a plastics company, even though I'm only 23 years old – shows what a go-getter I am.'

Kylie Minogue was the next most popular, with 45 replies to her ad in *Loot*. '21-year-old petite Australian girl, slim, blonde hair, into pop, jeans, telly, dancing, soaps and make-up, working in London 1990, would love to meet English boys/men. If you've got pen and paper, what are you waiting for? Photo if possible, love Yvonne!'

'I have never married and I am clean,' was one tempting reply, others being, 'I work nights in a supermarket and I'm completely bored' and 'You can tie my kangaroo down any time sheila (bad joke!).'

Among the men, Bernard Manning did best, with his ad in the *Sport*. 'Successful, hard-working club performer,

60ish, single, slightly overweight, wishes to meet kind, sexy woman, any age, to really lavish with jokes, money, romance. Pse write. Love, big kisses. Anywhere.' The respondents included someone who said they 'work locally and I drive a Skoda Rapide' and another who said, 'I can guess you're a comedian . . . I hope you are not coarse.' One was looking for a friend for their mother.

'Successful ageless Marxist feminist actress seeks committed "revolutionary" for close encounters of the politically sound kind plus Albanian holidays. On your marx, get set, go!' The ad for Vanessa Redgrave in *City Limits* managed to pick up five replies, including one from a 'Zen Marxist Comedian', another from a 'compulsive reader of anything from Gramsci to Hobsbawm', someone with a 'traditional warm red centre with a seriously green exterior' and a 'failed dialectical syndicalist with a degree in workers control'.

Cliff Richards' 'Preserved forties male into Elvis, Christianity, seeks woman before too late!' trawled only three replies from its insertion in *Time Out*, including one from a lady who said: 'I believe in the family, the police, good manners, God, and less graffiti. I do not know much about Elvis Presley but I have heard "Jailhouse Rock".'

Only one lonely heart found no comfort at all. Arthur Scargill received not a single reply to his ad. 'Militant Northern Trade Unionist, seeks politically-aware lass for stimulating conversations, meetings, conferences, pubs etc. Let's smash the new spirit of realism together!' ran the ad in *City Limits*. Sadly, no-one was tempted.

Loot turned down an ad for a Jason Donovan type: 'Successful male-model type, nice bottom, bleached hair; likes a singsong, having a laugh and making money. I hail from down under (Melbourne). I'm in London for several months. Contact me please, girls, Love, Jay.' The paper thought it a little improper, sending the postal order back together with the ad, with 'nice bottom' and 'likes . . . making money' underlined.

The authors of the hoax were intrigued by the subtle changes made to the ads before publication. Bernard

Manning's reference to living with his mother was deleted, while Kylie Minogue's, 'If your pen is out, what are you waiting for?' was toned down.

Recognising that many lonely hearts use dating agencies, Hind and Mosco sent off the Duchess of York's particulars to Dateline under the name of Belinda Hampton. Her computerised match was Anthony, who was 34, six foot one inch tall, interested in jazz, country and western and folk music, as well as listening to the radio, watching televised sport, do-it-yourselfing and pets.

When they sent Dateline details of Neil Kinnock – 'Welsh, working in politics . . . fun-loving, ambitious, generous, nervous' – they found he was matched with a 45-year-old primary-school teacher named Louise, remarkably similar to Mr Kinnock's own wife Glenys.

Dear Sir, I Am Disgusted

Another Hind and Mosco hoax involved sending off a number of complaining letters to see just how responsive companies were to grumbles from their customers. They complained to the BBC about the loudness of Terry Wogan's tie, to McDonalds about the size of the lettuce in a Big Mac, to Richard Branson about his beard, to Spurs about the quality of the tea at half-time at White Hart Lane and to the Archbishop of Canterbury-in-waiting about the way in which the Church was accepting women in high positions.

Buckingham Palace responded to a letter to the Queen about the decision to send Prince William to boarding-school along the lines of, 'I would not want him to repeat my tawdry experiences there.' 'I am commanded by the Queen,' wrote Robin Janvrin, 'to thank you for your letter and to inform you that Her Majesty has noted your comments on this matter.' When another letter was sent, grumbling about Prince Philip undermining the dignity of royalty by wearing an anorak, it got lost in the system.

The editorial executive of the *Sun*, Eddie Johnson, replied promptly after getting a letter grumbling about the quality of the Page Three girls: 'I'd like to know whether you're running out of horn-bags or whether you're trying not to be so saucy.' 'We are sorry,' wrote Johnson, 'that you think we are running out of hot girls. This could be associated with the long dry summer! Now that we're printing in colour we hope that they will appear a little warmer for you throughout the forthcoming winter.'

Supermarket chain Sainsbury's were the most responsive, replying politely to a letter complaining about the lack of bread late on Saturday afternoons.

'Derek Tomlinson' wrote back saying: 'I was not reassured by your generalised non-specific intention to "have a look at the bread order"', this time grumbling about muzak, the checkout girls and 'strategically-placed displays of sweets by the till to catch the kiddies' attention when mummy's paying'. He asked: 'Would it really be asking too much for you to reserve a bag of pretzels and a small brown sliced for me each Saturday?'

Instead of being told where to go, he received a reply suggesting that they meet to discuss 'a suitable arrangement for the reservation'.

BP responded promptly to a complaint of being overcharged for some chewing gum at a filling-station. Even though they then discovered that it had actually been bought from a Shell station, they sent a free box of gum anyway.

British Rail excelled themselves. They took two months to reply to a letter whining about litter on King's Cross station. Their reference for the note from 'Keith' was K3/15439/90-LD1/MM1210A/SCG/2/.

Porridge Makes Your Tadger Grow

The last great success *Punch* had was when Hind and Mosco mocked up a press release from The Institute of Gastro-Sexual Studies based in Zurich and sent it to the national newspapers.

'High Alkaline Diet Linked with Male Genital Growth,' it announced, explaining that ulcer sufferers had been being treated by the Institute with a diet of custard, yoghurt and porridge when an astonishing side-effect was discovered – a substantial growth in the size of the patients' penises. '62 per cent of ulcerated in-patients,' the release said, 'who adhered to a low-acid diet – custard, yoghurt, porridge – showed increases of up to 16 per cent in penile dimension.' The release pointed out that Dr Lionel Greene, the director of the Institute, was currently in London on a lecture tour and would be available for interview.

Recognising a good story when it saw one, the *Sun* tried getting in touch with Dr Greene. Although their phone call wasn't returned for almost 24 hours, the *Sun* decided that they couldn't wait. The first edition had a small story headlined 'PORRIDGE IS GOOD FOR YOUR OATS'. As the presses rolled, so the story grew. By the final edition, it was taking up ten paragraphs rather than the initial four, with a sub-heading of 'IT MAKES A CHAP'S ASSETS GROW' and had pride of place on the all-important Page Three, knocking Elton John's 'Battle with the Booze' story from the top.

Unable to reach Dr Greene, the *Sun*'s reporter had turned to other authorities on the subject. Tony Blackburn was quoted as saying, 'I eat lots of porridge and yoghurt and my member has grown by about half an inch a year. It is now over two feet.'

London's main talk radio station, LBC, took the story as its main topic on its middle of the night radio programme.

When Dr Greene finally contacted the *Sun*, he said that the Institute was looking for volunteers to come to Zurich to serve as guinea pigs. The *Sun*'s reporter confessed to Greene: 'I'll come straight with you, Doctor – I'm actually the Royal reporter. I was handed this yesterday because I was sitting in the office with nothing to do. I normally follow the Royal Family around. So, are we talking now about volunteers with ulcer problems or penis problems? Because obviously, being the *Sun*, the interest was in the side-effect on the penises . . . so we can say you're looking for 500 volunteers for penis growth. All right then, lovely, Doctor, lovely.'

'WANTED: 500 SOUGHT FOR PORRIDGE SWELL JOB' ran the story on Page Three the following day. 'The doctor who found that porridge helps men increase the size of their manhood, last night appealed for 500 *Sun* readers to take part in his research.' It was also the subject of a Franklin cartoon with a pair of Royal footmen bringing a giant bowl of porridge to the bed of Prince Charles and Lady Diana, on which was a headline 'DI WANTS MORE BABIES'.

For some reason, the rest of the nation's newspapers ignored the story completely.

Bunny Burgers

The American satirical magazine *Spy* is also partial to practical jokes. To celebrate Easter in 1992, writers Joe Queenan and Andy Aaron descended on various PR firms to see how far they would run with a completely ridiculous concept if they believed that a Japanese investor with an incredibly deep pocket was behind it.

Their idea was a new fast-food chain called Bunny Burgers Inc., which would sell ground rabbit, as well as french fried carrots, throughout 30 outlets in the US and Canada. Just in case this didn't seem ridiculous enough, diners could pick out their own bunnies before they were done away with, much like lobsters.

They contacted nine PR companies to 'assist us in determining whether the concept was feasible, public-relations-wise, and if so, what measures could be taken to mitigate public hostility toward the consumption of bunny meat at a time of burgeoning sensitivity towards the animals with whom we share this fragile planet.'

They printed up proper stationery and amended a Vancouver Stock Exchange prospectus about rabbit breeding to make it look like their own business plan. The company, according to its new prospectus, was targeting 'gastronomically adventurous diners' who liked the idea of leaner and more nutritious fast food.

The hoaxers were understandably concerned that the PR firms would simply tell them to get lost when they described what they wanted. Fascinated by the prospect of an account that could be worth several million dollars, not one did. In fact, they fell over each other for the account and Queenan and Aaron had to work hard to stop some from developing a prototype ad campaign on spec. They had obviously convinced the agencies completely, even though at one point during telephone discussions, they 'blew a Conair Prostyle Mini 500 portable hair dryer directly into the phone's mouthpiece' to back up their lie that they were in a private Gulfstream IV jet over Hawaii.

An actor and sushi chef posed as the mysterious Japanese billionaire bankrolling the project. He and one of the writers met the PR people in a $650-a-day suite in the Ritz-Carlton Hotel in New York 'that seemed big enough to have its own ZIP code'. The room also contained a pair of rabbits – the company's mascots – 'Bigwig' and 'The General'.

The public relations industry seemed in no way fazed by the project. 'It's new and it's different,' said one, 'and Americans like novel kinds of products . . . it's important to get the word "rabbit" out there . . . Americans love anything that's *chic*.'

One wanted to know, 'Would it interfere with the trademark of Playboy?' before telling them that they would have to abandon the ecologically-unsound Styrofoam containers that had been mocked up for the meeting. The containers had the Bunny Burger logo on and a pair of pink bunny ears sprang up as they were opened. The pranksters also played the PR people the jingle they had had recorded:

> Ooh, yummy yummy, got bunny in my tummy
> It's a Bunny Burger taste sensation (bunny!)
> Kinda like chicken, kinda like roast beef
> Pledge allegiance to the Bunny Burger nation
> They love it in France
> Come on and give it a chance
> Bunny Burger.

They were advised by one of those pitching for the account that, while he didn't think it a good idea to keep live rabbits in the restaurant, it would be great if the people behind the counter could be dressed in costumes with giant ears. The hoaxers decided to follow up his suggestion that they try the concept out on the public before proceeding any further.

A market research group canvassed eight Americans about Bunny Burgers, although initially they were not told what product it was they were discussing.

They didn't like the idea when it became clear what was being talked about. Asked whether, if they were on a desert island, they would rather eat bunnies or snails, they all opted for the snails. Even when the choice was bunnies or squid, they still wouldn't touch the rabbit.

They were then offered Bunny Burgers (in reality ground turkey meat) but, with the exception of one very large chap who wolfed his down, they did no more than nibble them,

most spitting them out. 'This could easily be the Edsel of the food industry,' said one. 'You'll have armies of kids trying to burn down the Bunny Burger place,' said another.

To round the hoax off, *Spy* set up a shop with staff in giant rabbit ears dispensing free Bunny Burgers. Even though there was a cage of rabbits clearly on view, over 100 Bunny Burgers were handed over. And while most people professed themselves to be horrified by the idea, many of them still ate their burgers. 'It's kind of like eating your dog,' one woman said. Chicken, liver and reindeer meat were other comparisons offered. Some passers-by denounced the whole thing vociferously. 'You guys are SICK!' screamed one sixteen-year-old girl. On the other hand, one chap said, after getting his first taste of a Bunny Burger, 'Can I take a couple home?'

Sadly, the conclusion of the market research company was that, 'If someone tried to go forward with Bunny Burgers, they would have picketers, protestors, riots outside the Bunny Burger stands, and so the product couldn't make it.'

Hi! I'm the President and I Use . . .

Spy contributors Alex Gregory and Peter Huyck noticed that even those American personalities who had once refused to endorse products had now succumbed, with Woody Allen promoting Seibu stores in Japan, Richard Dreyfuss boosting McDonald's and even Dennis Hopper advertising trainers.

The pair wanted to 'test the business world's limits of good judgement, sensibility, and taste'. Was there anyone who 'because of his or her position of power and influence should be kept above the crass commercialism of the battling brands?' They tried to ensnare various American corporations in a secret advertising venture that – brought out into the open – could be the biggest political scandal since Watergate.

What they were pretending to offer was the endorsement of President Bill Clinton himself, claiming that the legal costs of the Whitewater hearings had put the President in need of funds.

They invented the pukka-sounding L. Kensington Group and wrote to companies posing as Senior Vice-President Bradford C. Johnson. Asking that the contact be kept in the strictest of confidence, Johnson said that he had 'access to an unofficial "endorser" who has unparalleled visibility in the global market'. As an illustration of Clinton's past work in the field, genuine clippings from a couple of papers were included that showed Clinton naming New Balance trainers as his chosen running shoe. The money they were asking for the President's endorsement was deliberately pitched low so that they would know that 'any objections to our proposal would hinge upon scruples rather than budgets'.

Red Man Chewing Tobacco – 'The Flavour of America' – were told that, since being told to give up cigars by Hilary, Clinton had turned to their product. They were delighted and ended up offering between $15,000 and $20,000, for which they would like the President to be seen not only using the product, but also to be wearing a hat and T-shirt.

Subway, the second-largest restaurant chain in the world, got very excited at the idea of the President popping in for one of their sandwiches every time he was out jogging. It would be a *coup* for them if he switched his preference for fast food away from McDonald's but that didn't stop them haggling over price, with their promotions supervisor claiming that $10,000 was a little steep.

Ping Golf Clubs were delighted to be told that the President used their brand and appeared to have no qualms whatsoever about the planned cost of the endorsement. 'I'll try to draw in some parameters that give you some idea of what we're looking for – that we want to reach the avid core golfer and we want to do it in two magazines and we want to do it three times this year. And we'd want to mention the fact that the Zing 2 is the best thing he's ever hit.'

Weight Watchers were *extremely* interested in the idea of the President using them to show how he was managing to shed the pounds. A meeting actually took place with the General Manager of Corporate Affairs for Weight Watchers International and the Vice-President of Corporate Affairs at Heinz, which owns Weight Watchers. 'Not wishing to be self-serving,' the Spy men were told, 'but going on something like Weight Watchers has the advantage of being identified with regular people. It's the opposite of the expensive haircut.'

Spam were told that the President had been a fan of grilled Spam and melted Wisconsin cheddar cheese sandwiches all his life. But although excited by the prospect of his mentioning that fact on air, they were a little cagey and wanted more proof that the approach was genuine. Jimmy Dean Sausages passed, mainly because Mr Dean was great mates with George Bush. Ben & Jerry's Ice-Cream also turned them down, because it was 'already public that the President likes Ben & Jerry's ice-cream'.

Only when the L. Kensington Group approached Burger King did they encounter any problems with the idea of the President of the most powerful nation in the world endorsing consumer products. 'It doesn't make me feel good, the President of the United States doing this,' said Marketing Vice-President Paul Clayton. 'It just doesn't sit well with me.' But he agreed that it was a personal response and that he would refer the matter upstairs. The following Monday, both Burger King's public relations department and their ad agency rang wanting to discuss a possible endorsement.

Your Table's Waiting, Sir

With the best tables at the best restaurants seemingly impossible for the ordinary person to attain, *Empire* magazine decided to see what difference celebrity status made when ringing for a reservation.

It made a big difference. Ringing up 'in' Hollywood restaurants on busy nights, an ordinary Joe got absolutely nowhere but the big shots were immediately found tables. How they could face going to such appalling obsequious places is another question. *Empire* had only to drop names like Oliver Stone, Barbara Streisand, Michael Eisner and Roseanne for tables at swish places like Morton's, Chasen's and The Ivy to become mysteriously available.

There was no difficulty getting a booking at The Ivy for Macaulay Culkin and a group of ten friends to have a spot of cake and ice-cream, either. The restaurant was extremely helpful, even wanting to know, 'So . . . will you be needing a high-chair?'

The saddest call was perhaps that made on behalf of Barry Diller, within a day of him resigning as head of Twentieth Century-Fox. The restaurant was extremely brusque, refusing him a table at 7.30, claiming to have nothing for another hour. Even when the caller protested 'Hey, do you know who we're talking about here?' he was told that 8.30 was the earliest.

Spy ran the *Empire* piece, adding on a few calls they made to the top restaurants in New York. Although Le Cirque had no table for ordinary mortals, when they rang back immediately afterwards posing as Tina Brown's assistant, they were accommodated with ease.

When they called on behalf of Dan Rather, there was some problem over whether a table could be got ready in time, even when 'Rather' mentioned he wanted to bring Walter Cronkite. They rang again the next day apologising for not turning up because of a last minute crisis at work. Asking if they had a spare table that evening, *Spy* was told: 'I'll *build* one tonight. I can't say no twice.'

To Empire With Love

In a Henry Root-ish prank, *Empire* wrote a letter to 20 Hollywood stars saying: 'I just inherited $10,000 from my recently deceased aunt. Can you please send me a personally autographed photo of yourself to add to my collection? I'm enclosing a $10 check to cover the cost of postage and stuff.'

Signed photos 'To Matthew' came back from Robert De Niro, Arnold Schwarzenegger, Bruce Willis and Robin

Williams, with Williams writing on it: 'Congratulations dude! Spend it wisely.' Kevin Costner sent a signed photo but writer Matt Meuller was rather doubtful if Costner had even been near the photograph. Most sent back the cheques.

Mel Gibson's people sent back the cheque saying: 'Congratulations on your inheritance. Unfortunately, we do not accept payment from private individuals nor do we grant photo requests.'

After seven months, nothing had come back from Cher, Tom Cruise, Warren Beatty, Tom Cruise, Geena Davis, Michael Douglas, Harrison Ford, Jodie Foster, Dustin Hoffman, Jack Nicholson, Michelle Pfeiffer, Julia Roberts, Winona Ryder or Demi Moore, despite her husband's nice response. When Mueller contacted their publicists, every one denied any knowledge of a cheque having been received.

Only Patrick Swayze actually cashed the cheque (and sent a photo), but further investigations revealed that he had sent the money on to the California Autism Foundation.

Sex Lies and More Lies

In late 1991, Matt Mueller, again writing for *Empire*, revealed that he had sent what was, in essence, the script of *Sex Lies and Videotape* to 26 film production companies to see what their response would be. It was retitled *46:02*, one of the original titles, the lead character's name was changed to Sarah and the play was reset in Brighton rather than Baton Rouge, Louisiana. But while Mueller rejigged the first two pages, after that the screenplay reverted almost word for word to what Steven Soderbergh had written.

Nominated for an Oscar for Best Original Screenplay and winner of the Palme d'Or, one might have thought it would arouse some interest among film companies. What the hoax proved was how it was virtually impossible for an unknown writer to get a screenplay read these days. Letters informing him that unsolicited scripts could not be accepted were received from Palace, Merchant-Ivory Productions, Art Linson Productions, Samuel Goldwyn, Walt Disney, Warner Brothers, Hand Made Films, Imagine, Tri-Star, Paramount and Morgan Creek. Orion, Euston Films, MGM/Pathe, Geffen Films and Universal appeared to lose the script.

However, while First Independent said that their production slate was full and Cappa Productions (Martin Scorsese's company) wrote that the great man only worked on friends' projects, both Film Four International, Channel Four's film arm, and the British Film Institute, did give 46:02 a look. The BFI's script co-ordinator wrote: 'Thank you for submitting your script to BFI Production. It has now been read and discussed by the script-reading group and I am afraid it has been unsuccessful in reaching our shortlist. I would like to wish you every success in the future.'

Film Four were no more positive, 'I am afraid we were not enthusiastic enough about this project to wish to pursue it any further. However, we were glad to have seen it, and are sorry to be negative on this occasion.' Strange, really, considering that it is Channel Four that bought the rights to *Sex Lies and Videotape* for TV screening and shows it with such regularity.

Mueller's faith in the film industry was kept alive by four companies that rumbled him. Cinema Verity wrote back that: 'I found this piece as a whole uncomfortably close to *Sex Lies and Videotape*.' Working Title admitted to enjoying the screenplay but 'I finally felt that it was lacking in originality (and bears an uncanny resemblance to a recently acclaimed film!).'

Enigma, David Puttnam's company, were also rather dubious: 'It's an intelligent and well-written script, but it seems to me to bear more than a passing resemblance to *Sex Lies and Videotape*, and if my memory serves me right, some of the dialogue is remarkably close to the film's. This similarity in subject and approach would, I think, limit its chances of finding a home.'

Along with Twentieth Century-Fox's standard letter in response to unsolicited scripts came a post-it note on which was scribbled: 'P.S. I glanced through this script. For your information, plagiarism is illegal and despicable. I don't know who you thought you could fool by changing the names and the location of *Sex Lies and Videotape*, but I advise you to stop making a fool out of yourself.'

Here's a Quid

In Britain, the king of the letter writing hoaxers is Henry Root, a former Billingsgate fish porter who rose to own his own business, Henry Root Wet Fish Ltd. Having sold the firm, Root found himself with time on his hands and could think of nothing better to do with it than to write to a whole raft of people in the public eye, usually enclosing a pound note, offering advice and abuse and seeking to expose and extinguish unwholesome tendencies in modern society. *The Henry Root Letters* soon found their way into a bestselling book.

The Commissioner of the Metropolitan Police, Sir David McNee, was told by Root that 'ordinary folk are with you all the way in your campaign for greater police powers. Better that ten innocent men be convicted than that one guilty man goes free! That's what the lounge-room revolutionaries fail to understand. Don't be depressed by the fact that your "image" isn't too clever just yet. We have to face it that you come across a wee bit charmless. So what?' Root received back his requested photograph, together with the pound and a letter saying: 'Your kind comments are appreciated.'

Mrs Thatcher received many letters from Root, all of which were treated seriously and replied to with courtesy by Richard Ryder of her private office, despite Root comparing her with Joan of Arc: 'She put it over the French with their bidets and so-called soixante-neuf and so will you' or telling her: 'Don't worry about your voice. Don't listen to people who say you sound like a suburban estate agent's wife. What's wrong with suburban estate agents? They have a vote!'

When Root wrote to Esther Rantzen offering her some 'humorous' items for *That's Life* he received a letter from Rantzen telling him that: 'Hearing from viewers like yourself is a tremendous moral boost for us all – it really makes a great difference to me to know that you find our work enjoyable and worthwhile.' However, when Root was told that they didn't pay for unsolicited contributions, he wrote: 'You're a fat idiot and your show's a disgrace.' He received the reply from Rantzen: 'Hearing from viewers like yourself is a tremendous moral boost for us all – it really makes a great difference to me to know that you find our work enjoyable and worthwhile.'

To the Queen, Root suggested that instead of always opening things, Her Majesty should close a few things such as Soho's 'foreign' cinemas, the National Council for Civil Liberties, the National Liberal Club and 'the new white tile universities, which see it as their function to stuff the impressionable young students with half-baked left-wing notions'. A couple of weeks later he was sympathising with her 'about the trouble you're having with Princess Anne. My Doreen (19) is off the rails too, so I know what it's like.'

When publishers Jonathan Cape turned down his ludicrous synopsis for a novel starring 'bronzed, attractive, amazingly fit, 45-year-old Harry Toor, Chairman and Managing Director of Harry Toor West Fish Ltd', Root tried to get merchant bank Keyser Ullman to set up a takeover deal of the company for him, switching his favours to Hambros when he became suspicious of Keyser Ullman's bona fides. 'I would have thought it unlikely that it would be for sale on its own,' replied A.R. Beevor of Hambros. 'However, if you want to discuss this matter further, please do not hesitate to contact me.'

Root then contacted Lord Grade, asking if he wanted to join the consortium bidding for Jonathan Cape. On behalf of Grade, Jack Gill of Associated Communications wrote back saying, 'We actually looked at this particular company some twelve months ago and decided not to attempt to purchase it.'

President Zia of Pakistan thanked Root for 'your thoughtfulness in writing to me to convey certain very pertinent views'. Root had told the President to ignore the comments in Britain's liberal press. 'Most of us realise that a backward people such as yours needs, and appreciates, the smack of firm government.'

Policemen, politicians, newsreaders, publishers, lawyers, newspaper editors, television executives, football managers – they all received communications from Root and the majority replied, sometimes tersely but just as often in embarrassing detail.

Disgusted of West Brompton

On 15 August 1979, the *Evening Standard* published the following letter: 'I WISH to protest most strongly about everything – Henry Root, Park Walk, West Brompton.'

Only when Root wrote to the Senior Tutor of Magdalene College, offering to endow the college with a decent library if his boy could be guaranteed a place, was Root rumbled. He was accused of being 'either an ingenious hoaxer or labouring under a massive misapprehension'.

Root was in reality William Donaldson, a one-time theatre producer of shows like *Beyond the Fringe* and *The Bed Sitting Room* and author of an extraordinary book called *Both the Ladies and the Gentlemen* detailing his experiences as a brothel-keeper in Chelsea in the sixties.

Lazlo Toth

Donaldson readily admitted that the idea of Root came from a long-standing American letter prankster using the pseudonym of Lazlo Toth. As Mrs Thatcher found in Britain with Henry Root, American leaders have never been short of advice while Lazlo Toth has enough money for a stamp. The Toth correspondence goes back to the days of Lyndon Johnson and Richard Nixon and continues with President Clinton.

209

When Crown Prince Naruhito of Japan got married in 1993, Toth not only congratulated him, but also sent him a stars and stripes tablecloth. 'It was a little expensive, but I got it at half price. I'll admit it, because I bought it a day after the 4th of July (a big holiday here), and they lowered the price because of the stripes. I hope you and Princess Masako like it. And I hope the two of you will have many enjoyable meals on it.'

Like Root, Toth (in reality Don Novello) is fiercely patriotic. After flying with America West Airlines, for instance, he will dash off a letter to the Chief Executive Officer demanding to know the reason for 'your "assembled in Mexico" snack sacks . . . full of foreign style food and imported products . . . How about serving an "American" snack sack with: 1. a short rib. 2. corn-on-the-cob. 3. a small piece of watermelon. An American Combo! Made in America! Assembled by Americans! For America West Airline!

'An American! Born, Bred and Assembled in the U.S.A.!
'Lazlo Toth.'

Let's Not Be Beastly to the Germans

Even Germany has letter hoaxers. Winfried Bornemann, a schoolteacher in a small village, began his hoaxing career in 1983 when he wrote to a doctor asking to buy some medical instruments for 'leisure surgery' to remove a friend's appendix. When a group of doctors answered begging him not to do it, he caught the bug and before long had published a bestselling book of letters.

In 1987, he posed as Frau Carola von Gastern and Frau Gerda von Nussink, depending on his whim, and wrote to some of the world's top personalities. 'As an elderly woman living alone one thinks not of one's past but also beyond one's own being. In a word, I have a considerable fortune and no heir. For years I have been an admirer of your person and your artistic ideas and now I would like to name you as my sole heir . . . It would be a great pleasure if you were to accept this inheritance after my passing. I would hope that with this help you would be able to attend to your important work more intensively.'

Did the hundred or so people Bornemann wrote to turn their back on this kind offer? They did not.

Liza Minnelli was 'sincerely touched' and said that 'your generosity in naming me as your heir is astonishing, but if that is your wish and you are sure that is what you want, it would be my pleasure and my honor to accept.' It was Shirley Bassey's pleasure, too, as well as Meryl Streep's, John le Carré's, Barbara Cartland's, Pat Boone's, David Attenborough's, Sebastian Coe's and others.

Richard Nixon wrote back accepting, but saying that he wanted to divide the money among his favourite non-political charities while Jimmy Carter planned to spend the money 'in my efforts for peace, nuclear arms control and human rights'. Princess Anne wanted the money to go not to her, but to the Princess Anne's Charities Trust.

Bo Derek replied saying that she hadn't been able to find her benefactor's phone number, while Tony Curtis wanted to know when he could come and visit. Ian Paisley, too, was all set to pop over to say 'hello'.

Donna Summer was initially delighted to accept, telling her benefactor that she spoke fluent German, having lived in Germany for seven years and suggesting a meeting. She even gave out her home phone number. Six days later, someone had put her straight. 'It took me a while to figure out that this was a terrible joke . . . I think this is a very nasty and mean joke you play on people.'

Roald Dahl seemed on the ball, replying directly to Mr Bornemann: 'I have received your spurious letter in which you assume the name of a non-existent wealthy German lady. What you are doing is venal and wicked. I am guessing that you will sell the joyful replies you receive from well-known unsuspecting people over here, and you are thus to my mind nothing less than a criminal obtaining money under false pretences. I hope you fall down and break a leg on the way to the bank.'

10

The Wacky World of Work

Fools' Errands

The Stock Exchange is said to be the primary source of many of the jokes in this country. Yet brokers are just as keen on practical jokes as they are on the other kind. In the days when the Exchange still had a trading floor, young bloods would occupy themselves lighting the outside of newspapers being perused by old buffers reclining in armchairs. As the fire always took some time to take hold, the culprit could be on the other side of the floor by the time the paper really got going.

The old Wodehouse story mentioned earlier of the swapping of hats identical in all but size, convincing the owner his head was expanding and contracting was carried out for real on several occasions.

To this day, as in many other occupations, newcomers are sent off on fools' errands. In the case of trainee stockbroking dealers, they are usually told to find a price for the shares of companies like Icelandic Banana Plantations, Newton and Ridley Breweries, Venetian Tramways or whatever.

In other occupations, apprentices may be despatched to buy left-handed hammers, elbow grease, striped paint or any one of a hundred other ludicrous inventions of the mind. Such idiotic tasks can, however, have unforeseen consequences as we shall see later.

In New York, visitors to the floor of the New York Stock Exchange are likely to have their shoes surreptitiously scattered with white powder, for reasons that I have yet to fathom.

Ramping Both Ways

Many of the pranks are common both to London and New York and, perhaps, to many other financial markets around the world. One that has been played on more than one occasion on both sides of the Atlantic is, sadly, no longer possible now that the London Stock Exchange is an electronic market. In the days when there was a trading floor, the share wholesalers or 'jobbers' would conspire with some of the dealers and invent a fictitious 'hot' share. It would be something like an Antipodean mining company and it would be clear to observers who weren't in on the joke that it was a highly active share.

The price, perhaps just a few pence at the outset, would rise steadily throughout the day, with dealers trading in it vigorously. It wouldn't be long before news of the wonder share spread and, invariably, a few dealers and other investors not in on the joke would want to take a punt on it themselves. It looked like the equivalent of jumping into an open freight car: if it's going in the right direction, why not take a ride?

After moving upwards with a movement resembling a rocket, the time would come for the share to change direction. Suddenly, the price would start falling . . . and falling . . . and falling. Those who had bought shares, believing them to be real, would be desperate to get out while they still had a profit, particularly as they probably hadn't actually got the money necessary to buy the shares in the first place.

With the price falling rapidly, and everyone around the jobbing pitch where the shares were being traded clamouring to deal, the poor mugs were soon just desperate to get out with any profit, then to get out without too much of a loss and, finally, to get out at any price they could. Until they discovered it was all a hoax, they ended the day believing they had lost a small fortune that they didn't even have.

213

In *Liar's Poker*, Michael Lewis's book exposing the extraordinary behaviour of those who worked in the dealing room of Salomon Brothers, we read of a whole series of hoaxes played by the Swinging Big Dicks, pranks that were usually extremely cruel.

The hot foot, one of the oldest of American practical jokes was, at Salomons, turned into hot balls, with lighters applied to traders' nether regions, not by the young japesters in the office but by the head of the mortgage bond department himself, Lewis Ranieri.

When a dealer grumbled that the suit into the pockets of which somebody had poured Bailey's Irish Cream was his favourite, Ranieri simply produced $400 from his pocket and told him not to complain but simply to buy another one.

One of the favourite tricks at Salomon's was 'the suitcase goof', carried out on many occasions. This involved opening up a trader's weekend bag when they weren't around and replacing the clothes inside with pink lace panties or something similarly embarrassing.

As with all such pranks, it became a little more sophisticated as time went on. One trader, lording it over the others because he was going to Puerto Rico for the weekend, had his suitcase filled not with clothes, but with around ten pounds of wet toilet paper. Apparently he didn't discover the switch until he came out of the hotel shower, dripping, in Puerto Rico that evening.

The victim planned his revenge not upon the perpetrator of the gag, but upon the trainee that worked for him, one Gary Kilberg, which was standard practice around the office. When the poor chap had to bring a suitcase in to work he very sensibly hid it in a closet in the office of one of Salomon's big wigs, Henry Kaufman. A surreptitious phone call tipping Kilberg off that his suitcase ought to be checked was all it took to ascertain which room he was keeping it in.

When he returned a couple of days later, the traders were all laughing fit to bust, believing that his suitcase would have been full not of clothes, but of wet loo roll. But Kilberg's suitcase hadn't been touched. So whose were the very expensive clothes that the traders had hidden under their desks? They had come out of a suitcase with a large gold letter 'K' on it and their minds raced as they realised that several really important people at Salomons had surnames beginning with a 'K'.

The clothes were hurriedly shoved into a bag and dumped on a construction site across the road, every trader being sworn to secrecy.

Electric Buzzers Aren't Bunk

Businessmen who have made their pile often find themselves with too much time on their hands. This is often channelled into a predilection for practical joking. Despite his lack of sense of humour about almost everything else, it is said that Henry Ford was a keen user of the sort of hand buzzers which give the recipient of a handshake the impression of having had an electric shock.

Potty Hearst

Even a tycoon as august as William Randolph Hearst, the model for Orson Welles' *Citizen Kane*, was not averse to the odd prank when he was a student. He is remembered for having sent every single member of the faculty a chamber pot with a photograph of themselves pasted on the bottom.

Maxwell's Brick

The late Robert Maxwell was a benevolent employer and was, in turn, loved by all his employees. The tycoon was very proud of the fact that his office block in Holborn was one of only three in London on which helicopters were permitted to land.

It's said that on one occasion as they came in to land, Maxwell, ever the back-seat driver, asked the pilot what conditions were like. 'It's completely calm,' was the reply as the pilot glanced at the drooping windsock on the roof.

Seconds later, the pilot found himself fighting severe gusts of wind which were throwing the chopper from side to side.

He managed to bring the helicopter down, though with something of a bump, and received a severe tongue-lashing from the larger-than-life tycoon, who cast aspersions on his flying ability, his intelligence and his parentage.

As Maxwell strode off, the puzzled pilot went over to the windsock. Inside it, he discovered a brick weighing it down.

What a Blast

There's no doubt that some people have a strange sense of humour. The demolition expert Blaster Bates tells of the time that he had to blow up a tall chimney at a mill. To save time, he was asked to bring the chimney down on top of the engine house, the last remaining building standing. On one side of the engine house stood the old lavatory and, shortly beforehand, Bates found himself being taken aside by Reg, the clerk of works.

Reg confessed that his life had been made miserable by the chap who had ordered the job done and he wanted Bates' help to get his own back. They got hold of a tailor's dummy and dressed it in a jacket and trousers, but left the trousers around the dummy's ankles. Happy that it now closely resembled Harold Wilson, they sat it on the lavatory.

A wire was attached to the door and Reg made sure that, at the crucial moment, his tormentor was standing beside him, with the lavatory door clearly in sight.

Bates lit the fuse and, at the same time, pulled the door open. The chap suddenly saw, or thought he saw, somebody sitting on the loo and tried, desperately, to warn Bates. 'There's a bloke in the shithouse!' was his cry. 'He'll never make it!'

Indeed he didn't. The chimney came down right on top of it. They let the guy suffer for a moment or two before revealing the truth.

Dogs Go Free

British Rail has been the subject of many hoaxes over the years. In 1978, in a forlorn attempt to show that exasperating organisation just how ludicrous its multitiered fare policy was, someone went to the trouble of printing up a large quantity of leaflets. Looking like the genuine BR article and left lying around various ticket offices, they informed passengers that on Sunday 24 September, their dogs could travel on the railways for free.

'Owning a dog has its pleasures, the companionship of a faithful friend being one. But it also has its drawbacks. Many people who do not possess a car would like to visit friends or relatives but are deterred by the cost of taking their dog or having it looked after while they are away from home.'

The day of free dog travel was, apparently, by way of an introduction to BR's proposed 'Pets' Pass' scheme. The small print, full of detailed instructions about exactly how to qualify for the pass, made it look absolutely authentic. It specified that the owner must be over eighteen, that the dog must be over a year old, and that it must wear a collar with a disc showing its name and address. The owner would be held responsible for the good behaviour of his or her pet, and BR would not, of course, be held responsible for 'any injury, death or accident which may occur to the dog while it is being carried or which may occur on British Railways property'.

Bearing in mind just how authentic it looked, and how bizzare some of BR's promotions were and still are, perhaps it is not surprising that the Press Association picked it up or that several newspapers ran the story. That British Rail was mightily annoyed by it probably lifted the heart of every regular and long-suffering BR passenger.

What a Nana

In the late summer of 1994, Affitalia, an Italian company specialising in billboard advertising, spent $140,000 on adverts for a non-existent product called Nana, plastering 500 spare hoardings all over Italy with them. Their intention was to demonstrate to potential clients just how effective hoardings could be as a means of plugging consumer products.

Nana professed to be a revolutionary product, a pair of tights which were a miracle of modern cosmetic science, removing as they did excess hair from women's legs through 'continuous shearing action' while they were being worn. The campaign demonstrated how the tights worked by showing a before and after picture of a burly, moustached, bushy-eyebrowed bank robber first wearing the stocking over his head and then removing it to demonstrate that he had no hair left on his head, eyes or face.

Weirdly, the non-existent product, named after the 'film actress' Aike Nana who made a splash by stripping for photo opportunities in the fifties, was a massive hit. Shops were inundated with requests for the tights while a dozen wholesale knitwear companies desperately sought out the manufacturers through Affitalia.

When Affitalia did some research into the effectiveness of the campaign, they found that 40 per cent of the target group of women said they were aware of the product, with some professing that they had actually tried the stockings. There was even, revealed Affitalia, a small minority of those surveyed who claimed that they had 'tried the depilatory stockings but found they did not work very well'.

You 'Orrible Shower

Practical joking has always been a feature of military life, with the officer cadets at Sandhurst one of the keenest hoaxing groups in the Forces. Back in the sixties, they once stuck massive paper footprints over the wall of the New College building to make it look as if a giant had walked up it.

The adjutant at Sandhurst was less tham amused on arriving in the stables on one occasion to find that his magnificent white charger had been removed. In its place was a small Welsh pony.

More recently, cadets managed to divert traffic from the A30 near to Sandhurst onto the parade ground while, in 1994, shortly before the Sovereign's Parade, a platoon took themselves up to London and paraded down Pall Mall. Those up early enough to witness the sight saw 30 or so soldiers marching down the road in full military regalia. It must have been a splendid sight, but the top brass at Sandhurst weren't too happy about it and fined each of the men £50.

Don't Call Me Shirley

A friend who is a pilot assures me that hoaxing is rife on-board planes, with those on the flight deck taking particular delight in tormenting new cabin crew. Facing strong headwinds, he says that on several occasions they have managed to fool stewardesses by saying that they need all the speed they can get. Would the stewardesses please go through the cabins and adjust all the cold air louvres above passengers' heads so that they face towards the back of the plane, thus giving the plane an extra boost?

It is said that one pilot's favourite turn was to leave the controls of the plane in bumpy conditions to his co-pilot and to stroll past passengers in the back of the cabin holding the book: *How To Fly in Twenty Easy Lessons*.

11

People at Play

Channel Crossing

Some hoaxes can actually work for the common good. In the twenties, when swimming across the English Channel had just begun, Dr Dorothy Logan became concerned at the way in which cross-Channel swims were being carried out with inadequate supervision. She decided that the only way to bring this to the public's attention was by faking a swim herself.

In 1926, Gertrude Ederle, an American, had become the first woman to swim the Channel. The following year, Dr Logan came out of the water at Folkestone, having been seen off at Cape Gris Nez just over thirteen hours earlier. In fact, she had only swum the first and last mile or so of the journey, sitting in her support boat the rest of the way.

She let newspapers publish her new record, even accepting the £1000 prize money that the *News of the World* had put up to encourage a British woman to smash the American's record. But straight after the ceremony, she paid the money back, admitting what she had done to the embarrassed paper.

Although she was vilified by the Press and ended up being fined £150, she did achieve her aim. Thanks to her efforts, regulations governing cross-Channel swimming became considerably more stringent.

Long Distance Swimmer

One of America's great Olympic swimmers in the twenties was Norman Ross. He used to train in Lake Michigan and one day as he came back towards the Chicago beach from which he'd set off, he saw that a crowd of people was gathering.

Pretending to be exhausted, he dragged himself out of the water and shouted out: 'What city is this?'

'Chicago,' he was told by the crowd.

'Hell,' he cursed. 'I wanted Milwaukee!'

So saying, he threw himself back into the water and swam out of sight.

The Celestial Comet

Morris Newburger was a well-respected stockbroker, a partner in the firm of Newburger, Loeb & Co., a pillar of Wall Street and a model of conservative American propriety. Different reports place a different slant on his motivation to carry out a very untypical hoax. Some versions say that, as a keen American football fan, Newburger was irritated by the way in which newspapers insisted in wasting space on matches played in tiny towns or by insignificant college teams. Others say that he was actually a fan of small town football and was infuriated that the papers didn't devote *more* space to the subject.

Whatever the reason, Newburger took it upon himself in 1941 to invent his own football team, Plainfield Teachers, the college team of Plainfield, New Jersey. As the idea grew in his mind, so the day-to-day business of stockbroking seemed steadily less important. Steeling himself with a few stiff drinks, Newburger rang the sports department of the *Herald Tribune* and reported the information that Plainfield Teachers had just wiped the floor with the Benson Institute by the margin of twenty to nil. His news seemed to arouse no suspicion in its recipient, so he called *United Press, Associated Press* and the *New York Times* for good measure.

Lo and behold, when Newburger opened his paper the next day, there among the college football scores, was that for Plainfield Teachers. Newburger decided that he wanted to take the hoax further and decided to invent not only a whole team together with a fixture list, but also a sports reporter to handle the stories. Issuing reports 'from the desk of Jerry Croyden' on specially printed notepaper, Newburger rang in each week with the latest results, as Plainfield took on colleges like Scott, Fox, Winona, Ingersoll, Appalachian Normal and Harmony Teachers.

As it was his team, perhaps it wasn't too surprising that Newburger made sure that Plainfield won their matches with regularity. Such consistency needed to be explained, so Newburger conjured up a football wizard. Johnny Chung, also known as the 'Celestial Comet' was a 15 stone Chinese American who wolfed down bowls of rice at half-time and, so Jerry Croyden believed, it was obvious to everyone who saw Chung that he was destined for football stardom.

The sports departments of the newspapers rung by 'Croyden' didn't only repeat what they were given. They even elaborated on it. Herb Allen, a sports writer with the *New York Post*, penned an entire article on the wholly imaginary Chung, the 'indestructible Chinese', as he called him, warning that if Plainfield wasn't careful, 'Chiang Kai-shek would grab Chung for his own offensive'.

After Chung, Newburger's next invention was Plainfield's coach, Ralph 'Hurry Up' Hoblitzel, the man responsible for the innovative 'W' formation. Most of the players' names were those of Newburger's work colleagues and relatives. He himself, as Morris Newburger, was down as quarterback.

Although, thanks to Chung, Plainfield Teachers went from strength to strength, sadly for Newburger somebody at the *Herald Tribune* was tipped off, apparently by an employee of the phone company who overheard one of Newburger's telephone calls. Just two matches short of a grand slam, Newburger was rung by the paper to be told that they knew that Plainfield not only didn't have a team, but it didn't even have a college. Although he begged the reporter to let him continue the hoax until the end of the season, it wasn't to be.

In the middle of November, less than two months after it had begun, the *Herald Tribune* revealed the Plainfield Teachers as a hoax. Although Newburger had intended that the team should keep winning, his last release 'from the desk of Jerry Croyden' gave the stunning news that six of the team, including the 'Celestial Comet' Johnny Chung had been declared ineligible for the team because they had flunked their exams. As a result, the team had pulled out of the remaining games of the season.

What's the Weather Like Up There?

America's basketball players have turned their taste for practical jokes into a syndicated television show, *Pro Basketball's Funniest Pranks*, with rookies being the favoured target. It's very much along the lines of *Candid Camera*.

A newcomer to the Orlando Magic team, Dennis Scott, found himself trapped in a stuck lift at the Orlando Arena stadium with the pregnant reporter who had arrived to interview him. The reporter, actually an actress, suddenly went into labour while a camera hidden in the elevator recorded his reactions. She asked him to help him do her Lamaz breathing techniques, which he did. When she said she needed him to sing to her to calm her down, he made up a rag song on the spot.

Johnson Out for Nought

Cricket commentator Brian Johnson was very keen on practical jokes, although his propensity for giggling usually gave the game away. But he was sometimes on the receiving end of them too.

He was reporting on a match at Southport between the Indians and Lancashire for BBC2 and was given the task of interviewing the batsmen as they came back to the pavilion, an unenviable task because a man who has just been given out is never too keen on being asked his views about what has just happened.

Johnson jumped up from the deckchair in front of the pavilion where he was sitting when he saw that Wadekar was out. They had become good friends during the tour, with him calling Wadekar 'Wadders' and Wadekar calling Johnson 'Johnners'. He approached Wadekar with his microphone and confidently asked: 'What happened, Wadders?'

But instead of the expected smile, Wadekar's face was blank. Johnson repeated the question, only to find Wadekar saying, in very halting English, 'Sorry, I no speak English, not understand,' before trying to get past him on his way to the pavilion. 'But Wadders,' persisted Johnson, 'we've often talked together on the tour. Surely you understand. How did you get out?'

Wadekar continued to ignore him, however, and pushed past, muttering; 'Me no speak English. Sorry.'

Johnson, his face bright red, tried laughing off what had happened. But he was terribly embarrassed, as he well might be with several million people watching. He handed back to the commentator as quickly as he could.

Rushing into the dressing-room to find out what was going on, Johnson found Wadekar and the rest of the Indian team in fits of laughter, having pulled one over on one of the great sporting practical jokers.

What a Match

Newspaper drinking holes are full of hacks telling stories about drama critics writing about plays they never went to, only to discover the following day that the theatre burnt down. Cricket writer Neville Cardus, when the cricket correspondent of the *Manchester Guardian* in 1929, very nearly got similarly caught.

Believing, as did many others, that England were in such a dominant position against the visitors, South Africa, Cardus decided not to bother watching the last day's play at Leeds. Instead, he spent the day in Barnet, only to discover later that South Africa had fought like lions. He felt he had no choice but to write a report on that day's play, even though it had taken place a couple of hundred miles away.

It was a long piece and Cardus must surely have had his tongue in his cheek when he wrote lines like: 'The South African kicked back from a position so hopeless that few of us even took the trouble to be present at Leeds until we scented battle from afar.' It obviously passed muster, because the captain of the South African team told him that he 'must have had the glasses on all the time'. It was years before Cardus admitted his deception to anybody.

This Law is No Ass

In his book *The Best of Times*, Manchester United footballer George Best remembers that after a home game against Spurs in the 1964-5 season Denis Law came out of the shower to find that the toes of his socks and the sleeves of his shirt had been cut off. Law was livid and demanded to know who had done it. Eventually he was given the tip-off that it was Dave Gaskell, the goalkeeper.

Gaskell was still in the bath, so Law filled a bucket with ice-cold water and threw it over the yelling goalie. When Gaskell emerged, furious, from the bath, he was encouraged by the other players to carry on the tit for tat revenge. Nobby Stiles and Best told him that he should give Law a taste of his own medicine and pointed out that Law was currently occupying one of the lavatory cubicles. Gaskell filled up the bucket with more cold water and, standing on the seat of the next-door toilet, emptied it over Law who was sitting on the loo reading a newspaper.

Gaskell was laughing fit to bust when Law came back into the changing-room. He was wearing a suit and it was soaked right through. Law, though, didn't seem too bothered as he took off the shirt and the suit he had on. He dried himself off before putting on his own shirt, the one with the sleeves cut off, and the smart and very dry suit that was hanging on his peg.

As Best recalls: 'I can still picture Dave Gaskell's face to this day when he cottoned on that Denis had in fact been wearing *his* suit in the toilet cubicle. Mouth gaping, he stood for half a minute staring in disbelief.'

Volleyball Team Bounced Back

Passport Control at Fukuoka airport in southern Japan weren't impressed with the papers presented to them by the Philippine volleyball team. In front of them were 34 men and 22 women, resplendent in their navy-blue blazers, the Philippine flag adorning their breast pockets. They claimed to be the official volleyball team for their country at the Asian Games in Hiroshima, accompanied by trainers, manager and supporters.

Although the usual visa requirements were waived for those participating in the games, enabling athletes to be admitted on nothing more than the presentation of ID cards issued by the games' organisers, the passport officials noticed that these competitors' cards were smaller than the others they had been shown and, what's more, were green, whereas all the others they had seen were purple and green.

When the group's flight bags were opened, they contained not the expected volleyball strips, but jeans and casual wear. Further investigation revealed that the group of Filipinos had each paid £1300 to join the ingeniously disguised party of illegal immigrants who thought that they'd found an easy way into Japan. They were deported back to Manila and charged with forgery.

Anyone for Doubles?

In his droll account of life on the international tennis circuit in the golden years, *A Handful of Summers*, Gordon Forbes recalls that two Australian players over for Wimbledon were staying in a flat in the King's Road. They were delighted to discover that their ability to lay their hands on tickets to Wimbledon gave them amazing pulling power, although the other players were convinced that the pair would be too exhausted to change into their tennis gear when the championships began, let alone play a game.

One of the Australians met a girl who said her ambition was to lean out of the window overlooking King's Road on a Saturday afternoon, waving to her Chelsea friends passing by below, while being made love to from behind. The Australian readily agreed to help her dreams come true.

It was on Finals' Day at Queens that Forbes was told what had happened. As had been planned, at three o'clock she was in the Australians' flat, leaning out of the window and waving at any friend who went by. Although she was wearing a white lace shirt on top, what could not be seen was that below there was nothing – nothing that is except for the Australian tennis player doing his stuff.

After ten minutes, the doorbell rang. The Australian swore, saying that it must be his room mate, but that he'd send him away. Telling the girl not to move, he went to the door. As they had prearranged, the Australians then swapped places, with the other one taking up his friend's position and doing a passable imitation of him as he said: 'Bloody room mates can be very inconvenient at times.'

The *first* Australian dragged his clothes on and nipped out of the back of the building. Running round the block, he slowed to a walk as he strolled up the King's Road. As he passed underneath his flat window, he waved at the girl.

'For a second or two she actually returns the waving – then her eyes get wide, her jaw drops, and she ducks back into the room.'

According to the player who told the story to Forbes, the girl not only did not mind, but was delighted at the trick the pair had brought off.

12

Politicians, Royalty and the Nobility

The Practical Joking President

Although one might not have thought it of him, Abraham Lincoln was not above the odd prank. As a young man, the future President was once painting a room at home. With a pair of shoes, he made the marks of footprints up one wall, across the ceiling and down the opposite wall. The joke was not appreciated by his parents.

In later life, Lincoln loved to tell of a practical joke which was apparently very common, even in the God-fearing nineteenth-century Midwest. It involved drilling a hole under the bed in the hotel bridal suite and attaching it by a piece of string to a bell situated in the main lounge downstairs. As the honeymoon couple retired to bed, so the bell would start to ring and the laughter would begin. The more energetic the couple were, the more vigorously would the bell ring, the louder would be the laughter and the greater the round of applause when the bashful pair entered the room for breakfast the following morning.

Who knows if the story is true? The nineteenth-century French writer and 'abstract artist' Alphonse Allais (*see* Chapter 3) claimed that his friend Leon Dumachin had honeymooned in a hotel in Kleinsberg in Austria that had just such an apparatus installed for newly-wed couples.

Fortunately, he was forewarned that in The Three Kings Hotel there was a string attached to the bed which passed through to the ceiling of the bar, where a cork was attached. Watching the bobbing of the cork was the idea of a great night out for the locals.

It is claimed that, before celebrating their nuptuals, Dumachin took the string from the bed and attached it to the minute hand of a clock instead. Allais claimed when telling the tale that the slow progress of the cork was considered so fascinating that, before long, half the town was in the bar of The Three Kings, their eyes riveted to the ceiling.

Give the Man a Cigar

At a reunion dinner for alumni of Norton College in 1932, the grandson of Dr Horace Norton, the college's founder, stood up and gave a long and rather pompous speech. In it Winstead Norton paid tribute to a great American, General Ulysses S. Grant, the Civil War leader who had become the eighteenth President of the United States.

He used the speech to brag about the fact that the great man had, 75 years earlier, given his grandfather a cigar. Ponderously and self-importantly he told the audience that it was the self-same cigar that he was now holding in his hand and was now lighting. He felt honoured that there should be this connection between himself and one of the greatest statesmen their magnificent country had ever – BANG!

Three quarters of a century later, one of Grant's practical jokes had triumphantly paid off.

Roosevelt's Grandmother

Although you might have thought that anyone presented to the President of the United States would have their senses on full alert, President Roosevelt was convinced that nobody really listened to a word that he said.

He once proved this to his own satisfaction when he told everyone he was introduced to one evening that he had murdered his grandmother that very morning. The only person who remarked upon it at all told the President: 'She had it coming.'

Brief Encounter

Edward Frederick Lindley Wood, the Earl of Halifax, was a distinguished British statesman. A viceroy of India, then the foreign secretary during the early days of the Second World War, he later became the ambassador to the United States.

He was travelling to Bath by train one day and found himself in the company of two very prim middle-aged ladies of forbidding appearance who were strangers to each other. Halifax's tentative smile on entering the carriage was met by a stony-faced look from both of them.

When the train entered a tunnel, the compartment was plunged into darkness. Halifax rustled around in his seat in the dark, moaning and kissing the back of his hand loudly. As the train emerged into the daylight again, Halifax enquired: 'To which of you charming ladies am I indebted for the delightful incident in the tunnel?' He was delighted by the furious glances each gave the other.

Cole, not Dole

According to Alan Bennett's wonderful diaries, Alan Tyson, the 'genial snuff-taking aristocrat' who was a fellow of All Soul's Oxford, came very close to perpetrating what would have been one of the greatest of all practical jokes.

Although very much a story of its time, it appears that Tyson was deputed to show the Prime Minister, Margaret Thatcher, around the common room when she visited the college for a scientific symposium. The common room was stuffed full of paintings, drawings and photographs of dead Fellows, one of whom was the economist G.D.H. Cole.

Knowing that Mrs Thatcher would be very well aware who Cole was, Tyson planned to take Mrs Thatcher up to the painting and say, 'And this Prime Minister, is a former fellow, G.D.H. Dole,' reckoning that Mrs Thatcher would turn to him and inadvertently blurt out the popular slogan of the left at the time: 'Cole, not Dole.'

Sadly for posterity, Tyson lost his nerve when the moment arrived.

Be Ready in a Week, Your Majesty

Even the most exalted in the land are not immune from the attentions of the hoaxer. Our present Queen was once the victim of a practical joke, played on her by her father George VI.

During the last war, when she was plain Princess Elizabeth, she was keen to do something for the war effort and so she joined the Auxiliary Territorial Service. There, she was sent on a course on how to service and drive military vehicles.

The King arrived on a visit and found the Princess in an oily boiler suit, working under a car. He waited while she tried to repair the engine, mocking her for taking so long about it. Only when her embarrassment at failing to get it started was at its height did he reveal that he had taken out the distributor.

The Two Queens

Queen Mary had a rather alarming reputation among the aristocracy, who feared her habit of 'admiring' things that they owned. Once the Queen had taken a fancy to something, it invariably ended up in her possession. However, the Queen could hardly be made *persona non grata* and she was, in the pre-war years, very fond of being entertained by Charles Sackville at his home, the great country house of Knole. Once a residence of the Archbishop of Canterbury, this gigantic house is one of those few buildings designed with 365 rooms, one for each day of the year.

In the summer of 1936, a friend of Sackville had staying with him a man called Robin Moore, who was an amazingly good mimic. His special turn was impersonating Queen Mary as she gave her views on the abdication of Edward VIII to the Prime Minister Mr Baldwin. So entertaining was this thought to be that the group of friends thought it would be a brilliant wheeze to pop across to Knole and see whether or not Sackville, who had met Queen Mary so many times, could tell the difference between Moore and the real Queen.

Of course, they would happen to choose a time when the Queen was herself at the house. Wandering around the grand rooms downstairs, dressed in satin with a lorgnette to his eyes and a handful of Pekinese in tow, Moore was startled to find himself face to face with the real Queen Mary, similarly attired, staring at him through her lorgnette while her Pekes snapped away at the intruder's dogs.

As if this ghastly *faux pas* wasn't bad enough, the Pekes then decided, so the story goes, to enter into a pitched battle in which the leads were wound round the two Queens, pulling them together so that Moore could not even make a quick escape.

Not a Cat's Chance

Sir Charles Mappin, 4th Baronet, was a lover of practical jokes in his youth before the Second World War. Although few details remain, he once announced plans for the first Old Berkeley Square Cat Hunt. This would bring some of the joys of hunting to the capital and, at the same time, be of considerable benefit to local residents.

The idea was to use greyhounds to round up local stray cats. The police and the Royal Society for the Prevention of Cruelty to Animals fell for it hook, line and sinker.

Monkey Business

When you gaze at Waddesdon Manor in Buckinghamshire, you could be forgiven for thinking that you were in France. This reproduction of a French château, built by Baron de

Rothschild, was packed with a collection of French *objets d'art* to rival any in the country.

Its construction was long and costly, involving as it did the lopping off of the top of a hill and the building of a special railway line to import the materials from London.

Much like William Randolph Hearst with San Simeon and his fictitious counterpart *Citizen Kane* and Xanadu, Rothschild collected animals on a large scale. Visitors would be taken to the house from the station in a carriage drawn by four zebras and, as they passed through the grounds, they would see many other exotic creatures. These weren't only confined to the grounds outside, though. The unaware visitor might find himself face to face with a snake while, it is said, ladies were sometimes manhandled by the supposedly tame bear.

In the 1890s, Lord Salisbury was guest of honour at an important political dinner at Waddesdon, with some of the most important politicians in the land attending. As the guests went in to dinner, they were perplexed that there was an empty chair in between each of them, presumably for a further twelve guests who were yet to arrive. The doors at the other end of the room then opened, and in walked a dozen monkeys, attired in black tie and all the trimmings, who took their places in the remaining chairs.

13

The Odds and Sods That I Can't Shoehorn Into Any Other Category

The Cutting Off of Manhattan

There are some stories so bizarre and far-fetched, where people seem so extraordinarily gullible, that the tendency is to disbelieve them completely. Yet enough records exist for us to be sure that a former contractor called Lozier really did convince an amazing number of New York's citizens to help him move Manhattan Island before it snapped off!

Like many other workers with time on their hands, Lozier used to hang out at the Centre Market. It was a version of Hyde Park's Speakers' Corner, with people able to stand on a soapbox and hold forth on any subject under the sun. Lozier, an educated man, was one of the most active and vociferous of the speakers and immensely popular.

He must have been a magnificent orator, for in 1824 he got to his feet and begged for help in averting a disaster. He had been consulting with the mayor, who was extremely worried. It seemed that as a result of the heavy buildings that had been erected at the Battery end of Manhattan (the southern part), the island was actually tilting into the water. The city's experts were convinced that unless something was done quickly, part of Manhattan might simply break off and sink.

The solution that had been suggested to the mayor was a radical one – namely to saw the island off at its northern end, tow it out until there was enough room to turn it round, and then tow it back and reattach it, this time with Battery at the north end instead of Kingsbridge.

Even though as part of his argument Lozier pointed out just how rapidly technology was changing all their lives, with steamships now crossing the Atlantic and the ground-breaking Erie Canal currently under construction, it still seems remarkable that the assembled crowd still bit. But bite they did. So did many New Yorkers who weren't even present when Lozier spoke, for word of the scheme spread through the city like wildfire.

Several days later, Lozier turned up at the Centre Market and claimed that he had been told to sign up 300 skilled workers for the scheme. There was no shortage of applicants. He then went further and hired contractors to build the accommodation that would be needed for the workers, ordering food for them as well as some of the equipment that would be needed for the mammoth engineering project. Even though Lozier spoke of giant saws that would need 50 men to operate them, and rowlocks for the 250 feet long wooden oars that would manoeuvre the island, still nobody seemed to cotton on that they were being had. More workers were signed up to operate the saws and oars while bizarre breath-holding auditions were held to find those who would be capable of staying under water long enough to work on the sawing that had to be carried out below the water line.

After stalling for some time, Lozier finally fixed a day on which work would start. A crowd of several hundred people gathered on the day. Not just the workmen, but also many of their wives and children turned out, all led by a band. To add to the confusion, there were wagons with wood and tools as well as the food supplies.

The crowd waited at Kingsbridge, at the northern end of Manhattan, for the work orders to be handed out. But of course Lozier was not there. He had decided that it would be more sensible if he made himself scarce. It was some time before he felt it was safe enough to return.

It was in 1626 that the Indians sold the Island of Manhattan to Peter Minuit of the Dutch West Indies Company for what is reputed to have been around $24 worth of trinkets.

One of Minuit's co-purchasers was a man called Edwards. Years later a Dr Herbert Edwards set up the Edwards Heirs Association, ostensibly to pursue the claim in the courts that he, and other people with the name of Edwards, were rightfully entitled to a substantial part of Manhattan which had subsequently become worth rather more than $24. In reality, Edwards knew that there was not a cat's chance in hell of succeeding in the action, but he made a great deal of money from the subscription money that poured in from people with the same surname.

As with dicky companies and shareholder meetings, the Edwards Heirs Association held an annual meeting each year to report upon the state of the case. These turned into ever more boozy parties over the years as those present drank toasts to the success of their claim.

The scam went on long enough for Edwards to pass on the Association to his son. But even when the hoax was eventually uncovered, the members of the Association appeared not to mind. They enjoyed the annual shindigs so much that they continued to hold them every year.

Fairies at the Bottom of the Garden

Although we may be rather less romantically inclined now, there was a time when people were only too willing to believe in the existence of fairies. In 1919 two girls living in Cottingley in Yorkshire gave them proof. Frances Wright borrowed her father's camera and, in the garden, took five photographs of her friend Elsie Griffiths gazing at a bunch of happy, frolicking fairies.

One was shown to an expert in photography, Harold Snelling, who pronounced that it did not appear to be faked in any way. News of the Cottingley Fairies spread rapidly in a post-war Britain desperate for anything to cheer the spirits. An article written by Sir Arthur Conan Doyle, saying that real fairies had been photographed, appeared in *Strand* magazine in 1920. Before he wrote his article, Doyle had asked Kodak to examine the negatives, but they could find no 'evidence of superimposition, or other tricks'.

Doyle took a great interest in the fairies, and always hoped that the photographs were genuine: 'Children claim to see these creatures far more frequently than adults. This may possibly come from far greater sensitiveness of apprehension, or it may depend on these little entities having less fear of molestation from children.' In 1922, Doyle published a book on the subject, *The Coming of the Fairies*.

It wasn't until 1976 that the girls, girls no longer, admitted during a TV interview that they had faked the photographs. They had cut the fairies out of the *Princess Mary Gift Book* which had been published in 1915 and had fastened them to twigs and leaves with hat pins. 'How on earth anyone could be so gullible as to believe they were real,' said Frances Wright, 'was always a mystery to me.'

Crown Prince Jim

In 1947 the Crown Prince of Saudi Arabia, His Royal Highness Emir Saud, was touring the United States with a massive revenue and picking up many column inches from the royalty-obsessed American press. His visit to Hollywood was too good an opportunity for arch hoaxer Jim Moran (of which more in the next book) to pass up.

Moran, much like Cole years earlier, boned up on Arabian royalty and, with the help of three actors, the quartet was made up to resemble the real royal party as closely as possible, two taking the role of bodyguards and one becoming the Prince's companion. Unlike Cole's group visiting HMS *Dreadnought*, in this instance one of Moran's party actually spoke Arabic.

The swank restaurant Ciro's was delighted to receive a phone call booking a table for the Crown Prince. Late in the evening a large limousine pulled up and two bodyguards (in a day when such things were unknown in Hollywood) preceded the Prince to make sure that everything was to his liking. The Prince and his companion caused quite a stir with their entrance into the packed restaurant, even among the predominantly film-related customers eating there.

For much of the evening the Prince ignored anyone not at his table. After a time, though, he despatched one of the bodyguards to the bandstand to have a word with the bandleader, Jerry Wald. After the band played 'Begin the Beguine' for him, the Prince was observed by the goggle-eyed customers to take a large jewel out of a pouch and to have it sent to Wald.

Shortly afterwards, as the Prince's party were leaving, the pouch spilled, spraying the jewels out all over the dancefloor. When his servants made to pick them up, the Prince motioned for them not to bother with such trifles and the party continued on its way out of the restaurant.

There was a moment's silence after the door closed behind them, before everybody suddenly jumped from their chairs and grabbed for the jewels. Of course they were scrabbling around for nothing more impressive than costume baubles.

Unlike Cole, Moran made sure that his prank was faithfully recorded, tipping off a reporter from Associated Press about the whole thing in advance.

The USS Wyoming

A similar hoax to Horace de Vere Cole's *Dreadnought* lark was carried out in America five years later, in 1915, by Stanley Weyman. Unlike Cole, Weyman was of poor working-class stock, but was as fascinated by uniforms and medals as a jackdaw is by trinkets.

Attired as the Romanian Consul-General, although only 21 at the time, he was shown around the USS *Wyoming* on an official visit that he had arranged, being picked up by a launch and given a guard of honour. Sadly, Weyman was arrested shortly afterwards in the midst of repaying the ship's officers' hospitality by running up a massive bill at New York's Astor Hotel.

Bizarrely, he became a naval officer and later a 'doctor'. Even more weirdly, he ended up as doctor to Pola Negri, the silent film star who was heart-throb Rudolph Valentino's girlfriend when he died. It was Weyman who accompanied her to the massive funeral.

Hoaxing the President

In 1921 Weyman persuaded Princess Fatima of Afghanistan, who was visiting New York, that he was the State Department's chief protocol officer. He told her he could arrange for her to visit the President and collected a cash payment from her for doing so, in line with what he said was American custom.

Much of the $10,000 she paid him was used for hotel bills and for the hire of a private railroad carriage for the trip to Washington. Decked out in the uniform of a lieutenant-commander in the US Navy, Weyman did indeed manage to talk his way into the White House and even into the Oval Office, with the Princess, together with her three sons, getting to meet the great man. There are photographs of the group, smiling, taken on the White House lawn.

When it was discovered that Weyman was an imposter, he was sent to jail for two years, one of several periods of imprisonment he underwent for his activities.

It's a Puzzler

The word 'quiz' is said by some (though not by my dull dictionary) to have entered the English language as the result of a hoax. Around 1780 a Dublin theatre manager apparently bet a friend that he could introduce a new word into the language within just 24 hours.

He then went all over Dublin writing the word on every blank wall he could find. By the next day, everyone in the city was asking what the word meant. The chap won his bet and the word 'quiz' became common usage, although initially it meant an odd or unusual person.

The Cabbage Regulations

'The Lord's Prayer has fifty-six words. The Gettysburg Address has two hundred and sixty-eight. The Declaration of Independence has one thousand three hundred and twenty-two. So how come it took the Federal Government twenty-six thousand, nine hundred and eleven words to issue a Regulation governing the sale of cabbages?'

Although the wording varies, this information is frequently quoted by journalists and politicians seeking to show that bureaucracy in America has run rampant. It still surfaces with regularity, even though it is a well-known hoax, apparently conjured up by a bored mind during World War II. There is no such Regulation, nor has there ever been, but that hasn't stopped such august publications as the *Wall Street Journal* and the *New York Times* repeating it as if it were true.

Still, why let the truth stand in the way of a good story? Even if there isn't a twenty-six thousand, nine hundred and eleven word Regulation governing the sale of cabbages, there is probably one just as long governing the sale of some other vegetable or fruit, in Brussels if not in Washington.

There's No Business Like Snow Business

Another of those things held by most people to be true – namely that the Eskimos have anything up to 200 words for 'snow' – is a hoax. Growing gradually out of a book published in 1911 which misunderstood the Eskimo language, the myth was compounded by subsequent works of fiction, written largely from a point of ignorance, which seemed to vie with each other to make the Eskimo seem as exotic and different than they could be when compared to the average American.

In a Cleveland TV station's weather forecast in 1984, it was said that the Eskimos had over 200 words for snow. Even the *New York Times* put it at 100 in 1984. In fact, there are only two root words for snow, one referring to snow on the ground and one to snow in the air. All other words are based on these two, much as snowflake, snowmobile and so on are all based on the root word of 'snow' in English.

The LSD Tattoo Scare

From time to time in the eighties, the tabloids ran stories about the country's schools being swamped with tattoos which contained LSD and which would be absorbed when the tattoos were put on or licked.

Similar tales did the rounds in the United States, where leaflets were printed up warning schoolchildren of the danger. However the Drug Enforcement Administration, after much effort in tracking down the story, concluded that such LSD tattoos simply didn't exist and that the idea was just a hoax that mushroomed until it came to be generally believed.

The Devil's in My Washing Machine

In the early eighties, Procter and Gamble was the victim of a particularly weird hoax when rumours were spread that its corporate logo – a pretty rendering of the man in the moon – was actually a satanic symbol. The rumours, fanned by Fundamentalist church newsletters, became ever wilder, with talk that a proportion of the company's profits went to the Church of Satan.

Procter and Gamble received literally millions of letters on the topic from around the world. When it became clear to the company that the rumours weren't simply going to die down of their own accord, it hired private investigators to find those spreading the stories and prosecuted them. Only then did the rumours fade away.

Computer Hoaxing.

The growth of computer bulletin boards and, more recently, the Internet, provide the hoaxer with a means of disseminating information more widely and more quickly than ever before.

One long-standing hoax that seems to have been spread and kept alive in this way is the yarn about the Neiman Marcus Cookie Recipe, which says that anyone asking for the recipe of the cookies sold in the stores' restaurants is told by the company's employees that it will cost $250.

In fact, the whole thing is spurious. Neiman Marcus don't actually serve cookies in its restaurants and, in any case, the company has said publicly that it will give away the recipe of anything it does serve to anyone who wants it.

Flashers Beware!

More recently, the Internet was responsible for the dissemination of a story in America that drivers who flashed other road users to warn them that their headlights were not on were in grave danger.

The story had it that gang members had developed a new initiation rite and would drive around with their lights off. Whenever someone flashed their headlights to warn them, the gang member would follow them and kill them.

Although there has not been one documented case of this happening, word of it spread rapidly throughout the United States. Memos warning employees not to flash their headlights were pinned up on company noticeboards and even in public buildings.

The Aerial Gardener

Douglas Blake is an 'aerial gardener'. He plans his garden according to the view of it, not from the earth, but from the air. According to *The Sunday Telegraph*, visible at ground level are '. . . two oddly rounded rockery mounds, each one topped by a burst of red poppies, all this in a lawn bounded by two slowly curving paths. Nothing else at all, except for a heather bush, thick and wiry, cut into the shape of a triangle.'

'Now close your eyes,' says Blake, 'and think of that lot from 1000 feet up.' Claiming that his garden is a tribute to the female form, Blake claims to have got the idea from the Hellfire Club, to which one of his ancestors belonged. 'Of course, it's like Heathrow in the skies above it most weekends.'

Sadly, he abandoned plans to recreate in pink petunias the most prominent feature of the Cerne Abbas Giant, fearing that his back was not up to the spadework needed for constructing such a large structure. As he explained: 'Aerial gardening is not for the weak.'

I Can't Get My Ticket Through the Door

It is generally accepted that the longest place name in the British Isles is the town in Gwynedd which has such wonderfully long railway tickets: Llanfairpwllgwyngyllgogerychwryndrobwllllantysiliogogogoch. Its 58 letters translate as 'St Mary's Church in the hollow of the white hazel near to the rapid whirlpool of Llantysilio of the Red Cave'. In fact, the name is a hoax, dreamt up in the nineteenth century by local bard Y Bardd Cocos (John Evans) to fool gullible tourists. Its official name has only ever comprised the first twenty letters.

It has since been outdone by another railway, also in Gwynedd in North Wales. Cheesed off by the competition, the Fairbourne Steam Railway changed the name of its station to the 67-lettered Gorsafawddacha'idraigodanheddogleddollônpenrhynareurdraethceredigion, which means 'The Mawddach station and its dragon teeth at the Northern Penrhyn Road on the golden beach of Cardigan Bay'.

Fishy Name

There is a parallel to this in America, where some books list the longest place name as being the American Indian title for Lake Webster in Massachusetts: Chargoggaggogg-manchaugagoggchaubunagungamaug. The meaning is supposed to be: 'You fish on your side, I'll fish on my side, nobody fish in the middle.'

But, like Llanfair etc., the name is a hoax, perpetrated by Larry Daly, the editor of Massachusetts' *Webster Times*, as a joke in the early twenties. Until his revised name gained credence, the lake was rather more simply called Chagungungamaug Pond, which means 'boundary fishing place'.

Blinky RIP

One Jeffrey Vallance once persuaded a Los Angeles pet cemetery to bury a frozen chicken he had bought in a supermarket. Taking it along in a shoe box, he claimed that it was 'Blinky', a great friend of the family.

Once they caught a sight of Vallance's folding stuff, there was no problem and Blinky was buried with all the pomp and ceremony one might expect to be given to a frozen chicken who was a friend of the family. Nestling in a blue coffin with pink trimming, with a pillow for the bird's missing head, Blinky was lowered into the ground and probably still lies there, resting in peace.

What a Brick

In 1994, 25 or so people in Brussels took delivery of substantial parcels on which they had to pay excess postage costing some £6. On opening their parcels, they discovered an ordinary household brick and a telephone number.

Understandably furious, the recipients dialled the phone number, finding themselves talking to a military attaché at the Portuguese delegation at NATO headquarters in Brussels. They received so many calls that they had to disconnect the telephone. Although the security people at NATO did some investigating they got nowhere, other than discovering that most of the bricks had gone to middle-aged ladies.

14

April Fools' Day

The Spaghetti Harvest

The origins of April Fools' Day or All Fools' Day are now
lost in time, but it is celebrated, if that is the right word, in
an amazing number of countries.

Although there have been many practical jokes carried
out on TV, none is better remembered than *Panorama*'s
1 April programme of 1957 which was fronted by Richard
Dimbleby.

Things were very different in 1957. The BBC was, well,
the British Broadcasting Corporation, a universally well-
respected oracle around the world and Richard Dimbleby
was its most respected broadcaster, a man who could be
trusted implicitly. It was he who, in hushed tones, brought
us the details of the latest coronation, the opening of
Parliament or a state funeral. While his son may have helped
to make a fool out of Prince Charles, 40 years ago it simply
wasn't done to undermine the credibility of the premier
broadcasting company on earth by telling whoppers.

In those days *Panorama* had a massive audience, partly
because there was so little competition. There was no
video, no cable and no satellite, and independent television
had only been going for a couple of years. Why should
anyone have suspected the BBC's flagship documentary
programme?

So when Richard Dimbleby started talking about
spaghetti, still rather an exotic item to most British
households, the nation listened, and watched. 'It isn't only in

Britain that spring has taken everyone by surprise,' he told viewers. 'Here in the Ticino on the borders of Switzerland and Italy the slopes overlooking Lake Lugano have already burst into flower, at least a fortnight earlier than usual. But what, you may ask,' he continued as he walked through a Mediterranean cultivated area, 'has the early and welcome arrival of bees and blossom to do with food? Well, it's simply that the past winter, one of the mildest in living memory, has had its effect in other ways as well. Most important of all, it's resulted in an exceptionally heavy spaghetti crop . . . Many of you, I'm sure, will have seen pictures of the vast spaghetti plantations in the Po Valley. For the Swiss, however, it tends to be more of a family affair. Another reason why this may be a bumper year lies in the virtual disappearance of the spaghetti weevil, the tiny creature whose depredations have caused much concern in the past.'

Dimbleby brushed past the strands of spaghetti as he walked through the plantation, talking. The viewers then saw the spaghetti pickers taking it to be laid out and dried in the spring sun. Dimbleby explained that the uniform length of the spaghetti was the consequence of many years of 'patient endeavour by plant breeders who have succeeded in producing the perfect spaghetti'.

Abroad was then truly 'foreign' to most Britons and the majority of people watching the broadcast were completely convinced that every word Richard Dimbleby had uttered was absolutely true. The BBC received numerous calls from people wanting to know how they could grow their own spaghetti. The Corporation apparently advised them to 'place a sprig of spaghetti in a tin of tomato sauce and hope for the best'.

San Seriffe

It has now become customary for newspapers to vie with each other to see who can produce the best spoof on April Fools' Day. But this is a relatively recent practice, dating back to 1977, the year when the best of all newspaper April Fool jokes took place.

As with Richard Dimbleby and *Panorama*, the *Guardian* was perhaps the least likely newspaper to perpetrate an April Fools' hoax. It took itself – and still does – so seriously. Yet on 1 April 1977 it carried a supplement that would have looked all too familiar to readers of broadsheet newspapers, one of those interminably boring advertising-led puffs that are such a hazard these days, keen to tell you all about the automotive industry in Italy or gold mining in Peru or whatever. Train cleaners must hate them, for they are always scattered over carriages by commuters who have better things to do with their time.

This particular one was about the Island of San Seriffe and most of them were probably discarded, unread. And why not, considering that it began, as all of them do, with pictures of a tropical paradise and guff about, 'The ten years of independence which San Seriffe celebrates today have been a period of economic expansion and social development probably unrivalled by any other new nation.'

For those who actually took a moment to look at the supplement, and those perhaps who realised that *sans serif* is the name of a typeface rather than an island in the Indian Ocean, and who chose to read further, it provided considerable pleasure. For it mercilessly took the mickey out of innumerable past such supplements, in the *Guardian* as well as other papers, which had brushed the political complexion of loathsome military regimes under the carpet and whitewashed over the truth of life in innumerable banana republics so that advertisers would be happy to hand over cash.

San Seriffe, it seemed, was a small archipelago in the Indian Ocean whose two islands, Caissa Superiore and Caissa Inferiore (together resembling a semi-colon) had become prosperous almost overnight with the discovery of phosphates and oil. 'From a diet of mutton, goat cheese, and damson wine,' waxed the copy, 'it is a far cry to the international cuisine offered at many of the big hotels. The thatched huts still occupied by the irrepressible Flongs, an indigenous people at the tip of the southern island, are generations away from two international airports.'

The country was run by General M.J. Pica, shown in photographs to be a stereotypical military dictator, weighed down with medals, saluting his troops as he reviewed them from behind his sunglasses.

As with the real-life supplements, so there were adverts in this one. Kodak announced a competition to see who could send in photographs that best represented the beauty of San Seriffe 'from the serene, stately grandeur of the Cap Em Opera House to the hustle and bustle of the harbour at Port Clarendon'.

The name of the two islands was translated as Upper Caisse and Lower Caisse, which should have given the game away, particularly as pica, Cap Em, sans serif and so on were all terms used in printing.

Sadly, the San Seriffe supplement has never been equalled since in British newspapers' attempts for April Fool brilliance, with the *Guardian*'s follow-up piece the next year but a pale imitation of the earlier hoax. Nonetheless, two Labour MPs tabled a motion in the House of Commons, 'That this House commends the *Guardian* for the high standard of its spoof for two successive years on April Fools' Day, which in so many ways mirrors the problems and hypocrisy of the foreign policies of so-called advanced nations.'

Despite this motion, it doesn't appear to have stopped MPs jetting off to other politically dubious nations with sunny climates on 'fact finding missions'.

Your Bra's Interfering With My Vision

One of the few decent newspaper April Fool gags since the great San Seriffe spoof was carried out by the *Daily Mail* in 1982. An article reported that since a bra manufacturer had gone over to using, as the support for its bras, a specially treated copper wire designed to be used in fire alarms, their brassières had been causing interference with television sets.

Ten thousand of these bras were in circulation and when the body's heat, the wire, and the nylon material of the bra were combined, immense static electricity was produced, making TV signals go haywire.

Despite the date, the chief engineer of British Telecom sent out a memo saying that the women who worked in the company's laboratories should be quizzed as to whether they were wearing these brassières or not.

I've Got Dutch Elm Disease

Since the *Panorama* hoax in 1957, scepticism about the truth of what was seen on the box and heard on the wireless has not so much crept as bounded in, particularly with regard to news and current affairs programmes. Nonetheless, there is still amusement to be had on April Fools' Day.

In 1973 on the usually po-faced Radio Three, Dr Ronald Clothier, gave a learned lecture about Dutch Elm Disease. It was a fairly dry talk, taking listeners through the history of the disease in excruciating detail before informing them that a startling discovery had recently been made. It turned out that quite accidentally a researcher into the disease had discovered that rats exposed to Dutch Elm Disease had developed a resistance to the common cold.

Further experiments on human beings brought into contact with the disease found that it worked in the case of men and women too. There was, said Dr Clothier, an occasional problem with side effects in that one of the guinea pigs had found his red hair turning yellow. Further investigation revealed that, unlikely though it was that arboreal disease could be transferred to humans, the man *had* actually caught Dutch Elm Disease. It was, subsequent research revealed, likely to be a problem with red-haired people because they had a higher phosphorous blood count. Dr Clothier recommended that until science found a cure, it would be sensible for those who had red hair to avoid elm trees altogether.

Dr Clothier was, in fact, Spike Milligan, taking advantage of the fact that of the entire BBC, Radio Three was the least likely area to be involved in a practical joke. For Milligan, it was only one small episode in a lifetime of pranks. At one time he was fond of lying down in front of undertakers' premises and shouting out 'Shop!'

Fading Gravity

Three years later on BBC radio Patrick Moore spoke of the decreased gravitational pull that would result from Pluto passing behind Jupiter. He convinced hundreds of people that if they jumped into the air, they would feel as if they were floating back to earth. Many rang the BBC to say how happy they were to have experienced the phenomenon.

Big Ben Goes Digital

Four years later, in 1980, the BBC World Service caused consternation around the globe with their story that Big Ben's clock mechanism was proving so unreliable that it was going to be replaced and that, in keeping with the times, the clock-face would be going digital. What seemed to upset people more than anything else was the idea that the old, obsolete hands of the clock would be given away.

Operation Parallax

Capital Radio announced on 1 April 1979 that Britain's constant changing between Greenwich Mean Time and British Summer Time meant that we had grown increasingly out of step with the rest of the world, to the extent that 48 hours needed to be chopped out somewhere. As a result, the Government was launching Operation Parallax, under which the following 5 and 12 of April would be dropped altogether.

This caused consternation among worried listeners who wanted to know what would happen to people's birthdays, to staff payments and so on. One man said that he was due to sell his house on 5 April and he was worried that the sale might fall through.

The Left Switches to the Right

Ken Livingstone, while still leader of the Greater London Council, participated in a radio April Fool hoax. Livingstone said that he was irritated with the slow pace of Britain's integration with the rest of the European Community.

To show a lead, London planned to switch from driving on the left to the right, as on the Continent. Although it would lead to some inconvenience for a while as vehicles entered and left London, Livingstone said that once the capital led the way, he was sure that the rest of the country would follow suit shortly afterwards.

Ice, Anyone?

In Sydney on April Fools' Day in 1978, the radio station reported that Dick Smith had arranged to tow a giant iceberg into Sydney harbour. He planned to moor it near the Opera House where it could be cut into ice cubes which could be sold for ten cents each.

Curious Australians looking out at the harbour could see the iceberg, or at least what looked like an iceberg. In fact it was a barge covered with sheets of white plastic sprayed with foam. Smith admitted later that the stunt cost him $1500 to put together.

Blowing the Lid Off Politics

On 1 April 1933, the *Capital Times* in Madison, Wisconsin, reported that a series of explosions had blown the dome of the State Capitol building off. There was an accompanying photograph of the building without the dome, which lay on the ground nearby.

'Large quantities of gas,' said the report, 'generated through many weeks of verbose debate in the Senate and Assembly chambers, had in some way been ignited, causing the first blast.'

The article ended with just two words: 'April fool.'

On *That's Life*, Esther Rantzen and her cohorts leapt into the fray with their piece about the small, cuddly, furry creature (what else) called the Lirpaloof. Looking something like a hobbit, it's unlikely that this rather limp effort would have fooled very many people. But then, those people who get excited, like the *That's Life* team, by suggestive-looking root vegetables, may have different thresholds of belief than the rest of us.

That's Life did manage one pretty good April Fool gag when they introduced viewers to an old English sheepdog that could drive a car. Although the film was partly of a woman dressed in a sheepdog costume doing the driving, it is clear that many people believed what they were seeing. The BBC was inundated with irate viewers accusing the programme of irresponsibility, saying that dogs shouldn't be allowed to drive on public roads.

Freezing Crocodile

In 1994, a local county newsletter delivered on 1 April said that a freezing crocodile was stranded in the village pond in Sedgefield, in County Durham.

Over 50 people turned up with kettles of hot water to help the animal.

A Mars a Day

Advertisers have not been slow to follow the lead of the papers, TV and radio in producing April Fool spoofs. In 1994, for instance, Mars took out full page ads in newspapers announcing: 'New Biggest Ever Mars Bar.'

The 'Emperor' size was said to be 32lb of thick chocolate, glucose and milk. It was available for that one day only.

The BMW Series

The most consistently entertaining April Fool ads are those thought up by BMW. Although it is unlikely that many people are fooled once they finish reading the inventive copy, the ads usually cleverly involve technological innovations which are just about believable.

In 1983, newspapers carried a full page advertisement for a BMW which was 'The first open top car to keep out the rain even when it's stationary.' Realising that convertibles weren't practical all year round cars for Western Europe, the company's researchers had come up with a way to let people keep the roof open whatever the weather. A fast-moving car will generate an airstream to keep the rain off it, so BMW developed a way to develop an artificial airstream which would come on at low speeds when the sensors detected over 0.58 per cent of moisture by volume in excess of the atmospheric norm. 'BMW have always believed you should have total control over your car,' ran the ad. 'If you'd like control over the weather as well, please fill in the coupon below.'

The coupon, addressed to a Miss April Wurst, asked people to tick whether they'd like to test-drive it in light squalls, a torrential downpour or a car wash.

Another ad reported a new invention for BMW Series 3 cars, the glove compartments of which would in future contain a complete steering wheel and set of controls so that 'When You Cross The Channel, Our Steering Wheel Crosses Over With You.' It was developed by their engineer Aäp Rifühl so that, 'For the first time, British drivers will be able to drive abroad without getting on the wrong side of the natives.'

Another year's rather sweet ad recognised the importance to BMW owners of the chequered badge and reported that a windscreen wiper was being introduced to keep the enamel badge clean. Light sensitive sensors would switch it on when it became ever so slightly dirty, so that 'The BMW Marque Will Never Be Marked.'

One year, the April Fools' Day ad proclaimed 'A BMW You Need Never Wash Again.' BMW's senior molecular chemist, Dr I. Dehr, had made a technological breakthrough by impregnating the paintwork with a cleaning agent that could be activated by rain, keeping the car sparkling clean. It had taken some time to get rid of the problems of excessive foam but you could now send in the coupon to Uve Binhäd at BMW for details.

Two of the ads were for new dashboard gadgets. DWS professed to be a breakthrough in anti-theft technology. Standing for Driver's Weight Sensor, it compared the weight of the person sitting in the driver's seat with the pre-programmed weight of the car's owner and any authorised drivers. If they weren't the same, within a tolerance of 5 per cent either way, then the car simply wouldn't start. If the potential driver persisted, then the car alarm would go off, while a prerecorded message was transmitted on the police waveband, notifying them of the car's registration number.

Thanks to a sophisticated 365-day digital clock, the system could even take account of variations that would be expected after meal times, for instance, and it could compensate for the extra weight brought about by heavy clothing in the winter. Lady drivers who preferred passengers not to see their weight displayed on the console could contact their local dealer, who would carry out the adjustment for free. The coupons in this case needed to be sent to a Hugh Phelfrett.

Another dashboard gizmo was the UWAT system, designed for the ease of those who were poor linguists but who had to travel abroad. Recognising that the Englishman's habit of shouting loudly didn't work when you were on the road, desperate to work out what the sign up ahead meant before you were past it, the company brought in an automatic translation system, Urbien Waundab. Thanks to the insistence of the European Community in fixing a small black box to every road sign, you could set the UWAT to automatic and it would translate each sign for you as you approached.

My favourite of all BMW April Fool ads was perhaps the most plausible. It was headed 'WARNING: Are You Driving A Genuine BMW?' The ad cautioned BMW owners that counterfeit cars emanating in the Far East were being sold in Britain. It pointed out, however, that the counterfeiters had made a few important mistakes which would enable BMW owners to check whether their car was genuine or not. First they should check the positioning of the black and white quarters on the front badge. The counterfeiters had got them the wrong way round. There were several others: 'Is the oil dipstick no more than 450mm in length? Non-genuine dipsticks leave you short of 250mm'; 'All genuine BMWs have cigar lighters, whereas non-genuine BMWs have cigarette lighters'; 'Do the windscreen wipers make 253 sweeps per minute at their fastest speed? Non-genuine wipers only make 123 sweeps per minute'; 'With the driver's seat in the full reclining position, you should be able to raise your feet and lie them flat on the windscreen'; 'Check the fuel consumption. The average April fuel figures for urban motoring can be obtained from your local BMW dealer'; 'Check the aerodynamics by taping 6 inch strips of ribbon,

9 inches apart, to the side, bonnet, roof and boot of your car. While in neutral, take the engine up to 2,500 revs. The ribbons will not flutter if it's a genuine BMW (please note, the wind level should be at a minimum)'; 'The carpet pile should lie to the right, if it's a genuine right-hand driver BMW, and to the left if it's non-genuine.'

Although BMW claims to believe that, because of its bulging April postbag, people fall for these spoofs, I confess that I filled in the form for the above ad simply because I found it so wonderfully ingenious.

BMW has even carried out an April Fools' Day TV ad. In 1993, they introduced a special 'anti-tracking device for secret lovers everywhere', which was able to cover up tracks that the car had made in the snow. Two interlocking hearts made by tyre tracks, visible in the snow in the ad, were wiped out by the car which then drove off. Not quite as clever as the print ads, perhaps, but as believable as many other things in TV advertisements.

Rolling About in the Roller

Even Rolls-Royce have not been above the odd April Fool joke. One year they took out full page advertisements headed 'You Know All Those Stories About Rolls-Royce' which took the mickey out of the near legendary tales told about its cars. It was made all the more believable by the fact that it appeared on 31 March.

While we all know the one about being able to hear the ticking of the clock when travelling at 70 miles per hour, the piece gave us a few that most of us hadn't heard before, beginning with the most plausible, and becoming more and more far-fetched as they went on. Here are a few:

• Sir Arthur Windrush, Tory MP for Fen End had the ignominy of hearing his maiden speech in the House of Commons described by Aneurin Bevan as: 'The Rolls-Royce of speeches – it was smooth, inaudible and seemed to go on for ever.'

• Having lost his considerable fortune gambling, Viscount Arthur 'Dodgy' Rumplemere was arrested for drunkenness in 1923. Appearing in court he gave his address as a Rolls-Royce Silver Ghost parked on the Embankment. After serving ten days' prison sentence he returned to his residence and continued to live there until he died in 1952. The car was started without difficulty for the first time in 29 years, to carry Viscount Arthur to his last resting place.

• Incredibly, Nostradamus in 1548 made this prediction: 'From Albion's shore shall come a marvellous contryvance: a carriage silencieux bearing the arms of Rolles de Roi.'

• Until 1933 no Rolls-Royce was equipped with reverse gear. Sir Henry Royce was unwilling to have his car adopt what he regarded as an undignified mode of progression.

• On the exceedingly rare occasion when an owner has occasion to raise the bonnet of any post-war Rolls-Royce, he hears a discreetly modulated rendering of 'Land of Hope and Glory' played by the BBC Symphony Orchestra.

• Examine closely the number plates on the Silver Spirit. Each one is hand-painted by a student from the Crewe College of Art.

• In 1934 the far-sighted Mayor of Blackpool, Alderman Billy 'Progress' Bickerstaffe, decided to replace the entire Blackpool tram fleet with Rolls-Royce motor cars. Sadly, the company were not prepared to modify the car for overhead cables.

• In 1939, Adolf Hitler's attempt to buy the only Silver Wraith in the Third Reich was frustrated by a midnight phone call from Rolls-Royce's Conduit Street office, ordering the car into Poland. After a 300 mile drive, the car crossed the border pursued by an entire Panzer division. The date was 1 September. The rest is history.

• Extras fitted to Rolls-Royce cars have included a spiral staircase, an interior depicting the Battle of Lepanto, an integral Black and Decker Workmate, a nuclear fall-out shelter, and a one-twentieth scale model of the Leicester Square Odeon.

• The air conditioning on the Silver Spirit is so refined that owners have a choice of ten atmospheres ranging from dawn at Simla, to late evening on the Promenade des Anglais, to Sunday morning on the sea-front at Bournemouth.

• In the province of M'bnga in Lower Volta, a Rolls-Royce is worshipped as the supreme deity. It was brought to the area in 1911 by the missionary Sir Archibald Cameron, whose rudimentary knowledge of the M'bnga dialect led to some confusion between the appelations 'Silver' and 'Holy' Ghost. Sir Archibald was eaten before he could correct the unfortunate misunderstanding.

• Underneath the hallowed turf at Crewe Alexandra Football Club is buried an entire Rolls-Royce.

• In 1914 Major D'Avigor-Simpson, D.S.O., drove his Silver Ghost 23,000 miles across the Siberian wastes at temperatures as low as 50° below zero. After three months of such driving, he and his car skidded into the icebound River Yenesei, whence they floated into the Arctic Ocean. Three years later the car, frozen solid into the pack ice, was picked up by a Russian cargo ship. On reaching Murmansk the vehicle and its driver were thawed out. The Silver Ghost started first time; which is more than can be said for the gallant major.

• In 1967, Miss Gladys Moncrief, after a heavy dinner at the Shelbourne Hotel, Dublin, fell asleep at the wheel of her 1924 Silver Ghost on the drive home. The magnificent old car completed the remaining 23 miles of the familiar journey unassisted, and on arrival at the family residence summoned Miss Moncrief's sister Amelia with a series of gentle toots on the horn.

The ad concludes with a note: 'Each word in every Rolls-Royce advertisement is checked by a Committee of four: the Editors of *The Times* and of the *Oxford English Dictionary*, a lineal descendant of Peter Mark Roget and the Archbishop of Canterbury. The process takes about four months.

'In 1911 the normally humourless Henry Royce played an April Fool joke on his employees: he presented them all with exploding cigars. The date of his prank (due to Royce's failure to purchase a new calendar) was in fact March 31st – but none of his staff dared to point this out.

'Subsequently, the incident gave rise to a tradition of premature April Fools' jokes at the Rolls-Royce factory which continues to this day.'

Welcome to Chicago

My favourite April Fool prank of all occurred in 1992 and may have resulted in a few moments' panic among passengers flying into Los Angeles International Airport.

Ten miles away from the airport, clearly visible to any plane coming in to land at Los Angeles, is the Hollywood Park race track. On this particular April Fools' Day, somebody had erected a massive sign on the roof of the race track stand.

It read simply: 'WELCOME TO CHICAGO.'

15

The Home-Grown
Variety

All Work and No Play

Everyone seems to take life and work much more seriously
today. Gone are the days when people kept themselves going
at work by playing pranks on each other. An article in the
American workplace I read lamented the fact that groups of
workers that used to be renowned for playing practical jokes
now behave in a completely po-faced manner.

Even firemen (or firefighters, this being a PC report)
who were once infamous for thinking up practical jokes
while waiting for the alarm bell to ring, were now, said the
piece, more likely to be boning up on the latest course they
had to go on. 'In the cost-efficient, time-conscious world,
there's little time for the good old practical joke.'

Only among professional sports players could the writer
of the article find a group where practical joking was still
being kept alive as an art form. Baseball players are
apparently still in the habit of giving each other a hot foot
to liven up a long game.

An English professor at Vanderbilt University who
specialises in humour was quoted as saying that practical
jokes began disappearing from the workplace when
women started entering it. 'Women have a low tolerance
for that kind of thing . . . They see it as boyish or bullying.'

Although it appears to be mainly men who indulge in
hoaxes and practical jokes on a regular basis, women are

not always above it, particularly when it comes to the question of revenge, and especially with regard to affairs of the heart.

Boiling Over

Jilted lovers are renowned for wanting to get their own back. A friend who had a relationship with a well-known chef simmered for some time when he ditched her for a new model.

Finally, she hit on a solution. She got several of her friends to book tables in his restaurant under assumed names and using bogus phone numbers, with one of them even booking the private room upstairs. Not one of them intended taking up the booking, of course, and she contented herself with imagining the fury of the master chef as he contemplated his empty establishment.

The Revenge of the Prawn

Although it has now acquired the gloss of an urban legend, presumably there was once a girl who wreaked revenge on the rat who threw her over by unscrewing the end of the curtain rod in his living-room and stuffing it full of frozen prawns before putting the end back on again.

Good though the story is, it has taken on a life of its own and is now often told with the addition of a new girlfriend moving in, only for the couple to find the gradually increasing stench completely unbearable. So bad does it become that they decide to move to another flat and the old girlfriend just happens along as the removal van is being packed. She is gratified to witness the curtain rod being loaded into the van along with the rest of the furniture.

A variant on this is to hide a fish somewhere in a car where, gradually, its aroma will make itself increasingly evident. This prank has also often been played in offices, usually by someone on the point of leaving. To get their own back on the person who has made their life a misery during working hours, they will secrete the fish at the back of a desk drawer or inside the false ceiling.

At the First Stroke

One lover's revenge story tells of the girl (it usually seems to be women getting their own back on men) who is given the elbow by her pilot boyfriend just as he is about to go on an overseas trip. She is told to be out of the flat by the time he returns.

When he gets back, he is happy to see that there is no sign of the ex or her belongings. He is a little puzzled, though, as to why the phone should be off the hook. As he lifts it he hears those familiar words: 'At the first stroke, it will be . . .' but in an unfamiliar accent. His ex had cleared out her stuff six days earlier, her parting shot being to ring the speaking clock – in New York!

The Bells, The Bells

It is possible to bring about *coitus interruptus* without actually being one of the two parties involved. One chap was asked by a friend for the loan of his flat during the day. The friend was involved in an affair but he couldn't find anywhere else to go that was discreet enough.

The flat owner was rather reluctant to get involved, but his friend was so persuasive that eventually he agreed. Handing over the keys, the flat owner was made to promise his friend that he would not go anywhere near the building at the pre-arranged time.

The friend set the scene beautifully, with an ice-cold bucket of champagne, flowers and the hi-fi playing suitable music. It all worked and the couple then moved through to the bedroom.

That was when things started to go wrong. Just as they were settling down to business, an alarm clock went off. Then another, then another. The flat owner had gone out and bought himself ten alarm clocks and hidden them in the bedroom. They were all set for different times but just close enough to each other to put the loving couple off their stroke.

The afternoon was not the success that the friend had been hoping for.

A Mustard Wheeze

Although told by one friend that she had actually carried this next prank out on some fink who had dumped her, I remain sceptical about its veracity, despite – or perhaps because of – having heard exactly the same story from several other sources. I don't know if it really does work, but the story has it that if you scatter mustard and cress seed on a deep pile carpet – the more expensive, the better – and sprinkle it with water, then the cress will take root and grow. I remain dubious but welcome news of any confirmed sightings.

This is one I have never dared to try myself, being something of a wimp, but I love the idea of it.

You need an office by a bus route to play it and, what's more, you need a clear view from your office of a bus stop that has a telephone box close by. Once you've noted the number of the phone, you're ready.

Dial the number just as someone is about to use the telephone. Although whoever picks it up will initially be suspicious, you should tell them that your friend/wife/husband/colleague always takes the bus at that time and that you've got an urgent message for them. You know it's a dreadful imposition, but would they mind calling them to the phone?

Any suspicion that they're being had should evaporate when you describe the exact appearance of somebody in the bus queue, together with the clothes they are wearing. For some reason, the idea of someone going up to a complete stranger in a bus queue and telling them that there is a phone call for them is considered a source of great amusement in many offices.

The Phone Swap

One practical joke that I used to enjoy greatly in my days of working in an office is rather harder to carry out these days, thanks to the newfangled telephones with which most offices are now equipped.

However, if you do happen to chance upon a desk on which there are two separate telephones, each with their own bell, then you have at your disposal the basic ingredients for one of the neatest of all office practical jokes. All you have to do is swap the handsets over, making sure that the wires are tidied away so that your handiwork is not visible.

Then, when there's a phone call to either of the phones, the poor sap will pick up the handset sitting on that phone. However, as the handset actually belongs to the other phone, they will hear only the dialling tone. Believing they've simply wrongly identified the ringing phone, they'll replace the handset in their hand and pick up the other one. However, by doing so, they're cutting off the caller.

It's a terribly simple prank to carry out and, I readily confess, gave someone of my limited intelligence great pleasure when I was supposed to be working.

Office Pranks

There are those who believe that it is amusing to smear the earpieces of telephones with charred cork but this seems to me to be on a par with putting burnt cork or shoe polish on the eyepiece of a telescope or a pair of binoculars. It may well work, but it's surely the sort of thing you ought to have grown out of by the age of twelve?

Similarly, sawing the legs off a desk and chair, which I have heard of, would seem to be destructive rather than funny. However, I do find the idea of moving somebody's desk, chair and their personal effects into the lift or the lavatory rather more appealing.

The Photocopier

Photocopying machines are a boon to the practical joker. One of the more pleasing pranks you can play is to photocopy something mildly embarrassing, making sure that the machine is set to a very light setting, so that the image is quite faint.

Then take the photocopy and put it back into the photocopier's paper tray, a little way down from the top. Whoever uses the machine will find – as late as possible, you hope – that in the background of some terribly dull report is the latest centrefold from *Women Only* or *Penthouse* or whatever.

Keeping Idiots Amused

The practical joke I recall most vividly from my schooldays is both simple and childish. To my surprise, I discovered recently that despite its whiskers, it can still work wonderfully, even on adults.

On a sheet of paper, you write: 'How do you keep an idiot amused for hours?' At the bottom, put: 'PTO.'

Write the same on the other side and then count how many times your mark turns the paper over and over in bafflement before giving up.

It turns out that we weren't being as original as we thought. In the American state of Georgia, there is a town called Talking Rock. It got its name from a giant rock on one of the trails used by pioneering settlers. On it was painted the words 'Turn Me Over'. Many curious travellers did just that, although it took considerable manpower and effort to manage it. On the underside were the words 'Turn Me Back That I May Fool Another'.

You've Got To Hand It To Them

Hardly sophisticated, but surprisingly effective, is shaking hands with a dummy's hand in place of yours. This works best if you're wearing gloves, but even without them, you'll usually get a satisfying look of shock as the person you're greeting momentarily thinks they've pulled your hand off.

In-Car Entertainment

Being so cautious myself, I would worry too much about accidents to play hoaxes in moving cars. Others think it the height of sophisticated humour to put a stupid mask on the back of their head and to drive with their head out of the window. Although the driver can see perfectly well what they are doing, motorists behind them become a little concerned that the car in front is being driven by a nutter looking backwards instead of the direction they are heading.

Another neat car trick, so I'm told, is for someone in the back seat sitting behind the front passenger to wind down their window. After waiting a little, when the car is travelling at some speed, they should lean forward and knock loudly on the front passenger window.

Eggsellent Joke

Those who feel that they are brave enough to play practical jokes on the cook in their household can have a fine old time with eggs. Forget all the tricks that involve piercing eggs and trying to get the yolk out. Far too much like hard work.

Instead, simply hard boil an egg in advance of it being needed and replace it in its box. Then watch while whoever is doing the cooking cracks a couple of normal eggs and then tries neatly to break open a hard-boiled one.

Is It a Bird, Is It a Plane?

Although it doesn't sound as though it should work, it is all too easy to get a large group of perfect strangers to stare in a particular direction. Next time you're out walking with a friend, simply stop in your tracks and look up at something that appears to fascinate you. Indulge yourself with a little bit of pointing, too, if you feel you want to throw yourself into the part.

It sounds bizarre and unlikely, but almost invariably other people will slow down or stop and look in the same direction. Once you've attracted a suitably large crowd, you can just melt into the distance and observe the first law of crowd psychology, namely that no-one in a crowd is willing to admit they can't see what all the others are seeing.

Levin in Mufti

I recall having a rather eccentric Welsh friend at college. He was a great collector of official forms. I would frequently receive missives from abattoirs about the defective carcases I had been sending them, from crematoria about terrible mistakes that had been made with my relatives and from various council bodies demanding to know why I hadn't complied with some weird regulation or other.

Andrew was someone who had no concept of the meaning of the word 'embarrassment'. An evening out with him could be mortifying if you didn't want to attract attention to yourself. I can remember standing outside the Cottosloe auditorium at the National Theatre one night when Andrew suddenly said, in a voice that could clearly be heard by everyone, 'Look, there's Bernard Levin.'

Like everyone else, I turned around to look while pretending that I wasn't really looking at all. But I couldn't see Mr Levin and I confessed as much to Andrew in a hushed voice.

'Look, over there,' he said, in an exasperated voice, waiting for everyone to turn round and look with me. 'Over there, in the purple dress.'

He had the temperament of the ideal practical joker. He was incapable of being embarrassed, despite the angry stares of what must have been 50 or 60 people. I, on the other hand, was mortified, and sought refuge in the lavatory until the play was about to start.

My friend Gail once carried out a superb practical joke, though I doubt if I would be able to carry it off without laughing. She was expecting a friend, Martin, for dinner the next day when he happened to let slip that he was going to be eating that night at the house of a vague acquaintance of hers.

Gail found out her phone number and found out from her exactly what she was planning to give Martin, right down to the Orange Matchmakers and coffee. As this woman had recently returned from South America, she wanted to try out various native dishes, so it was a somewhat exotic menu, particularly for someone of Gail's culinary abilities.

Nonetheless, when Martin and she sat down to dinner the following evening, in front of them was a corn and green pepper starter. Martin had a gratifyingly surprised look on his face, but said nothing.

However, when the main course came out – chicken in chocolate sauce – he burst into laughter. He headed out for the kitchen and there found the South American pudding waiting, just as he had had the previous evening.

Sadly for Gail, while the joke got a great laugh from its victim, Martin admitted that he hadn't actually enjoyed the meal the night before.

The Professionals

If you can't think of your own practical jokes, you could always pop into your nearest joke shop, which is likely to stock a few. Of course, if you have friends who fall for things like hand buzzers, whoopee cushions, fake vomit and so on, then it says more than you should be willing to admit about the sort of friends you have.

Another alternative is to use a professional. With Alan Abel's fees probably a little out of your reach, you could always try Tom Antion of Prankmasters: 'Professional Tricks Orchestrated Anywhere in the Free World.' He charges from $75 for playing practical jokes on people, although he'll never agree to one in which his victim suffers pain, substantial humiliation or monetary damage. Antion thinks that the victims ought to be flattered: 'If someone did it to me, I would think, "Wow, someone really went out of their way to spend time on doing something specifically for me, rather than giving me a pair of socks or a tie or something."'

A journalist writing a piece on Antion found that meeting the Prankmaster inspired him. He and his wife were going out at the weekend to see a film with their friends Robb and Joan. It was usual for Robb to drive them in Joan's car so, while they were in the cinema, he arranged for Joan's bright red 1988 Toyota Corolla to be replaced by Robb's own dark grey 1986 Toyota.

With the help of Joan, who provided spare keys for each car, and her sister, who switched the car while they were watching the movie, they made the swap. When they emerged, Robb simply unlocked the car and they all got in. Only when the other three reckoned that they could mention it without laughing did they switch the subject away from the film they'd seen, *Crazy People*. 'You guys may think I'm crazy,' said the hoaxer, 'but I could've sworn we drove Joan's car to the movies.'

All of them agreed that the effort involved in setting up the hoax was well worth it for the look on Robb's face when he realised that the car he was driving was not the one he'd left outside the cinema.

Spannering

In Britain, a company called Spanner In The Works will bring an element of chaos to parties and functions. Usually posing as waiters, they will offer guests canapés such as jelly baby and radish on a cocktail stick or perhaps carrot and banana, which they claim to be a Tahitian delicacy often served by Egon Ronay at his cocktail parties.

One of them will pretend to be a wine waiter, getting himself steadily more sozzled as the evening wears on and becoming ever ruder to the diners, examining their thinning hair with a large magnifying glass and taking a mini vacuum-cleaner to the dandruff on their jackets, before collapsing and having to be dragged out of the room. Their waitress will flirt outrageously with the men, making assignations in the car park that are kept, not by her, but by the poor chap's giggling mates.

One of them usually dons the garb of a maintenance man and will disrupt the dinner by working clumsily on chandeliers, fuse boxes or by drilling holes with an electric drill. He might slip and shove the drill bit through an 'old master', to the guests' horror. Or he could tear down a carefully-prepared fake fuse box that will explode and leave him twitching on the floor.

Frank Carson has declared them 'the funniest thing since me' but then perhaps you need to see 'Spannering' in action to truly appreciate their craft.

Amorous Couples

Although kissograms and stripograms are somewhat passé now, other outfits try to be a bit more inventive. Comic Ivor Dembina once set up a company called Pranksters which used a group of actors to carry out stunts that could be extremely complex. They staged an armed robbery, for instance, in the middle of a prize-giving ceremony for a group of computer salesmen. Their top of the range stunt was a police raid involving twenty uniformed policemen.

Another outfit, Sleazy Telegrams, was once hired to carry out a de Vere Cole-like stunt. They posed as a jilted bride and her furious mother disrupting a wedding at Willesden register office.

In America, a company offers Amorous Couples. These people turn up at sedate parties and, before long, can't keep their hands off each other. To the consternation of the other guests, they get steadily more and more involved until conversation comes to a halt.

271

16

The Rebounds

A Pipkin of an Idea

Practical jokes sometimes have unforeseen consequences. They may rebound on the pranksters or they may turn out to be of considerable benefit in one way or another.

At the American company General Electric the research department had an initiation rite which involved pulling the leg of newcomers, asking them to come up with a method for frosting the inside of lightbulbs. One victim, pretty unbelievably named Marvin Pipkin, not only managed it, but in doing so invented a lightbulb that lasted far longer than the unfrosted variety.

In the Cathouse

In 1978 Joey Skaggs put an ad in *Village Voice*, New York's equivalent of *Time Out*.

CATHOUSE FOR DOGS
featuring a savoury selection of hot bitches. From pedigree (Fifi the French Poodle) to mutts (Lady the Tramp). Handler and vet on duty. Stud photo service available. No weirdos, please. Dogs only.
By appointment.

The ad was taken seriously enough for Skaggs to decide to open a real brothel for dogs. But when the newspapers picked up on the story The American Society for the

Prevention of Cruelty to Animals investigated and soon got the District Attorney to shut Skagg's operation down.

Ghost Artists

Hugh Troy, the great practical joker who we've come across so often in this book, thought he'd come up with a great hoax when he put an advertisement in the *Washington Post* in 1947 for a fictitious company called Ghost Artists. The idea was that the company's artists would paint a picture in any style for those people who were too busy or untalented to paint for themselves.

TOO BUSY TO PAINT?
CALL ON GHOST ARTISTS, 1426 33RD STREET, NW
WE PAINT IT – YOU SIGN IT!
PRIMITIVE (GRANDMA MOSES TYPE),
IMPRESSIONIST,
MODERN, CUBIST, ABSTRACT, SCULPTURE . . .
ALSO, WHY NOT GIVE AN EXHIBITION?

To Troy's surprise, he was inundated with enquiries. Although papers (including our own *Times*) made great fun of people who were so gullible as to fall for such a thing, artists down on their luck saw the prank in another light, viewing it as a great business opportunity.

Shortly after the ad appeared, genuine ghost artists willing to carry out the job for real placed their own ads along the same lines and were soon making a good living.

Pocket Sundials

When *Design* magazine published a plan for a luminous, pocket sundial that could be used at night, the BBC programme *Tomorrow's World* wasted no time in getting in touch with the inventor. Although Fred O'Brien had simply wanted to see if the magazine would publish such a ludicrous idea, he told the programme that it worked through the process of 'photosynthetic sound' and that a

Japanese manufacturer was very keen to start producing it. Sadly, he had to inform them later, plans had collapsed because in the Land of the Rising Sun the angle of the sun was such that the sundials were three and a half minutes out.

When a manufacturer contacted O'Brien to see if he could make them, he was not in the least bit fazed to be told that it was a hoax. Before long he had produced 150,000 luminous sundials that could be carried around in the pocket for the Hong Kong market. O'Brien was entitled to half of all profits made.

According to *The Sunday Times* in March 1981, a bemused Mr O'Brien said, 'I could make more money from a joke that backfired than from my more serious work.'

Brushing Up

J.B. Morton, who wrote the Beachcomber column as we learnt earlier, once wrote an article in his column about the electric toothbrush. He talked about it as a completely ludicrous device, much as W. Heath Robinson drew startlingly useless but visually delightful gadgets that could be of no possible use to man nor beast.

Although Morton meant it as satire, he lived long enough to see it became an everyday household object.

A Texan Welcome

In the sixties, novelist Graham Greene and his friend John Sutro wrote to *The Times* about The Anglo-Texan Friendship Society, a body which they said existed to strengthen the cultural and social ties between Britain and the State of Texas but which they had of course merely conjured up in their minds.

The initial letter set off a correspondence to which, among others, the Attorney-General contributed. Intended as a hoax, it wasn't long before a real Anglo-Texan Society was brought into being, with officers appointed and a busy schedule of events organised. It also wasn't long before they were having high-powered cocktail parties at which people like the Duke of Edinburgh were spearing the sausages and cheese with silly little sticks.

Greene and Sutro didn't hang around as members of the society for too long, but their absence didn't stop it. It just went from strength to strength.

Ivor Tune for You

During the Second World War, a competition was organised among British composers to write a march for the underground movement in France. In the midst of rehearsing one of his shows, Ivor Novello was interrupted by a bowler-hatted man who reprimanded him in front of his cast because whereas the others, Sir Arthur Bliss, Vivian Ellis and Ralph Vaughan Williams, had all handed their entries in, they had as yet had nothing from Novello.

Furious at the man's attitude, Novello told him to wait until the end of the scene they were rehearsing. When it finished, he walked across to the piano and scribbled some notes down on manuscript paper. With a final 'harrumph', the man departed.

The actors were naturally curious to know what the music written in such a hurry sounded like. 'I've no idea,' said Novello. 'I just wanted to be rid of him so I took the first sixteen bars of "Keep The Home Fires Burning" and jotted it down backwards!'

The music not only won the competition but was duly recorded with a full orchestra and choir and adopted by the French resistance.

Cementing Relations

Although it has now attained the status of an urban legend, it would be nice to think that there really was once a cement-mixer driver who began to suspect that his wife was having an affair while his work on distant construction sites kept him away from home for days at a time.

Her new clothes and recently acquired habit of wearing scent convinced him that his suspicions must be right, especially as she often didn't answer the phone when he called.

He fibbed about when his next job was due to end, returning earlier than his wife expected. As he had surmised, there was a car parked in his drive that didn't belong to him, a flashy open-top sports car. Through the net curtains, he could see a chap talking to his wife.

The man saw the same flaming red as the sports car. He'd show whoever it was that he couldn't fool around with his wife and get away with it. He backed his cement-mixer up against the car and started it up. The cement began flowing and was filling up the insides nicely when his wife stormed out of the house and began screaming at him.

It turned out that the chap was a car salesman and the car a present from his loving wife for her husband's forthcoming birthday. To help pay for it, she'd taken up working as a waitress in the evenings. As they stood arguing, the cement began to harden.

One of the best books about hoaxing is *The Compleat Practical Joker* by the American humorist H. Allen Smith, first published in 1953. In the first edition, page 47 was left blank except for a tiny hand indicating that you should turn to the next page.

When the book was reprinted by Doubleday in 1975, the hand was omitted, the publishers thinking it a nice practical joke to leave the page completely blank. Unfortunately, bookshops were inundated with people who believed that they had a faulty copy and wanted it to be replaced by a perfect one.

The next edition of *The Compleat Practical Joker*, published by William Morrow in 1980, abandoned the idea of the blank page.